THIRD SERIES
Modern Collector's Dolls

by

Patricia R. Smith

COLLECTOR BOOKS

Published by Collector Books
Box 3009
Paducah, Kentucky, 42001

Distributed by

Crown Publishers, Inc.

419 Park Ave. South
New York, New York 10016

DEDICATION

Series III is dedicated to all my pen pals who have helped me in so many ways. Their friendship, assistance and trust have made this Series much easier to put together.

ALL PHOTOGRAPHS BY DWIGHT. F. SMITH
except those of Maish, Flack & Houston or unless noted.

COVER DOLL; SWEET AMY, School Girl
made by Deluxe

I would like to thank the following for loaning their dolls and many pieces of literature that helped to date and identify them: Jaynn Allen, Louise Alonso, Frances & Mary Anicello, Joan Amundsen, Joan Ashabraner, Sally Biethscheider, Margaret Biggers, Peggy Boudreau, Ruth Brocha, Alice Capps, Bessie Carson, Ruth Clark, Pearl Clasby, Barbara Coker, Edith, DeAngelo, Sibyl DeWein, Helen Draves, Cecelia Eades, Marie Ernst, Thelma & Joleen Flack, Linda Fox, Bev. Gardner, Helen Garrett, Adele Gioscia, Susan Goetz, Edith Goldsworthy, Martha Gonyea, Ellie Haynes, Maxine Heitt, Robbie Heitt, Phyllis Houston, Virginia Jones, Elaine Kaminsky, Kimport Dolls, Tilly Kobe, Angie Landers, Donna Maish, Marge Meisinger, Jay Minter, Barb Mongelluzzi, Grace Ochsner, Pat Raiden, Julia Rogers, Dodi Shapiro, Diana Sorenson, Donna Stanley, Pat Stewart, Mary Partridge, Karen Penner, Carolyn Powers, Mae Tetters, Teri Schall, Shelia Wallace and Kathy Walter.

My very special thanks go to Laura Zwier for the interview of Cushman and Glass and to a very delightful lady Miss Mollye who interviewed herself!

EDITOR: KAREN PENNER

CONTENTS

New and Revised Information

Series I: Page 140: The 1965-1966 11½" (12") Cinderella by Horsman Dolls came packaged with only one doll body and had an extra head that had the hairdo of Rich Cinderella. The 12" Rich Cinderella was also sold in a package by herself. The same flyer from Horsman Company shows a 16" Mary Poppins doll. The above flyer was sent to me by Mrs. J. C. Houston.

Series I: page 161: Ideal Baby Big Eyes also came with flirty sleep eyes. Marks; (-5/Ideal Doll.

Series I: page 188: 17" "Jolly" of Jolly Toys was also used as "Happy" of the twins, "Happy & Nappy," in 1963. They came with a white/pink wooden swing set.

Series I: page 113: 13" "Junie" of 1968 was also marketed as "Jackie" in 1969.

I find that I made a mistake in saying that the last Gerber Baby was made by the Uneeda Doll Co. I wish to thank Mrs. Frank Wilson for the correct information and will quote a letter, received by Frank Wilson, from Mr. Ralph Merrill of the Gerber Products Company: 'Our records show that we have had three Gerber Baby dolls. The first doll was offered twice. 1. 1956: Sold: 300,000. Made of rubber by Sun Rubber Company. 2. 1965: Sold: 75,000. Made by Arrow Toy Company. 3. 1972: Sold: 58,000 white and 90 black (this was the first time Gerber offered an ethnic doll). Made of vinyl by AMSCO INDUSTRIES.'

Sasha dolls are being made at the Freidland Group in Trenton, England. The firm owner's wife, Mrs. Sara Doggart is the "guardian angel" who watches over the production of the dolls. Mrs. Doggart keeps tract of the quality of the dolls they are producing, to keep the standards high as the designer of the dolls: Sasha Morgenthaler insists upon. These dolls were first "mass-produced" in 1965. The original, hand done ones are still available at $250.00 to $350.00 prices. Fisher of America has taken over the rights to distribute the dolls in the United States. For many years they have been a part of the Creative Playthings line.

Series I: Page 143: The Horsman "Princess" doll caption name was reversed and the doll's name is actually "Gloria Jean."

Series II: Page 178: 29" "Miss Echo" was made by the American Doll & Toy Company 1963.

Kenner's "Baby Alive" was featured by Simplicity Patterns (1974-Dec.) in its counter catalog, Holiday Catalog and Fashion News. It is shown modeling 6 dresses designed by Simplicity especially for her. More than 100,000 catalogs featuring Baby Alive were distributed.

6" "WHIMETTES" by the American Character Co. included: Pixie, Swinger, Granny, Mini Mod, Jump'n and GoGo.

To show how the use of names can be confusing: BABY SUSAN: one made by the Marlin Co., one by Eegee (1958), one by Natural Doll Co. and yet another by the Belle Co.

Lorrie Dolls are made by the Eugene Doll Company.

Princess Grace Dolls Inc. is also the Mego Corp.

There were four different "Blythes" in the Kenner series. Each had a different set of eye color changes.

The Alexander Baby Ellen is the Black version of Sweet Tears.

Mattel's #2 "Barbie" is the same as the #1 except there are no metal cylinders in the feet and legs forming holes for a stand. She does have the white eyes and painted brows. She has a heavy solid torso. MARKS: PATS. PEND. MCMLVIII.

Eege Company also used mold codes of "VS" and a "V" on the lower back.

Susy Smart was made by Deluxe Reading Corp.

The American Character 1963-64 Tressy Series included Cricket, Mary Makeup (Girlfriend), a Bonus Tressy and called "Pre-Teen" Tressy. She is 14" tall, a standard size doll and has the grow hair feature. She is shown in this book.

The little Uneeda dolls shown on page 313 and 314 of Series II were also marketed under the names: Ping & Pong.

The Ralph A. Freundlich, Inc. Company made the 1940 "Baby Sandra" doll (Sandra Henville). The doll was produced in different screen costumes that included: "East Side Of Heaven," "Unexpected Father," "Little Accident" and "Sandy is a Lady."

I have been asked many, many times "Just how is a doll conceived and made?" Wanting to answer the questions, I wrote to 102 different doll companies, mould makers and doll designers. I received "resumes" back from only three, and these three have the fewest dolls to offer than any company in the industry! (Kamar, Tomy & Gabriel).

I did receive a reply from the Perfect Doll Moulds Corp. Mr. Mark M. Schaffer outlined what "made" a doll:

1. The type of doll is conceived.

2. The doll is sculpted.

3. Wax models or plaster models are made according to the method of molding to be used for the various doll parts.

4. The proper molds are made for rotation, blow, or injection molding.

5. The doll parts are produced from the molds and assembled.

Care

TO CLEAN CLOTH BODIES: Use a paste of cornstarch and water. Add a drop or two of ammonia. The paste should be of the same thickening as you would use for making gravy. Smear the paste over the entire cloth area and let it dry. As it dries it will turn a yellowish color. Use a vegetable brush, gently but also thoroughly, to brush paste from body.

TO CLEAN COMPOSITION: Another of the many suggestions is to use VASELINE INTENSIVE CARE lotion.

TO GET RID OF "STICKY" VINYL: Go over it with nail polish remover. This from Rua Belle Green. It sure works for her.

TO CLEAN HARD PLASTIC: Yet another suggestion: Use Liquid Wrench. Wipe on and off quickly.

Metal plate holders for holding plates upright can be used to hold plastic or composition in a sitting position.

New and Revised Information

The product "No More Tangles" can be used very successfully to clean old mohair wigs. Remove wig from doll, then spray on the "No More Tangles." Rub wig with soft cloth or pad made of tissues to remove dirt. Also makes the wig easy to comb.

Q tips can be used to clean ears, noses or other hard to clean places. Dip the Q tip in "Jubilee" Kitchen wax cleaner to clean plastic and compo dolls.

Doll shoes can be made out of felt with lace or pearls, etc. for bows.

For Bride dolls: Second hand stores usually have a Bride's dress for sale.

Clean bisque or porcelain with milk and cotton pads.

MAKE RAG DOLLS, stuff with sawdust, paint features with hobby enamels, OMIT HAIR. Dip doll into wax to which 1 teaspoon of powdered alum for each cup of wax has been added. When doll has desired wax look let it cool and harden before gluing hair on or wig. Dolls with stitched joints can be posed while still very warm and let cool for a permanent position. Doll will have a very lovely and different skin tone.

When fragile antique lace needs washing, baste it first to a clean white cotton fabric then wash by hand, dipping gently through warm suds, then rinse well, to remove all soap and dirt. Then lay between layers of a towel and press firmly to nearly dry it.

To put snap fasteners on easily, put all snaps on one side first. Then use a piece of chalk on each fastener and rub against opposite side of material. This will insure your getting the snaps exactly opposite.

For mildew on vinyl use Crisco. It will generally remove it and won't damage the finish.

When gluing wigs on doll heads always use Rubber Cement as it will peel off at a later date without damaging the wig or head.

In combing out old matted doll wigs use a metal dog comb, the kind with the long wire teeth. Divide the hair into small sections by running your fingers through the hair and find the seam circles from the bottom to the top. Then carefully comb out the sections...you will lose some hair...a lot of hair...there is usually too much hair in a wig anyway, proceed until all is combed out. THEN the wig can be washed dipping up and down gently, as not to tangle, in luke warm water suds, use a mild soap. Rinse: recomb when partly dryed and set hair, using curlers and wave lotion. Also Dippety Doo works good. Let dry thoroughly. Comb out and spray with hard hair spray. Put on a net and let dry.

Use Johnson's furniture PASTE WAX and coat composition with it. This not only prevents further cracking or crazing but it also makes your doll sparkle.

Rub a little Johnson's Baby Oil into palms of hands then apply to doll's hair. As you comb or brush the hair will shine.

If you have a glued wig of snythetic shiny type that is sticky to the touch, you can eliminate this by sprinkling Johnson's Baby Powder on it. Then rub the excess out with a towel and brush with a bristle brush. The baby powder acts as a dry shampoo and it will make the doll smell better. After this you can set or style the doll's hair with a slight dampening with water.

How to Use Price Guide

The prices in this book are the retail prices of the dolls, if bought from a dealer. Prices change by demand and supply and doll prices are no different and once in awhile the prices shoot up due to stimulated interest in a particular doll or doll company.

The CONDITION of the doll is uppermost in pricing. An all original and in excellent condition doll will bring top dollar and sometimes more, where one that is dirty or damaged or without original clothes will bring less. The cost of doll repairs has soared and it is wise to judge the damage and estimate the cost of repair before you buy or sell a damaged doll.

An all original means, original clothes and original wigs/hair. This type of doll is what the prices in this book are based on. The prices shown are top dollar prices for excellent and original dolls. IF YOUR DOLL IS LESS THAN ORIGINAL, DISCOUNT FROM THE PRICES SHOWN TO ALLOW FOR CONDITION.

Another factor in pricing is size. For example a 16" Dionne Quint will be worth more than a 7½" one, or a 11" Shirley Temple may be worth a lot more than a 13" one.

No one knows your collection better than yourself and in the end YOU must decide if a certain doll and asking price is worth it. If you don't think so, then you will pass it by.

A PRICE GUIDE IS JUST THAT   A GUIDE

Alexander Doll Co.

For complete information about the Alexander Doll Co. refer to Series I, page 11. The following is a list of some of the most desirable dolls by this company.

1925: Blue Boy, Pinkie (rag)

1933: Alice in Wonderland, Little Women

1935: Little Colonel (often mistaken for Shirley Temple), Jane Withers

1936: Dionne Quints, Five Little Peppers (book: Little Genius), Little Lord Fauntleroy, Doris Kranne in "Romance" (Movie), Geraldine Farrar in Carmen, Pitty Pat and Tippy Toes from Eugene Field's Poem and were of cloth and made in three sizes, Susie and Bobby from a comic strip.

1937: Princess Elizabeth in three sizes, Scarlet O'Hara from "Gone With the Wind," Melanie, Margaret O'Brien, Neva Wet, Tweeny Winkle, Princess Alexander, McGuffey Baby, McGuffey Anna (McGuffey Readers), Snow White, Annie Laurie, Little Shaver (cloth from Elsie Shaver painting), Madelaine du Bain in French 1880 costume (exclusive for F.A.O. Schwartz) reissued 1938-39.

1938: Flora McFlimsey (books by Mariana) re-issued in 1952, Dickens character dolls, Mother and Me, Sonja Henie in three sizes. Re-issued in hard plastic/vinyl in 1951.

1939: Madeline, Jennie Walker

1940: Butch McGuffey, Madeline as a blonde

1941: Lov-Le-Tex dolls

1942: Fairy Princess in four sizes

1943: Southern Girl, in four sizes, Kate Greenway in four sizes, Carmen in six sizes, Bride in five sizes, Baby Genius in five sizes with molded hair, also wigged in three sizes, So Lite Dolls (cloth, wigs of yarn and in five sizes) Special Girl (soft body and cry Mama voice), Country Cousins.

1949: Mary Martin from "Sound of Music"

1951: Clara Belle (Clown from Howdy Doody Show), Portrait Group (two dolls in formal dress with chairs), Slumber Mate, Maggie in three sizes, Violet a fully jointed plastic doll and made in 1952, 53 and 54, Penny (teenager from comics), Christening Baby in three sizes, Sunbeam a new born infant in three sizes, Bonnie a toddler in three sizes, Bitsey in five sizes, Honey Bun in three sizes, Kathy in three sizes, Littlest Cherub, Nina Ballerina in three sizes, Wendy Bride in three sizes, Rosamund Bridesmaid in three sizes.

1952: Tommy Bangs, Stuffy, Cynthia in three sizes

1953: Mary Muslin (pansy eyes that wink), Sunflower (clown with flower eyes and a pompom nose), Ruffles the Clown, Alexander-kins, Quiz Kids, Benny Walker, Story Princess, Glamor dolls, including Queen Elizabeth, Gody period, Edwardian Period, Victorian Period, Blue Danube, Gardian party dress (opera), Snow Baby, Commodore Peary's daughter (1903 dress), Bride

1954: Flower girl, Mary Ellen in three outfits, Bonnie Baby (rooted hair), Christening Baby, Kathy, Bible Character dolls, Nina Ballerina

1955: Romeo & Juliet, McGuffey Anna-re-issued

1957: Cissy, Cissette, Sleeping Beauty, Mary Belle, Kathy Tear, Sheri Lewis, Elise, Lissy, Dumplin

1960: Betty Walks (flirty eyes), Joanie (Joni) 36" & flirty eyes, Little Genius re-issued, Cissette, Portrait series: Bride, Belle of the Ball, Maid of Honor, Creole Beauty, Queen Elizabeth II, Gody Girl

1961: Baby Genius, Wendy, Kitten, Caroline, Jacqueline, Timmie, Mary Sunshine, Madeline, Little Lady, Betty Talks, Maggie Mix-up, Mimi (30"), Pollyanna

1965: Leslie, Katie (12"), Baby Ellen

1966: Laurie, Sound of Music, Little Orphan Annie (with poem by James Whitcomb Riley), Pussy Cat, Alice in Wonderland re-issued, Sweet Tears, Children around the World, USA, Ballerina Girl, Granny, Bride, Scarlett, Amish Boy & Girl.

Due to the continuing cost rise in making dolls, the Alexander dolls have cut some of the quality from the clothes as well as the dolls themselves and since 1974, the 8" dolls no longer have "bend knees."

Alexander Bi-centennial dolls will be released in 1976. Madame Alexander chose the 6 First Ladies to be issued: **Martha Washington, Dolly Madison, Abigail Adams, Martha Randolph, Elizabeth Monroe and Louisa Adams.**

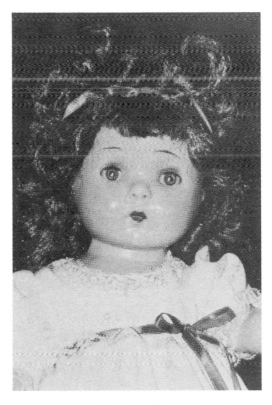

Alexander--19" "Betty." All composition. Blue sleep eyes (also came with brown eyes), Eyeshadow. Marks: None. Had paper tag on front of dress: Betty/Madame Alexander. 1935. $75.00. (Courtesy Karen Penner)

1

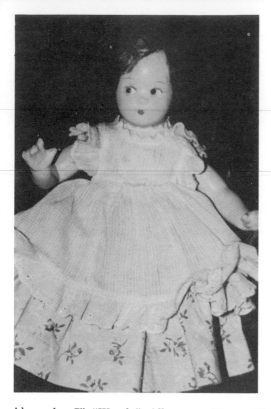

Dionne Quint Prices

7½" baby with molded hair. $200.00 set. Each $25.00.
7½" baby with wigs. $225.00 set. $28.00 each.
8" Toddler with molded hair. $200.00 set. $25.00 each.
8" Toddler with wigs. $225.00 set. $28.00 each.
11" Baby with molded hair. $75.00.
11" Toddler with wig. $75.00.
14" Toddler, wig and sleep eyes. $85.00.
16" Toddler, wig and sleep eyes. $85.00.
17" Toddler, wig and sleep eyes. $85.00.
17" Toddler, wig and sleep eyes. $85.00.
17" Cloth body, baby legs, with molded hair and sleep eyes. $95.00.
19" Toddler, wig and sleep eyes. $95.00.
20" Toddler, wig and sleep eyes. $95.00.
23" Toddler, wig and sleep eyes. $100.00.
24" All stuffed pink stockinette body and limbs. Molded felt face mask. Painted features. $125.00.

Alexander--7" "Wendy" All composition with dark brown mohair wig. Painted blue eyes. Painted on white socks/black shoes. Bent right arm. Dress is red roses on yellow with white pinafore. Marks: Mme/Alexander, on back. Madame Alexander, etc. on tag. 1936. $35.00. (Courtesy Pat Raiden)

Alexander--Set of all original 8" toddlers. $200.00 set.

ALEXANDER

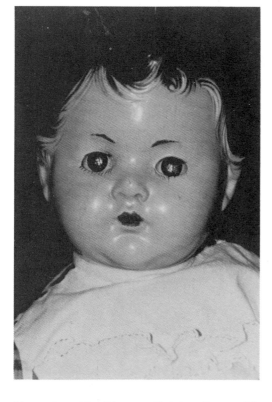

Alexander--17" Dionne Quint. Composition shoulder plate with jointed neck. Cloth body with composition bent baby legs. Original tagged dress. Marks: Alexander, on head. $95.00. (Courtesy Alice Capps)

Alexander--8" "Wendy Ann" All composition. All original. 1936. $35.00. (Courtesy Jay Minter)

2

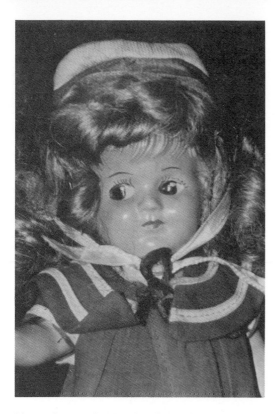

Alexander--8½" "Little Colonel" All composition. Painted brown eyes. Wig over molded hair (hair pushed back to see bangs). Original. Marks: Tag: Picture as on "Little Colonel" Book/Trademark/Little Colonel/Alexander Doll Co./New York. 1936. $55.00. (Courtesy Marge Meisinger)

Alexander--Full view of "Little Colonel" 8½". Original. 1936. (Courtesy Marge Meisinger)

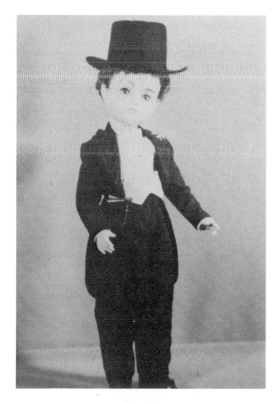

Alexander--21" "Prince Phillip" All composition. Blue sleep eyes. All original. Tagged clothes. $95.00.

Alexander--23" "Pinkie" Cloth and composition. Blue sleep eyes. All original. 1937. $65.00. (Courtesy Mrs. J.C. Houston)

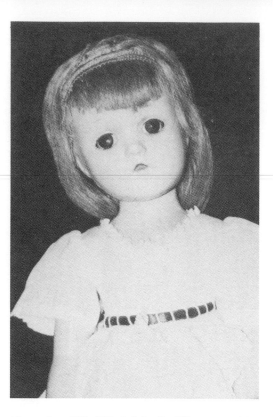

Alexander--14" "Madelaine" All composition. Brown sleep eyes/lashes. Painted lashes below eyes only. Eyeshadow. Blue skirt with roses. Pink top. Marks: Mme Alexander, on head. Tag: Madelaine/Madame Alexander, etc. 1939. $85.00. (Courtesy Marie Ernst)

Alexander--17" "Madelaine" All composition. Brown sleep eyes/lashes. Eyeshadow. Blonde human hair wig worn off. Lashes below eyes only. White dress/red ribbon trim. Knee length pantaloons. Hoop skirt. Marks: Mme Alexander, on head. Tag: Madelaine/Madame Alexander. 1940. $75.00. (Courtesy Marie Ernst)

Alexander--21" "Bride" All composition. Tag: Created by/Madame Alexander. 1941. $75.00. (Courtesy Marie Ernst)

Alexander--14" "Sonja Henie" Shown in original ski clothes. $75.00. (Courtesy Jay Minter)

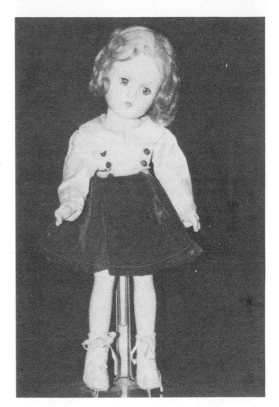

Alexander--14" "Sonja Henie" Closed mouth version. All composition and all original. 1942. $65.00. (Courtesy Jay Minter)

Alexander--14" & 9" "Mother & Me" All composition. Mother: Blue sleep eyes. Me: Brown painted eyes to side. Gowns are blue. Marks: Madame Alexander. 1942-43. $125.00 set. (Courtesy Jay Minter)

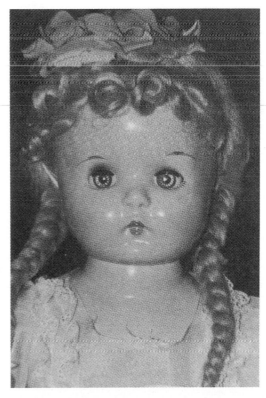

Alexander--23" "Special Girl" All composition with cloth body. Blue sleep eyes. Straight long legs. Marks: None. 1942. $85.00. (Courtesy Marie Ernst)

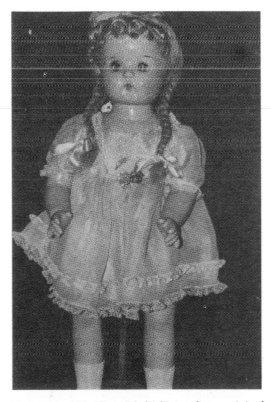

Alexander--23" "Special Girl" to show original clothes. 1942. (Courtesy Marie Ernst)

5

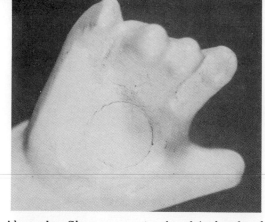

Alexander--Shows magnets placed in hands of the Miss Victory doll by F.O.A. Swartz Co.

Alexander--20" "Miss Victory" All composition. Blue sleep eyes. Magnets in hands. Red skirt/white top with blue trim. Marks: Princess Elizabeth/Alexander Doll Co., on head. Tag: Madame Alexander/New York, etc. Replaced wig. 1944. $90.00 (Courtesy Marie Ernst)

Alexander--24" "Maggie Walker" All hard plastic walker, head turns. Blue sleep eyes. Original red satin dress. Shoes not original. Marks: Alexander, on head. Tagged clothes. $45.00.

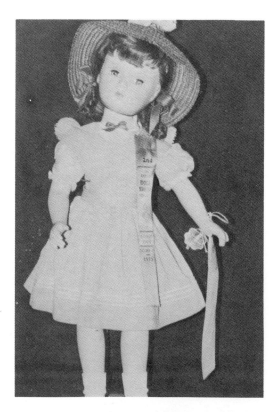

Alexander--21" "Margaret O'Brien" All composition. Original. 1946. $185.00. (Courtesy Barbara Coker)

Alexander--This is a movie still of Hedy Lamarr. Refer to the color photo of the doll made for the 1949 movie Samson & Delilah, although this is an unconfirmed, by Alexander, doll.

Alexander--15" "Amy of Little Women" All hard plastic. Original. 1948. $60.00. Complete set $275.00. (Courtesy Sally Bethscheider)

Alexander--Shows back hair view of the 1948 Amy.

Alexander--17" "Bride" All hard plastic with dark skin tones. Dark red glued on wig. Blue sleep eyes. Original clothes. Marks: Alexander, on head. ca. 1950. $40.00

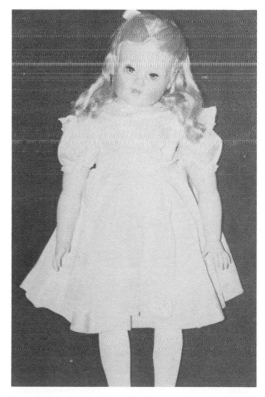

Alexander--29" "Alice in Wonderland" Stuffed vinyl with blue sleep eyes. Original. Marks: Alexander, on head. Tag: Alice in Wonderland/ By Madame Alexander. 1951. $115.00. (Courtesy Mae Teters)

7

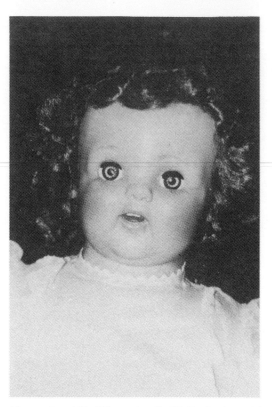

Alexander--15" "Margot Ballerina" All hard plastic. Blue sleep eyes. Orange hair. 1952. $55.00. (Courtesy Jay Minter)

Alexander--18" "Honeybun" Cloth body with vinyl limbs and head. Glued on Saran wig. Open/closed mouth with two inserted upper teeth. Cryer in lower back. Blue sleep eyes. Marks: Tag: Madame Alexander, etc. 1952. $42.00. (Courtesy Bessie Carson)

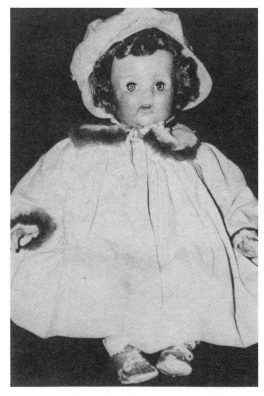

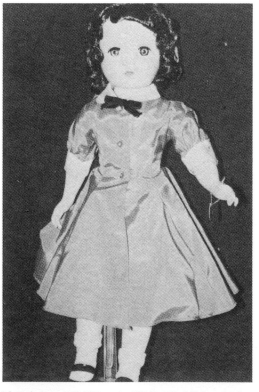

Alexander--18" "Honeybun" Shows original coat/bonnet, both are yellow with real fur trim on collar and cuffs. (Courtesy Bessie Carson)

Alexander--17" "Maggie Walker" All hard plastic. Brown sleep eyes. Red dress. Tag: Fashion Academy/Mme/Alexander/Award. 1953. $45.00 (Courtesy Jay Minter)

Alexander--8" "Jo" All hard plastic. One on right is a walker. Left one earlier than other. $45.00. (Courtesy Jay Minter)

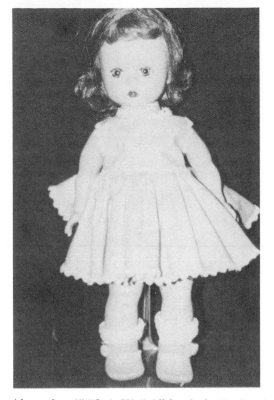

Alexander--8" "Quiz-Kin" All hard plastic. Bend knees. Has knob in back that makes head move. 1954. $55.00. (Courtesy Jay Minter)

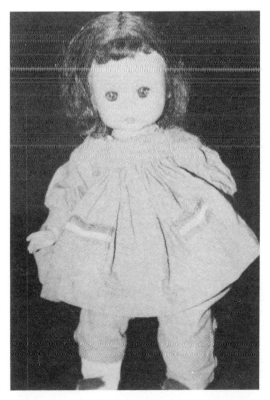

Alexander--8" "Madelaine" All hard plastic. Bend knees. Tag: Madelaine/Madame Alexander, etc. 1954. $35.00. (Courtesy Jay Minter)

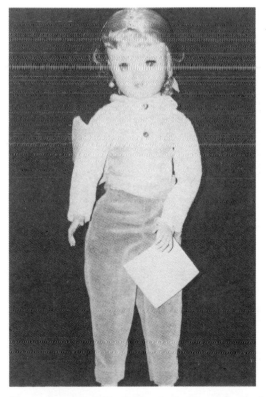

Alexander--16" "Elise" Hard plastic with vinyl oversleeve arms and jointed at the elbows. Original. 1957. $45.00. (Courtesy Jay Minter)

9

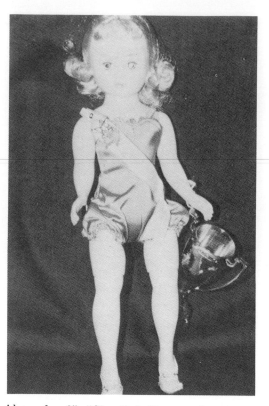

Alexander--8" "Maggie Mix Up" All hard plastic. Blue sleep eyes. Freckles. Usually came with green eyes. 1960. $55.00. (Courtesy Jay Minter)

Alexander--9" "Cissette" Beauty Queen. All hard plastic. Jointed knees. Bluish grey outfit. Yellow-gold band with gold eagle emblem. Gold cup. 1961. $40.00 (Courtesy Jay Minter)

Alexander--8" "Scotland" All hard plastic with straight legs. Green sleep eyess. 1961 to date. This one is 1974. Currently available. (Courtesy Marie Ernst)

Alexander--8" "Italian" Bend knees. 1961 to date. $18.00. (Courtesy Marie Ernst)

Alexander--8" "Italy" Variation of costume. Bend knees. 1961. $18.00. (courtesy Jay Minter)

Alexander--8" "Tyrolean Girl" Hard plastic. Bend knees. 1962-1973. In 1974 this became "Austria." $18.00. (Courtesy Jay Minter)

Alexander--12" "Pamela" Plastic and vinyl. Blue sleep eyes. Came with change of wigs that attach with a velour strip. 1962. $60.00 (Courtesy Jay Minter)

Alexander--12" "Smarty" Orange/red rooted hair. Blue sleep eyes. Open/closed mouth. Marks: Alexander/1962, on head. Tag: Smarty/ Madame Alexander. Original. $35.00.

11

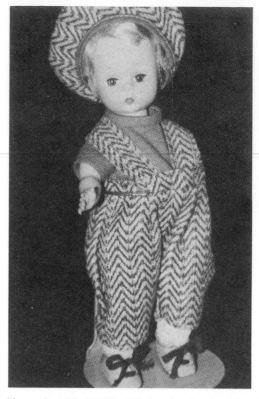

Alexander--8" "Bill" All hard plastic. Bend knees. 1963. $45.00. (Courtesy Jay Minter)

Alexander--11" "Smarty & Baby" All original. Baby is Hong Kong plastic. Blue sleep eyes. 1963. $45.00. (Courtesy Jay Minter)

Alexander--8" "Irish" Bend knees. 1964 to date. $18.00. (Courtesy Marie Ernst)

Alexander--8" "Irish" Has different shawl. Bend knees. 1964. $18.00. (Courtesy Jay Minter)

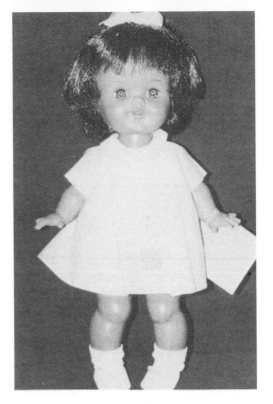

Alexander--12" "Janie" Black rooted hair. Blue sleep eyes. Freckles. Marks: Alexander/1964, on head. Tag: Janie/created by/Madame Alexander. Original. $35.00.

Alexander--11" Plastic and vinyl. Open/closed mouth. Tag: Madame Alexander, etc. 1964. $32.00. (Courtesy Jay Minter)

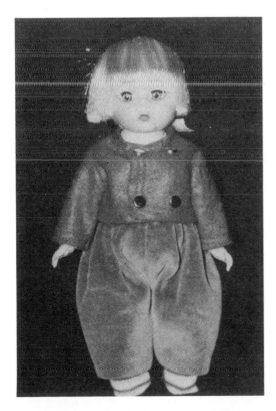

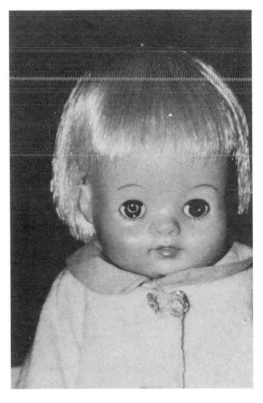

Alexander--8" "Dutch Boy" Hard plastic. Bend knees. 1964. $30.00 (Courtesy Jay Minter)

Alexander--7" "Littlest Kitten" All vinyl. Blue sleep eyes. Marks: Alex. Doll Co., on head. 1963-64. $25.00. (Courtesy Alice Capps)

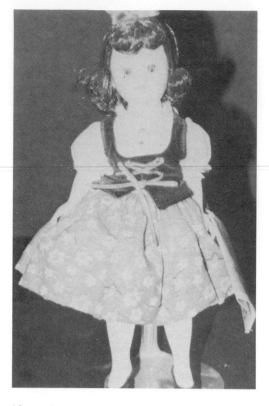

Alexander--9" "Brigetta" Of Sound and Music.
1965. $45.00. (Courtesy Jay Minter)

Alexander--8" "Gretl" of Sound of Music. 1965.
$35.00. (Courtesy Jay Minter)

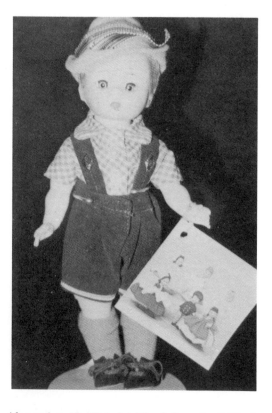

Alexander--9" "Lissl" of Sound of Music. 1965.
$35.00. (Courtesy Jay Minter)

Alexander--8" "Friedrich" of Sound of Music.
1965. $35.00. (Courtesy Jay Minter)

Alexander--8" "Miss Muffet" Hard plastic. Bend knees. 1965. $18.00. (Courtesy Jay Minter)

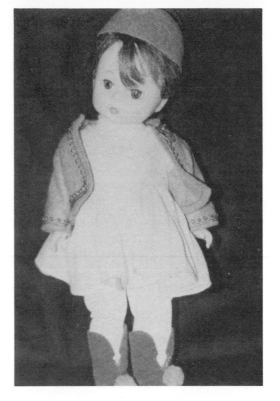

Alexander--8" "Greek Boy" Hard plastic. Bend knees. 1965 to 1968. $50.00. (Courtesy Jay Minter)

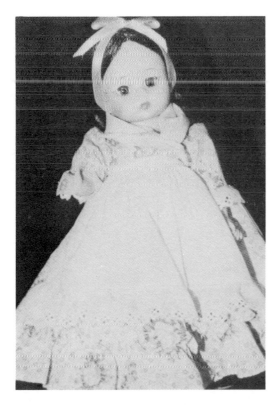

Alexander-8" "Argentine Girl" Hard plastic. Bend knees. 1965. Discontinued 1972. $35.00. (Courtesy Jay Minter)

Alexander--8" "Mary, Mary" Hard plastic. Bend knees. 1965. $18.00. (Courtesy Jay Minter)

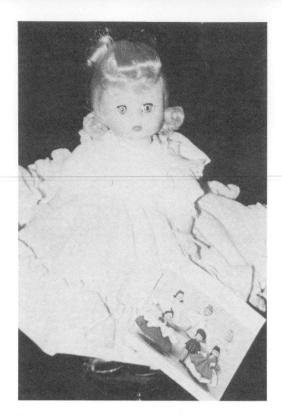

Alexander--8" Newer "Mary, Mary" Hard plastic. Bend knees. $18.00. (Courtesy Jay Minter)

Alexander--8" Newer "Amy" of Little Women. Hard plastic. Bend knees. $18.00. (Courtesy Jay Minter)

Alexander--8" Older "Meg" of Little Women. Hard plastic. Bend knees. $25.00. (Courtesy Jay Minter)

Alexander--17" "Elise Bride" 1966. $35.00. (Courtesy Marie Ernst)

Alexander--17" "Leslie" Bride. 1966. $50.00.
(Courtesy Marie Ernst)

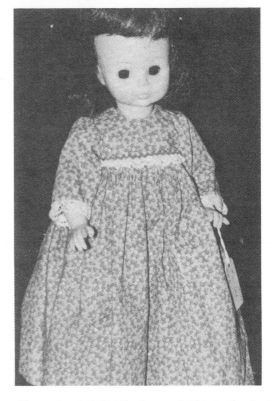

Alexander--14" "Little Granny" This is the first
"Granny." Black eyes. Plastic and vinyl.
Original. Tag: Little Granny/Madame Alexan
der. 1966. $45.00. (Courtesy Marie Ernst)

Alexander--8" "German" Bend knees. 1966 to
date. $18.00. (Courtesy Marie Ernst)

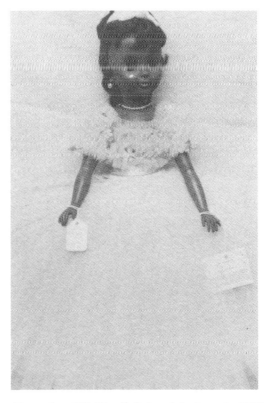

Alexander--17" "Leslie" In pink formal. 1967.
$50.00. (Courtesy Marie Ernst)

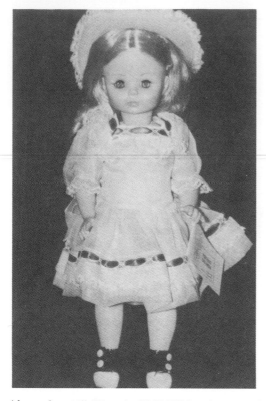

Alexander--14" "Renoir Girl" White dress with red trim. 1967. $55.00. (Courtesy Jay Minter)

Alexander--8" "Canada" All hard plastic with un-jointed knees. 1968 to date. Currently available. (Courtesy Marie Ernst)

Alexander--8" "Portugal" Bend knees. 1968 to date. $18.00. (Courtesy Marie Ernst)

Alexander--8" "Korea" Bend knees. With "Maggie" face. Eyes are partly closed. 1968. Discontinued 1970. $45.00. (Courtesy Marie Ernst)

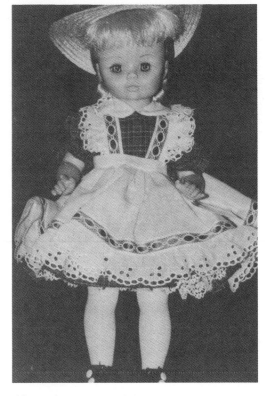

Alexander--17" "Leslie" In blue formal. 1968. $50.00. (Courtesy Marie Ernst)

Alexander--14" "McGuffey Ana" 1968. $45.00. (Courtesy Marie Ernst)

Alexander--8" "Vietnam" Bend knees. 1968. Discontinued 1969. $45.00. (Courtesy Marie Ernst)

Alexander--8" "Turkey" With bend knees. 1968 to date. $18.00. (Courtesy Marie Ernst)

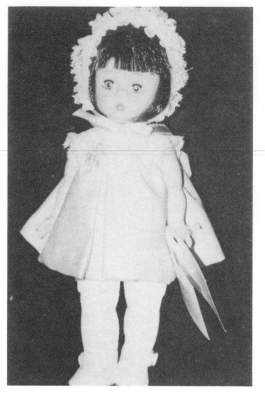

Alexander--8" "Easter" Hard plastic. Bend knees. 1968 only. $60.00. (Courtesy Jay Minter)

Alexander--8" "Greece" All hard plastic. Bend knees. 1968 to date. $18.00. (Courtesy Jay Minter)

Alexander--8" "Morocco" All hard plastic. Bend knees. 1968 to 1970. $45.00. (Courtesy Jay Minter)

Alexander--10" "Melinda" Jointed knees. Bright blue taffeta with white lace and trim. White straw hat with flowers. Tag: Gold paper tag over regular one: Melinda/By Madame Alexander. 1969. $50. (Courtesy Peggy Boudreau)

Alexander--21", 14" and 11" "Jenny Lind" All in pink. 1969. 21" $125.00; 14" $50.00; 11" $65.00. (Courtesy Marie Ernst)

Alexander--8" "Indonesia" Bend knees. 1970 to date. $18.00. (Courtesy Marie Ernst)

Alexander--14" "Sleeping Beauty" Long curly hair. Plastic and vinyl. 1971. $35.00.

Alexander--21" "Melanie" 1971. $125.00. (Courtesy Jay Minter)

Alexander--21" "Cornelia" 1972. $125.00.
(Courtesy Jay Minter)

Alexander--21" "Gainsboro" In blue with over-
lace. 1972. $125.00. (Courtesy Marie Ernst)

Alexander--8" "Czechoslavakia" Hard plastic.
Bend knees. 1972. $18.00. (Courtesy Jay Minter)

Alexander--8" "Belgium" Hard plastic. Bend
knees. 1972. $18.00. (Courtesy Jay Minter)

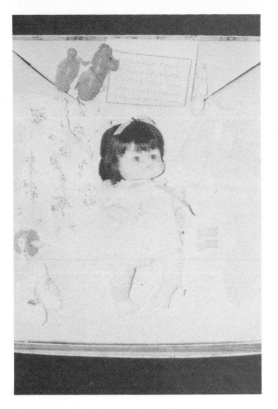

Alexander--9" "Sweet Tears" All vinyl. Open mouth/nurser. Discontinued in 1973. $25.00. (Courtesy Jay Minter)

Alexander--21" "Renoir" 1973. $125.00.

Alexander--8" "United States" Hard plastic. Straight legs. 1974. Some first issues had misspelled tags that read "Untied States." Most were recalled. Currently available. (Courtesy Jay Minter)

Alexander--21" "Melanie" Red and white. 1974. $125.00. (Courtesy Marie Ernst)

23

Alexander--21" "Cornelia" In blue with black trim. 1974. $125.00. (Courtesy Marie Ernst)

Alexander--14" "Pinky" Plastic and vinyl Blue sleep eyes. 1975. Currently available. (Courtesy Phyllis Houston)

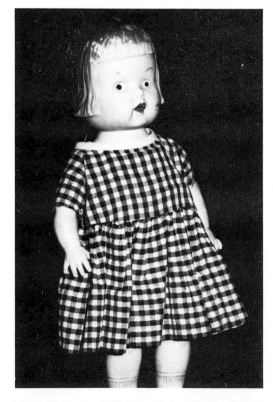

Allied Doll Co.--10" "Wendy" All vinyl with molded hair. Painted features. One piece body, arms and legs. Molded on shoes and socks. Marks: Allied Grand Doll/Mfg. Co. Inc. 1958. $3.00.

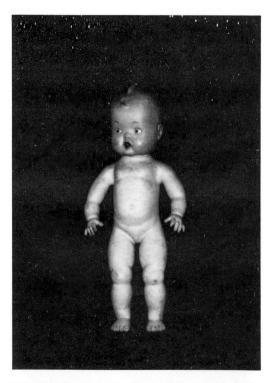

Allied Doll Co.--11" One piece vinyl body. Painted blue to side eyes. Molded hair, topknot with hole for ribbon. Marks: Allied Grand Doll/ Mfg. Inc. 1958. Large "A," on backside. $3.00. (Courtesy Carolyn Powers)

Shows an all original "Little Colonel" Shirley Temple. (Courtesy Marge Meisinger)

14" "Miss Teenage America"--Pageant Doll. Plastic body and legs. Vinyl arms and head. Painted features. High heel feet. Marks: 3426/Kaystan Co./1972/Hong Kong, on back. Original. Medal says: Miss Teenage America. (Courtesy Marie Ernst)

11½" "Walking Jamie"--Brown decal eyes/lashes. Red hair, but came in various colors. Fuzzy, wired poodle. Felt nose and tongue. Plastic eyes. Marks: 1967 Mattel Inc/U.S. Patented/Pat'd Canada 1967/Other Pats. Pend/Japan. Dog is unmarked. (Courtesy Bessie Carson)

 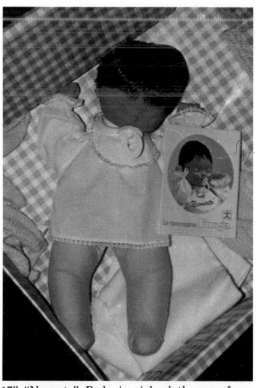

19" "Baby Dawn"--Early vinyl head. Latex one piece body. Brown sleep eyes/lashes. Open/closed mouth with molded tongue. Beautiful modeled ears. Marks: Uneeda, on head. 1953. (Courtesy Bessie Carson)

17" "Neonato"--Body is pink cloth over foam. Vinyl gauntlet hands. Vinyl head. Not a nurser but comes with a pacifier. Marks: Furga, in square/122ol. (Courtesy Virginia Jones)

Allied Doll Co.--10½" "Bonnie Buttons" All vinyl with blue sleep eyes. Open/closed mouth. All original. Marks: 39AE 1 A, on head. 1964. $6.00. (Courtesy Marie Ernst)

Allied Doll Co.--10" "Susan" Plastic body, arms and legs. Vinyl head with rooted dark brown hair. Blue sleep eyes. Original clothes. Marks: No. 2112, on head. Made in Hong Kong, on back. Box: Susan/1967 Allied Doll & Toy Corp $1.00.

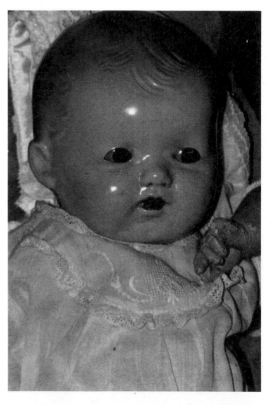

Allied Doll Co.--22½" "Valerie" White version in Name Doll/Mfg. Unknown section of Vol. I, page 230. Also sold as "Meri" in a 19" version in 1970 and came with a 15 pc. "mod" wardrobe. Marks: KT, on head. Made by Allied Doll. Same mold (different marks) used by P&M Sales as "Belinda." See Vol. I, page 237. $7.00.

For complete information on the American Character Doll Co. refer to Series I, page 34. American Character--13" "Toddle Petite" Composition head. Rocker sleep eyes. Open/closed mouth. No eyebrows. Molded yellow hair. Rubber body, fully jointed. Tag: Petite/Doll/Toddle. ca. 1936. $38.00. (Courtesy Marie Ernst)

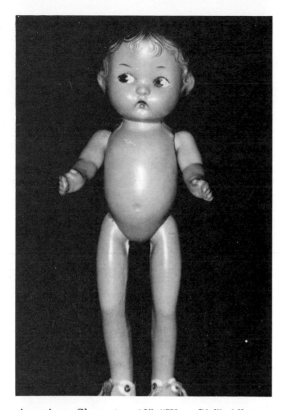

American Character--10" "Wee Girl" All composition. Painted brown eyes. Molded, painted black hair. Marks: Noen. 1940. $20.00. (Courtesy Mary Partridge)

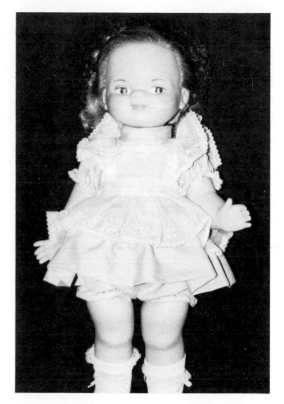

American Character--23" "Chuckles" All vinyl with elastic strung legs. Painted brown eyes with molded lashes and lids. Also came with painted blue eyes. Marks: Amer. Doll & Toy Co/ 1961. $40.00. (Courtesy Barbara Coker)

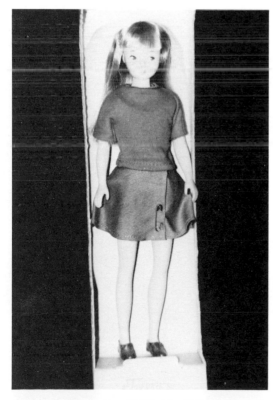

American Character--9" "Cricket" Tressy's little cousin. Sold as a Sears exclusive, later when sold as "little sister," she had the grow hair. Original olive green skirt. Red sweater (snaps on back) with green piping at neck and sleeves. Brown tennis type shoes. Marks: Amer. Char./ Inc/1961, on head. $10.00. (Courtesy Bessie Carson)

American Character--Grow hair Tressy shown in "Miss American Character" outfit. White dress with two large pink flowers. Red roses and silver cup. Pearl tiara. Navy Blue streamer says "Miss American." 1963. $12.00. (Courtesy Bessie Carson)

27

16½" "Patsy Joan"--All composition and all original. 1946. Marks: Effanbee, on back. Tag: This is/Patsy Joan/The Lovable Imp/With Tiltable Head/and Movable Limbs/an Effanbee Durable Doll. (Courtesy Frances & Mary Jane Anicello)

17" "Hedy Lamarr"--All hard plastic. Black Saran hair, curls drop down neck. Not original clothes. Doll was to have been issued with the 1949 movie "Samson & Delilah." Not confirmed by Alexander Doll Co. Refer to the Alexander section for a photo of Hedy Lamarr. (Courtesy Bessie Greeno)

16" "Robbi"--An original doll by artist Judi Kahn. Won a Blue ribbon in competition at Rockford, Ill. in 1973.

9" "School Girl"--All felt with jointed shoulders and hips. Mohair wig. Painted features. Tag: Old Cottage/Doll/Hand Made/In/Great Britain. (Courtesy Marge Meisinger)

12" "Batgirl"--All vinyl with same body as posable Tammy. Green eyes/shadow. Marks: 1965/ Ideal Toy Corp./W-12-3, on head. 1965/Ideal, in oval/2 M-12, on hip. (Courtesy Lisa Lineberger)

8" "Capt. Kirk" (William Shatner) and "Mr. Spock" (Leonard Nimoy). Action figures by Mego Corp. 1975.

8" "Mr. Scot" (Scotty), "Dr. McCoy (DeForest Kelley) and "Klingon" (Kang* Michael Ansara). Action figures by Mego Corp. 1975. All are marked 1974 Paramount/Pict. Corp. on head and have MCMLXXI on the back.

American Character--13" "Pouty Miss Marie" Plastic body and legs. Vinyl arms and head. Black pupiless sleep eyes to the side in "googly" fashion. Marks: Amer. Char. Inc./1965, on head. $20.00. (Courtesy Bessie Carson)

American Character--13" "Marie Lee" Plastic body and legs. Vinyl arms and head. Sleep eyes that change from blue to light brown, depending on light direction. Original. Marks: 3/American Character/1966, on head. $20.00. (Courtesy Jayn Allen)

American Character--13" "Marie Ann" Plastic body and legs. Vinyl arms and head. Dark red hair. Blue sleep eyes/lashes. Marks: American Character/1966, on head. $20.00. (Courtesy Jayn Allen)

American Character--8" "Little Joe Cartright" All rigid vinyl with molded clothes. Marks: Portugal, on back. Little Joe was played by Michael Landon. $35.00.

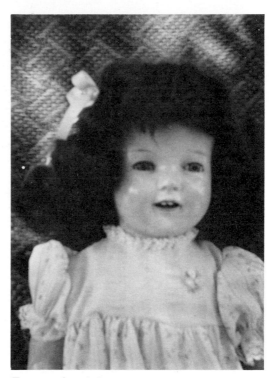

Amsco--12" "Buffy" (T.V. series) Make up and hairdressing head. Marks: 1971/Amsco Ind. Inc. Hopefully "Buffy" will look like this as a young woman, as the head is much too old looking for a child star. $35.00. (Courtesy Phyllis Houston)

For complete information on the Arranbee Doll Co. refer to Series I, page 43.

Arranbee--23" "Nancy" Cloth with composition shoulderhead. Narrowed blue tin sleep eyes. Molded hair under wig. Open mouth/2 teeth. Marks: Fiberoid, on head. Arranbee, on body. $40.00. (Courtesy Flacks)

Arranbee--12" "Nancy" All composition. Jointed arms and legs. Painted hair and eyes. Original clothes and trunk. Marks: Nancy, on back. 1930-1936. $32.00. (Maish Collection)

Arranbee--19" Cloth with composition head, arms and legs. Blue sleep eyes. Original. Box marked Salesman Sample. 1937. $30.00 (Courtesy Jay Minter)

31

14" "Snuffy Smith"--All cloth with nylon pressed face mask. Removable clothes. Painted features. Felt ears and sewn on shoes. Tag: This is an original comic strip doll that all America loves. Copyright King Features Syndicate Inc. By Columbia Toy Products/Kansas City, Missouri. (Courtesy Virginia Jones)

19" "Capt. Kangaroo"--Cloth stuffed with vinyl head and painted features. Marks: 1961 Robt. Keeshan/Assoc. Inc. (Courtesy Shirley Puertzer)

One of the most desirable of the Barbie early clothes. The Candy Striper. (Courtesy Bessie Carson)

17" "Simona"--All vinyl. Had long inset lashes. Marks: Furga, Italy. 1968. (Courtesy Virginia Jones)

Arranbee--16½" "Miss International" All composition with blue sleep eyes. Open mouth/four upper teeth. Marks: Design/Pat. Pend., on head. Came with four outfits, Swiss, American, Mexican, and Dutch. 1938. $35.00. (Courtesy Mary Partridge)

Arranbee--26" "Baby Nancy" Composition head with 3/4 composition arms and legs. Deep blue-green sleep eyes. Open mouth with two upper and lower teeth. Marks: Arranbee. 1939. $40.00. (Courtesy Flacks)

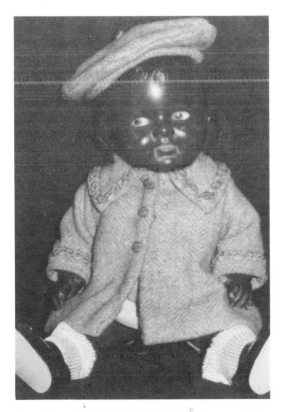

Arranbee--14" "Bessie Toddler" All composition. Fully jointed. Painted side glancing eyes. Closed mouth. Dimpled cheeks. Molded hair with three outfits of silk hair. Marks: R&B on head. 1940. $35.00.

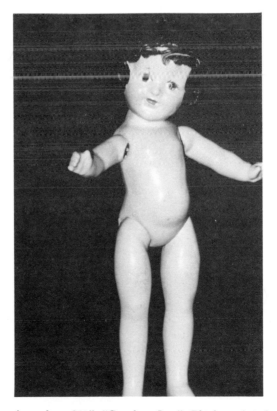

Arranbee--8½" "Carolyn Lee" Black painted molded hair. Smile/closed mouth. 5 year old played in Virginia with Fred McMurray and Madelaine Carroll. 1941. Arranbee also produced sets of five labeled "Quint." Doll also used for "Round World" series. Marks: R&B/Doll Co., on backs. $22.00. (Courtesy Marie Ernst)

Arranbee--15" "Happy Time" Hard plastic head. Glued on mohair wig over molded hair. Rocker blue sleep tin eyes. Cloth body, composition arms and legs. Marks: R&B/250, on head. ca. late 1940's. $10.00

Arranbee--18" "Swiss Girl" All composition. Blue sleep eyes/lashes. Original. Doll by Arranbee. Tag: National Mission/Gift Shop/156 Fifth Ave/N.Y.C. 1946. $38.00. (Courtesy Marie Ernst)

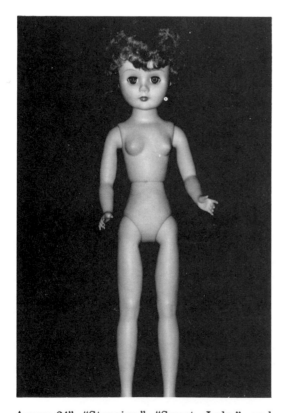

34

Arrow--24" "Stunning," "Sweet Judy," and "Marlene" Excellent quality rigid vinyl. Jointed waist. Softer vinyl head. Blue sleep eyes. Painted fingernails and toes. Marks: ◇ 55. Some are marked and some were used by Premium Doll Offer Companies. Refer to Volume I, page 227. $30. (Courtesy Bessie Carson)

Arrow--24" "Marlene" Dress. Also sold in 1957 by Alden's as "Shirtwaist Sally."

Averill--13½" All cloth with pressed face mask. Lashes are set in a slit. Felt coat, cotton dress. ca. 1940's. $65.00. (Courtesy Phyllis Houston)

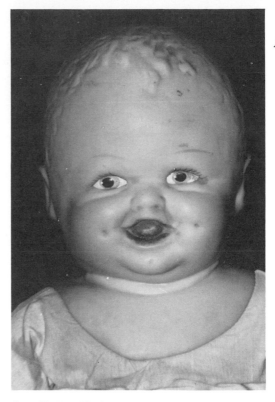

Averill--20" Cloth body and legs. Early vinyl guantlet hands and head with vinyl sew to cloth at neck. Painted blue eyes. Open/closed mouth with molded tongue. Averill. 1945. $55.00. (Courtesy Virginia Jones)

Azark-Hamway--12" "Kit Carson" Plastic body and legs. Vinyl arms and head. Jointed knees and waist. Marks: Hong Kong, on head and back. Made by Azark-Hamway in 1973 for 1974 market. Still available in some areas.

Teen--11½" "Calamity Jane" Jointed waist. Posable hollow legs. Painted blue eyes/lashes. Pink lips. Brown skin tones. Made by Azark-Hamway. 1973. Marks: Hong Kong, on head and body. Still available in some areas.

35

Baby Berry--18" "Christopher Robin" Stuffed orange cloth body. Pink cloth arms and legs. Vinyl head with molded orange hair. Painted blue eyes. Marks: None. $30.00. (Courtesy Margaret Biggers)

Bauer & Black--21" "Miss Curity" All composition. Blue sleep eyes. Original. 1946. $35.00. (Courtesy Marge Meisinger)

Belle--22" "Perfect Companion" Walker, head turns. Hard plastic with vinyl head. Rooted red hair. Blue sleep eyes. Jointed knees. Arms positioned to go no higher than shoulder. Marks: AE/553. 1953. $7.00.

Belle--19" "Ballerina Belle" Hard plastic arms and legs. Jointed knees and ankles. Walker, head turns. Vinyl head and arms. Rooted blonde hair. Sleep eyes. Marks: AE/200/21. 1956. $8.00.

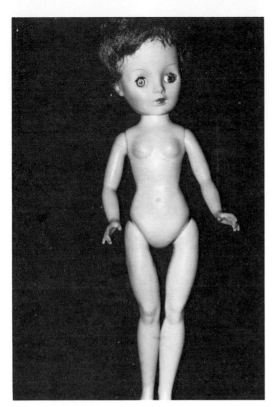

Belle--14" Plastic disc jointed legs. Marks: 15 BAL HH, on lower back. 1957. $4.00.

Belle--8" "Baby Gem" All vinyl with blue sleep eyes. Lashes under eyes only. Open mouth/nurser. 1956. Came dressed in baby dress reflecting the birthstones of the year, also had a glass stone of the same color tied to the arm. Marks: None. 1958. $4.00.

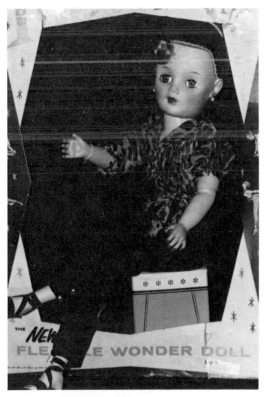

Belle--19" "Twixie, The Twisting Pixie" Hard plastic with vinyl head and vinyl arms that are jointed at the elbow. Jointed waist with series of raised dots all around bottom half. Jointed knees and ankles. High heel feet. Original. Marks: P-16, on head. 1958. $20.00. (Courtesy Edith De-Angelo)

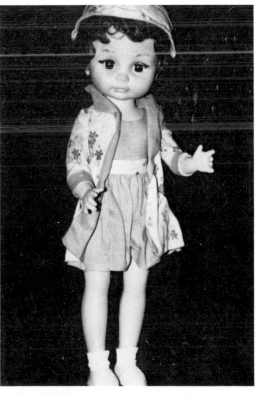

Belle--14" "Melinda" All plastic with vinyl head. Black sleep eyes with black eyeshadow. Rooted brown hair. Staples on hat and removable clothes. All original. 1961. $5.00. (Courtesy Marie Ernst)

37

Blumberg--15" "Sally" All vinyl with blue sleep eyes/lashes. Sold with suitcase/clothes. Marks: 26/AE, on head. 1958.

Camay--15" "Trease" All soft polifoam. Rooted blonde hair. Blue sleep eyes. Original dress. Marks: Made in Taiwan, in a circle/15/10, on head. 15/Made In Taiwan, on back. 1969. $4.00.

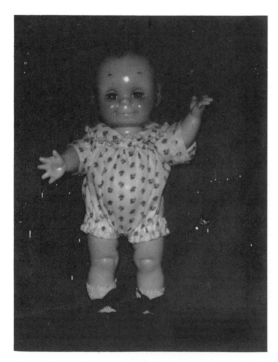

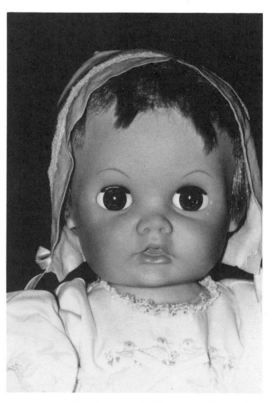

For information on the Cameo Doll Co. refer to Series I, page 57.

38

Cameo--16" All Hard plastic. Sleep eyes. ca. 1952. $75.00. (Courtesy Adele Gioscia)

Cameo--20" "Baby Mine" Sleep eyed version. Open/closed mouth. Molded tongue. All vinyl body that is the same as Miss Peeps and jointed the same. Marks: Cameo, on head and back. $50.00. (Courtesy Alice Capps)

Carlson Dolls--7½" "George Washington" Very good quality hard plastic head. Jointed shoulders and neck. Blue sleep eyes/molded lashes. Excellent clothes. Marks: None. Tag: Carlson/Dolls/A Collector's Item. Not An Ordinary toy. Manufactured/With the Founders of America In/Mind to Keep/Americans Aware of Our Heritage. (Courtesy Edith DeAngelo)

Charm--4" Half doll of hard plastic with blue sleep eyes. Hoop skirt is over a wire frame that is a lamp. Marks: Charm Lamps/Rock Island, Ill. $4.00. (Courtesy Marie Ernst)

Cloth--18" "Crib Mate" Buckram face mask. Large googly eyes/paper discs. Tuffs of mohair. Chenille body. Tag: Thompkin Co./1939. $5.00.

Cloth--23½" "Scarecrow" From the Wizard of Oz. All stuffed cloth/"gunny-sack" face. Tag: Knickerbocker. 1939. $65.00. (Courtesy Donna Stanley)

39

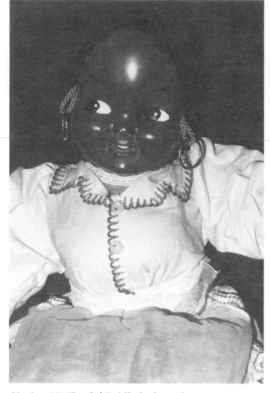

Cloth--18" "Beulah" All cloth with buckram face mask. Painted features. Yarn hair. Bust made of "yarn dust." Dimples. Original. Marks: It's the Beulah/Doll/Mfd by Juro Novelty Co. ca. 1940. $50.00. (Courtesy Virginia Jones)

Cloth--16" "Honey Lou, the Airforce Colonel" Cloth with pressed face mask. Dimples. Original. Tag: Honey Lou/A Gund Product. Other side: J. Swedlin, Inc. 1943. $30.00. (Courtesy Marge Meisinger)

Cloth--16" "Poncho" (Of Cisco Kid, Played by Leo Carrillo). Cloth with highly painted buckram face mask. Hat missing. ca. 1944. $75.00. (Courtesy Kimport Dolls)

Leo Carrillo who was famous for his roles as "Pancho" of the Cisco Kid series of movies. His was a much loved man in Hollywood and Santa Barbara, California.

Cloth--15½" "Little Lulu" Cloth with pressed face and felt clothes. Tag: Georgene Novelties Inc./Corp. 1944/Marjorie H. Buell. $45.00. (Courtesy Marge Meisinger)

Cloth--23" All stuffed cloth with plastic face mask. Marks: None. $3.00.

Cloth--6" Yarn and cloth Indian. From the collection of 5-year old Angie Landers.

Cloth--10½" "Papa Bear," 9" "Mama Bear," 6½" "Baby Bear" & 6½" "Goldilocks" All cloth, printed. Do it yourself kind that are sold in kits. $4.00 set.

Cloth--23" "Desmond" & 20" "Rhoda" (Short for Rhododenron) All cloth with removable top clothes. Tag: Gund. Wrist Tag: An Exclusive Creation/By Gund Mfg. Co. Other side: Gund Mfg. Official Licensee/Al Victor. 1971. $40.00 pair.

Cloth--38" Display doll. All felt with stitched individual toes and fingers. Separate thumbs and ears. Fur black hair. Plastic eyes. Wired to be posable. $25.00. (Courtesy Elaine Kaminsky)

Cloth--23" "Wednesday" For "Wednesday's child is full of woe." Made by Aboriginals Inc. for Cartoonest Charles Addams. Cartoon called "Addam's Evils." 1962. $50.00. (Courtesy Elaine Kaminsky)

Cloth--18" "Tiny Tim" All cloth with felt features. Body and limbs are wired for posing. Tag: Tiny Tim, on jacket. $18.00.

Cloth--12" "Sister" All printed cloth. Do it your-self kind. 1957. $3.00.

Cloth--12" "Sister" All printed cloth. Do it your-self kind. Without skirt and apron. 1957.

Cloth--15" "Mailman" Printed cloth. Jacket missing. Tag: Toy Innovations, Ltd./Family Friends. $2.00.

Cloth--This uncut boy doll is in 2 tones of green. Came from the "Wee Bit O' Ireland" Store in Seattle. $6.00. (Courtesy Bessie Carson)

Cloth--Uncut linen doll. Colors are blue and green. This girl doll came from a store in Seattle called "Wee Bit O' Ireland." $6.00. (Courtesy Bessie Carson)

Cloth--7½" "Pocket Doll" Stuffed stockinette. Original well detailed removable clothes. Tag: Pocket Doll/Boucher Associates/San Francisco. $9.00.

Cloth--7½" "Brave Cowboy" All cloth stockinette face. Excellent clothes detail. Small eyes only. Marks: Pocket Doll/1962, 1970 Wolfpit Enterprises, Inc. These "pocket" dolls are from Joan Anglund's books. $9.00.

Cloth--16" "Grandpa" All cloth. Tag: Joyce-Miller Original/Copyright/Sears Roebuck & Co./Grandpa. $18.00.

Cloth--26" All cloth and plush. Key wind music box in backs. Sold exlusively with Nemis-Markus. 1965. $35.00 set. (Courtesy Jay Minter)

Cloth--14" "Tom & Becky" "Country Cousins" All cloth with removable clothes. "Bean" filled lower legs. Tag: Amsco Ind. A Milton Bradley Co./Country Cousins. There are four of these, the other two are Jenny (blonde) and Katie (Brunette). Still available in some areas.

Cloth--17" "Spanish" A UNECEF Doll. Tag: Mary, Many Face/Aurora Products/Corp. All cloth with flip up skirts. $12.00.

Cloth--17" "Oriental" Mary Many Face.

Cloth--17" "African" Mary, Many Face.

Cloth--17" "Scandinavian" Mary, Many Face.

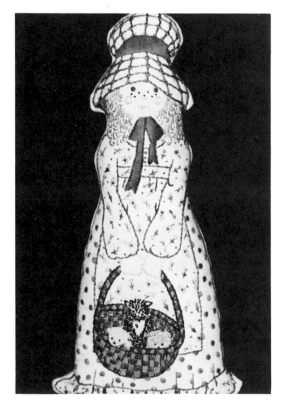

Cloth--17" "Holly Hobbie" Embroidery. Made from Simplicity Pattern #6248. Made by Barbara Baker.

Cloth--16" "Official Levi's Rag Doll" Only the jacket is removable. Glued red yarn hair. Marks: Tag: Levi's Denim/Rag/Doll. Other side: Knickerbocher. Tag on jacket: Levi's. 1974. Still available.

Cloth--12" "Korean" Baby, Many Face/173/
Aurora Products. This UNECEF doll has flip up
skirts that changes faces. $16.00.

Cloth--12" "Nigerian" Baby, Many Face.

Cloth--12" "Mexican" Baby Many Face.

Cloth--6¼" "Nancy" Asst. #9223. All printed
cloth. Tag: Nancy/Knickerbocher. Box: Copyright United/Feature/Syndicate/Inc. 1973.
$4.00.

Cloth--6½" "Sluggo" All printed cloth. Vest removable only. Marks: Tag: Sluggo/Copyright United Feature Syndicate 1973. Other side: Knickerbacher. $6.00.

Cloth--13" "Becky Thatcher" All cloth with embroidery features. One of the "official" Hanibal, Mo. dolls. This one is made commercially by 70 year old Mrs. Quattrocci and she has been making these dolls for over 30 years. $6.00.

Cloth--8" "Floppy Sox" Removable top clothes and scarf. Plastic eyes and felt hands. Tag: Floppy Sox/Knickerbocher. Still available.

Cloth--8" "Floppy Sox" Felt hands. Removable top clothes and bonnet. Plastic eyes. Tag: Floppy Sox/Knickerbocher. Still available.

8" All hard plastic with floss blonde glued on wig. Sleep eyes with long molded lashes. Head fits flush onto neck. Walker. Marks: A Hollywood Doll, around a star. (Courtesy Bessie Carson)

Two originally dressed Ginny dolls by Vogue. (Courtesy Marge Meisinger)

Tiny Betsy McCall dressed in "Sunday Best" (B-41). Made by American Character Doll Co. (Courtesy Jay Minter)

Vogue's Ginny doll dressed in two original outfits. (Courtesy Marge Meisinger)

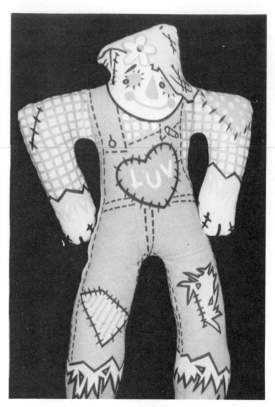

Cloth--8" "Floppy Sox" "Sock" doll with felt hands, plastic eyes. Removable top and bonnet. Tag: Floppy Sox/Knicherbocher. Still available.

Cloth--17" Brock Candy "Sam The Scarecrow" $10.00. (Courtesy Robbie Heitt)

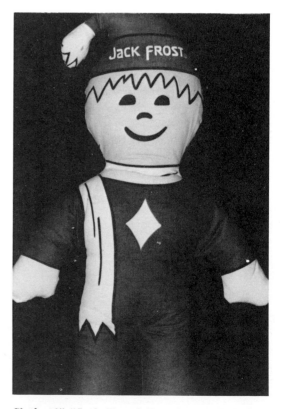

Cloth--17" "Dig 'Em Frog" All printed stuffed cloth. Premium (1973-74) from Kellogg's Corn Flakes. Marks: 1973 Kellogg Co., on back of right foot. $4.00.

Cloth--18" "Jack Frost" Premium Doll. $8.00.

Cloth--18" "Tony, the Tiger" Kellogg Co. 1973. $12.00. (Courtesy Robbie Heitt)

Cloth--14" "Sugar Bear" $9.00. (Courtesy Robbie Heitt)

Cloth--19" "Archie" $12.00. (Courtesy Robbie Heitt)

Cloth--27" "Jolly Green Giant" & 10" "Sprout" Giant, $18.00. Sprout, $7.00. (Courtesy Robbie Heitt)

Deluxe--Dawn on her "Floral Stand." Came in pink, yellow, green and blue. Will hold 3 dolls. Doll comes with each stand. Bendable knees. Marks: K11A, on head.

7½" "Muffie"--All hard plastic. Walker head turns. All original. Marks: Storybook/Dolls/California/Muffie. (Courtesy Bessie Carson)

7½" Early brown eyes "Muffie" by Nancy Ann Storybook Dolls. All hard plastic. Not a walker. Brown sleep eyes with no brows or lashes. Painted lashes above eyes. No Muffie name on doll, use purse (paper to identify. Marks: Storybook/Dolls/California. (Courtesy Bessie Carson)

9" "Court Man & Women"--All felt. Jointed at shoulders and hips. Removable clothes. Mohair wigs. Painted features. Marks: Old Cottage/Doll/Hand Made/in/Great Britain. (Courtesy Marge Meisinger)

Hong Kong--7" "Bo Bo" Plastic with vinyl head. Sculptured, painted eyes. Painted clown's face. Rooted hair but bald on top with hole for hat. Posable head. Original. Marks: Made In/Hong Kong, on head and back. (Courtesy Marie Ernst)

11" "Trine"--All rather orange vinyl. Rooted red hair. Painted green eyes. One molded tooth. Marks: The V/bee/W. Goebel/1957/Charlot BYJ/2901/Made in Germany.10, inside ears. O2, back of left leg. 01, back of right leg. Charlot Byj is the designer. (Courtesy Virginia Jones)

Sambo restaurant advertising dolls. See Squeeze Toy section for marks.

17" "Mary Hoyer"--All hard plastic. Marks: Original/Mary Hoyer/Doll, in circle on back. Dress tag: Handmade/Annie Kilborn. Information on the Mary Hoyer Doll Co. is located in Series II, page 182. (Courtesy Mary Partridge)

"Police Nurse" See teen section for black/white photo and description.

Cloth--20" "Jack Frost" Premium doll. $5.00.

Cloth--12" "Chocolate Man" from Nestles as a premium doll. $5.00.

Cosmopolitan--8" "Ginger" shown in Disneyland dress. Doll: $5.00. Outfit: $5.00. 1955. (Courtesy Marge Meisinger)

Cosmopolitan--8" "Mousketeer" Another version of the outfit shown in Series II. Doll: $5.00. Outfit: $3.00. 1954. (Courtesy Marge Meisinger)

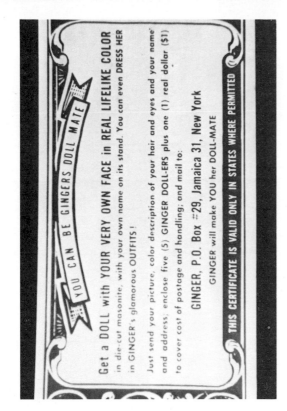

Cosmopolitan--Ginger Doll-er. With this certificate, a child could have a die-cut masonite doll with her own face. She had to send a picture, give color of hair and eyes. This "doll" could wear Ginger's clothes. 1956.

Cosmopolitan--Shows a Ginger Doll Mate. 1956.

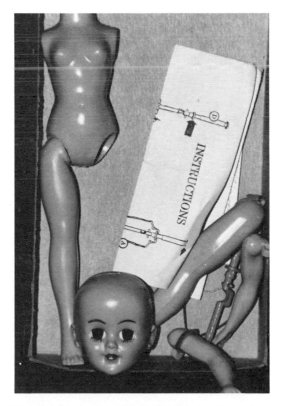

Cosmopolitan--Shows box top for the 10" "Make-Ur-Own" doll kit.

Cosmopolitan--10" "Make-Ur-Own" Complete Walking Doll Kit. All hard plastic. Dark blue sleep eyes/long molded lashes. High heel feet. Came with wig and shoes. 1956. $8.00. (Courtesy Bessie Carson)

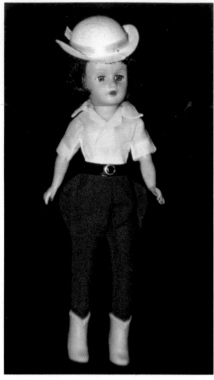

10½" "Miss Nancy Ann"--All vinyl with jointed waist. Blue sleep eyes/molded lashes. Tagged riding habit. Marks: Nancy Ann, on head. (Courtesy Bessie Carson)

16½" "Mary Jane"--All hard plastic. Walker, head turns. Flirty, sleep eyes/long molded lashes. Marks: None. (Courtesy Margaret Biggers)

4" All wood. One piece body, legs and head. Jointed shoulders only. Pegged to fit into stand. Nailed on clothes. Oil painted features and hair. Marks: Patent Pending, on bottom of base. (Courtesy Mary Partridge)

11½" "Cleodine"--All vinyl. Sleep eyes. Squeeker in head. Nurser. Marks: Turtle in diamond/Schildkrot/Germany, on back. Turtle mark/63, on head. 1958. (Courtesy Virginia Jones)

56

Cosmopolitan--Shows "Zip" the monkey, pet for the Ginger doll, in the six outfits he was able to wear. The monkey is all vinyl with jointed shoulders and hips. Has sleep eyes. Marks, if any, would be CBS Television Enterprises, or Columbia Broadcasting System.

Cosmopolitan--Zip of Television fame, shown holding one of his own vinyl images and a Ginger doll. 1956.

Cosmopolitan--14" "Merry" Plastic and vinyl with rooted blonde hair. Blue sleep eyes. High heel feet. Was originally dressed in red gown with white "fur" trim. Marks: AE 1406/41, on head. Backward AE, lower back. 1960. $3.00.

COSMOPOLITAN

DAKIN

Dakin, R--15" "Dream Doll, Aloha Alice" All stuffed nylon net. Painted features. Glued on dark blonde wig. Original. Tag: Dream Dolls/R. Dakin & Co. 1956. $6.00. (Courtesy Virginia Jones)

Dakin, R.--8" "Pebbles" Plastic with vinyl head. Marks: R. Dakin Co./Product of Hong Kong, on back. Trademark of Screen Gems/Hanna Barbera Corp./Productions Inc./1970, on head. $3.00. (Courtesy Maxine Heitt)

57

DAM TROLLS

Trolls, in Scandanavians language are what leprechauns are to the Irish or genies are to the Persians. In Norse mythology trolls are little creatures and at the same time, in Icelandic literature they are giants who dwell underground. Trolls are very kind to humans but are said to be mischievious and do things like stealing food and in some cases anything that is not nailed down. They are supposed to be able to make themselves invisible, can foretell the future and, if believed in very strongly, they can bestow great wealth and great strength upon people. Because of the nature of beliefs, the trolls are both loved and feared by Scandanavian people.

In 1952, Helena and Martti Kuuskoski of Tampere, Finland, "invented" the modern day version of the troll. Helena was the designer and since they were poor, the Kuuskoskis made two doll-size clowns, stuffed them with sawdust and put them under the Christmas tree for their two children.

Helen Kuushoski made a few more of these clowns and tried to sell them at the local shops and couldn't find anyone who wanted them but one shop keeper gave her an idea, he told her to make them smaller and put a string through the head so they could be hung in an automobile, and that is what she was trying to do when she accidently "put everything together" and up came the troll design. It was an instant success. It was not long before the Kuuskoskis had over 100 people working making these lovable creatures.

It did not take long for the trolls to enter the United States and they were very popular and reached a peak about 1966. Trolls have been used for many advertising ventures and premiums. All trolls are collectable and the most desirable seems to the DAM ones as they are the original design of the Kuuskoskis. Second are the ones that have a horsehoe on the feet; they too are the original design.

Dam Things--Troll shown dressed as "Sappy Claws" Marks: Dam, on back. $3.00.

Dam Things--3" "Nite Out Troll" All vinyl with inset, stationary brown eyes. Glued on white mohair wig. Glued on sequins earrings and necklace. Original clothes. Marks: '64/Dam, on back. 1964. Made by Thomas Dam, Denmark, Dist: Scanda House. $3.00.

Dam Things--7½" "Troll Bank" All vinyl. Jointed neck only. Inset stationary green eyes. Green mohair glued on wig. Marks: USA Feeler Co., on head. Wrist Tag: The First National Bank of Odessa. Used as a promotion item. Original. Made for Feeler by Dam, Things, Ind. 1967. $7.00.

Dam Things--Troll shown in outfit called "Lover Boy-Nik. Marks: Dam, on back. $3.00.

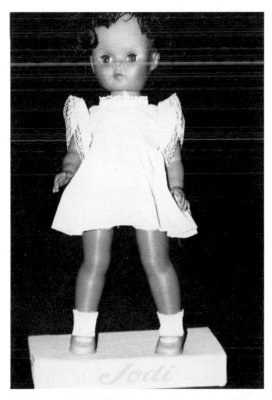

Deluxe Topper--Deluxe Topper, Deluxe Reading, Topper Corp., Topper Toys & Deluxe Toy Creations are all the same company. Refer to Series I, page 61 for full company information. Complete Dawn series shown in Series II, pages 63 to 69. For the two year production of the Dawn dolls, 56 outfits were made. I have tried to show as many as possible, although I was only able to buy 33 of them.

Dee Dee--15" "Jodi" Plastic with vinyl arms and head. Brown sleep eyes/lashes. Original. Marks: AE/7, on head. $3.00.

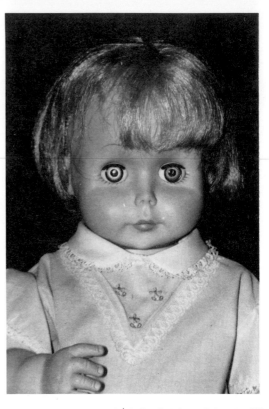

23" "Sweet Amy" School Girl Doll. One piece body, arms and legs of latex. Vinyl head. Blue sleep eyes. Was $16.98 new. Accessories: Schoolbag, blackboard, eraser, chalk, coloring book, jigsaw puzzle, flag. Marks: A-1, on head. Made by Deluxe Toy Creations, part of Deluxe Reading (out of business). $25.00.

Deluxe Reading--16" "Schoolgirl Writing Doll" Plastic with rigid vinyl arms and head. Arms move in all direction, fingers especially molded to hold crayon. Came with and without freckles. Marks: 1963/Deluxe Reading/2. $8.00. (Courtesy Mrs. John Eades)

Deluxe--"Dawn's Sofa Telephone" White and blue. Battery operated conversation between Angie and Dawn. Phone case marked: QEN/ Pat. P. 69528/71647/72768/51406/53452/Made In Japan. Has record that is reversable. $15.00.

"Dawn and Her Fashion Show" The stage, etc. was made by Irwin Toy Limited of Canada. Doll by Topper. Marks on Doll: 586/H11A. Dress is gold top with silver and gold threaded, 2 tier pink skirt. $12.00.

Deluxe Topper--Dawn's "Dress Shop" Lever operated, makes her turn. $12.00. (Courtesy Sibyl DeWein)

Deluxe--Dawn's Beauty Parlor. Pink/lavender/ white chair that swivels and tilts back. Pink/ lavender hair dryer that adjusts. Pink/lavender stool. Pink/lavender/white sink and stand marked: Cat. No. 1031/Made by/Topper Corp./ Elizabethport, N.J. $10.00

Disney, Walt--6" (Size of head only) "Grumpy" All dark brown rubber. Molded beard. Painted features. Marks: Gund/W.D.P. 1938. $12.00.

Disney, Walt--11" "Minnie & Mickey Mouse" All rubber. Marks: 50/Walt Disney Prod./Sun Rubber Co./Barberton, Ohio. ca. 1945. Mickey: $20.00. Minnie: $25.00. (Courtesy Maxine Heitt)

61

Disney, Walt--26" "Mickey Mouse" Hard plastic walker, head turns. Vinyl face mask with felt ears. Vinyl molded on shoes. Marks: 207, on back of hands. 1954. $65.00. (Courtesy Barbara Coker)

Disney, Walt--7" "Dumbo" Plastic and vinyl. Marks: Walt Disney Productions/R. Dakin Company/Product of Hong Kong. 1973. $2.00.

SMALL WORLD DOLLS

Boys and girls could take a "boat trip around the world" at the UNICEF exhibit at the New York World's Fair. Walt Disney designed this wonderful exhibit called "It's A Small World" which was dedicated by the Pepsi Cola Company to all the World's children.

The Tower of the Four Winds soared over the UNICEF exhibit that contained the life sized figures that were dressed in native costumes of 12 foreign lands.

By May 1965 8" replicas of the life size figures appeared to be advertised as Ambassadors for peace. Each was dressed in authentic foreign costume. Each doll came with the name and address of a pen pal and each came with an international 15 language dictionary plus pen and stationery. The dolls were made by Pressman-Lipson and extra costumes of any nation were sold at $1.89 each.

The original Pepsi Cola UNICEF exhibit had 12 figures and Pressman released 15 foreign costumed dolls. I have only been able to locate 13 and do not know what the other 2 are: Japan, Switzerland, India, Holland, Africa, France, Chile, Spain, Russia, Ireland, South America, Scotland, Turkey. I would venture a guess that they were England and Germany.

Disney, Walt--8" "Small World Doll-Scotland" Plastic and vinyl. Painted features. 1965. $10.00 (Courtesy Marge Meisinger)

Disney, Walt--8" "Chile" A Small World Doll. Plastic and vinyl. Painted features. 1965. $10.00. (Courtesy Marge Meisinger)

Disney, Walt--8" "Small World Doll" Country unknown. Plastic and vinyl. Painted features. Hat belongs to "Chile" Doll. $10.00. (Courtesy Marge Meisinger)

Doll Artists

As long as there have been dolls there have been doll artists, even if it were just an uncle making a wood doll for his favorite niece. In modern times that we are interested in (1935-1976) the mass amount of dolls have been designed by many artists and the best known are people such as Bernard Lipfert, Eloise Wilkin and Mollye or the largest and one of the most respected is the Marvin Glass Co. who has over 70 designers working for them. These "type" of artists are referred to as "commercial," I guess because they sell a lot of dolls; but at any rate there is a group of American doll artists that are referred to as just "doll artists" and it is not "acceptable" to refer to them as "commercial" although many sell a pretty gigantic amount of "dolls" and many of their creations are not really dolls but figurines. There seems to be a very thin line between the two. (figurines and dolls).

The difference seems to lay in the fact that the-"commercial" artists are filling the needs of the American public and the magic of childhood where as the American Doll Artist is filling the collector needs of the COLLECTOR. In fact, the most sought after artist dolls, by the collectors, are the ones made by artists who have died, retired, are very ill or getting ready to be ill. This seems to please collectors as they know the prices will increase on the dolls. Second in desirability is the "limited" edition dolls. Here I am referring to original designs.

As in every case there are exceptions and a few of these American Doll artists stand out for their ability to capture what "dolls" are all about. The first on my own list would be any dolls made by Dewees Cockran. They are all delightful children who not only appeal to the child but also to the

adult. Dewees has always been accepted as an American Doll Artist even though she certainly was "commercial" during the 1930's when her designs were used by the Effanbee Doll Co.

There are many other of these artists that appeal both to children and adults but there are a great many that in no way can it be said that there is "children" appeal as no adult, in their right mind, would allow a child to play with such dolls, for they are truly display manikins for elaborate clothes.

The name of the American doll artist group is the National Institute of American Doll Artists (N.I.A.D.A.). It was formed in 1963 with 11 Charter members and Helen Bullard was its founder. Prior to its existence, there were a great many artists at work, such as Madame Alexander, Grace Storey Putnam, Bernard Ravca (native of France), Dorothy Hiezer, Dewees Cockran, Gertrude Florian, Emma Clear and Maggie Head, just to name a few. Some of these artists would be denied membership to N.I.A.D.A. on various grounds.

The requirements for artist membership is supposed to be based on high standards, meet the organization's aims, have "genuine" originality and be professional in craftsmanship and the creations should not be "commercial."

New members are presented as candidates through sponsorship of one of the artist members. This artist member familiarizes herself with the work and BACK-GROUND of the applicant, provides a completed questionnaire and arranges for the doll examples to be delivered to the artist meeting (held at the National Convention of the United Federation of Doll Clubs as ALL members of

N.I.A.D.A. must be members of the Federation) at which time judging takes place. The dolls and <u>background</u> material of the candidate are carefully considered and vote is taken.

These "accepted," by N.I.A.D.A., artists use many medias to get across their idea of dolls. They work in felt, ceramic, porcelain, composition, papier mache, wax, cloth, latex, wood, stone, clay, bronze, sheet metal, paper, plastics, etc.

It is to be assumed that N.I.A.D.A. artists are the "amateurs" and the commercial artists are the "pros," set up such as Olympic competitors are amateurs and major league members are pros. At any rate let's look at some of the pros: Marvin Glass Co., Eloise Wilkin and Mollye Goldman.

Marvin Glass, the owner and President of Marvin Glass & Associates played a major part in innovating new styles and concepts in the toy industry for over 35 years. He built a company that employs over 75 designers, engineers, scientists, model makers and artists. A complete unit for the design of toys.

The following was taken from a Press Release from the firm of Aaron Cushman and Associates Inc., the Public-Relations firm that handles the Marvin Glass account. The time of this release was at the death of Marvin Glass, in January 1974.

MARVIN GLASS

'Mr. Glass was the outspoken champion of safe toys, the first to openly take a position in opposition to war toys and always upheld the ingenuity, integrity and technological superiority of the American toy manufacturer. In February 1970, Glass was honored at the British International Toy Fair in Brighton, England when he was named Toy Man of the Year.

Credited with being the father of automated toys, Marvin Glass was also known as the originator of proper names for toys and the creator of the first toy to participate with children in play, the first toy with selective sound, the first talking puzzle, the first three dimensional game and the first games based on the use of the electric light.

Mr. Glass's designs have put 500 toys on the market in the past 10 years. During his lifetime he held several hundred patents.

Mr. Glass felt that toys were as much a part of the entertainment world as the theatre. He saw the toy as a catalyst between the child and the world of fantasy. To him the word "toy" had become a misnomer denoting something frivolous, inconsequential and even rudimentary and he felt this image was inaccurate. To Glass, modern toys were important products of highly sophisticated design requiring advanced technologies and were often forerunners of adult tools, appliances and vehicles.

Glass organized his company in 1941 with capital of $80.00. The son of an engineering consultant, he was raised in Evanston, Illinois and he was making toys in his childhood--cardboard animals, a submarine that shot wooden torpedoes and models of pirate ships. He was educated at military prep school in Wisconsin and the University of Chicago.

His pointed and poignant views on dolls, games and toys made him the subject of numerous national magazine articles. Consumer publications, including Time, Newsweek, Business Week, Fortune, Coronet, Playboy, Better Homes & Gardens and similar magazines as well as newspapers nationwide, recognized him in print as the nation's leading designer.'

Since the death of Marvin Glass, the new head of the firm is Anson Isaacson. Mr. Isaacson has been active in the toy industry for over a quarter of a century and it was in 1954 that he became associated with the Ideal Toy Company in the engineering department. From there he rose through the ranks first as manager of the plastics devision and then became vice president of product development. It was in this position that he met Marvin Glass, the independent toy designer.

In 1964 Isaacson left Ideal to become president of the troubled A.C. Gilbert Company. Three years later the company was liquidated and Isaacson started his own marketing consulting business with Marvin Glass as one of his clients.

Isaacson joined the staff of Marvin Glass & Associates in 1971. When Marvin Glass died in 1974, Isaacson was elected managing partner of the firm. In this position, he and eight general partners of the company work closely, continuing the design philosophy and goals that were initiated by the late Marvin Glass.

No single individual is responsible for a completed product from Marvin Glass & Associates. A new concept may be the result of the input of many staff workers, artists, engineers, designers, etc. The General Partners are involved and aware of the progress in all stages of development to final completion of model or proto-type.

Toy manufacturers do not come to Marvin Glass asking for a new toy or doll development. When Marvin Glass comes up with a new concept, a proto-type is made up, and they go to any manufacturer who they think would be interested in it and sell them the manufacturing rights.

It was the personal observation of Laura K. Zwier, who

conducted the interview with Jeffrey Breslow, a General Partner of Marvin Glass & Associates, for me, that Marvin Glass seems to be an 'invention' factory. The manufacturers have their own product development departments, but will also buy new concepts from an outside source if they feel it will be a highly marketable product.

All work is done under closely guarded conditions to prevent possible disclosure of product ideas in stage of development to possible competitors. This is reflected in the new headquarters building of Marvin Glass & Associates at 815 North LaSalle in Chicago as the workshops and design studios are off limits to anyone besides authorized staff members. A unique closed-circuit television system is used to identify arriving visitors.

The exterior of the Marvin Glass & Associates building

The following is a list of some of the dolls designed by Marvin Glass & Associates and does not include them all:
Tiffany Taylor for Ideal Toy Co. (refer this Vol.)
Lazy Dazy for Ideal Toy Co. (refer to Vol. I)
Kissy for Ideal Toy Co. (refer to Vol. I)
Real Live Lucy for Ideal Toy Co. (refer to Vol. II)
Tubsy for Ideal Toy Co. (refer to Vol. I)
April Showers for Ideal Toy Co. (refer to Vol. I)
Dusty for Kenner (refer this Vol.)
Nancy Nonsense for Kenner (refer this Vol.)
Polly Pretend for Amsco (refer to this Vol.)
Baby Peek-A-Boo for Hasbro (refer to Vol. II)
Lainie for Mego (refer to Vol. II)
Peggy Pen-Pal for Horsman (refer to Vol. II)
Pirate Series for Lesney (refer this Vol.)

To sum up the design concepts of the Marvin Glass & Associates would be look at a couple of their doll designs: for example, Tiffany Taylor reflects current real-life interest in changing hair color, and in interest of safety, it is done by non-chemical means; Dusty represents the new athletic freedom of today's women. She can simulate the action of various sports, wears a casual hairdo and make up.

Now let's take a look at an individual American Doll Artist. The following is reprinted with permission. Originally written for United Federation of Doll Clubs publication "Doll News."

Contemporary Collectables:
The Work of Eloise Wilkin

by Pat Stewart

When my first son was about a year old (1950), I bought a little Golden Book entitled "Busy Timmy" to read to him. This I did over and over until the pages were tattered. That book inspired my personal admiration society for Eloise Wilkin, the illustrator of Busy Timmy. Through the years that followed there were 3 more children and many more Little Golden Books bought and read in our house but Busy Timmy remained the favorite, by now really worn to a frazzle! A second favorite came on the scene with my daughter; this was "Baby Dear" and produced in conjunction with it was a doll, the original Baby Dear from Vogue Dolls Inc. In the meantime I had begun to collect dolls and was later invited to join a doll club.

About four years ago at a club meeting someone brought in a current book illustrated by Eloise Wilkin and a number of other ladies expressed their admiration for her work. They had been saving her books as I had. We decided we wanted to know about her, so I wrote many letters to try and contact her. Then one day there was a letter from Mrs. Sidney J. Wilkin with my questions answered and a handwritten list of books she had illustrated. We formed the Eloise Wilkin Fan Club and had our first meeting on February 29, 1968.

Eloise Burns (Wilkin) was born in Rochester, New York. She spent most of her childhood in New York City. At 11 she won a prize in a Wanamaker drawing contest for New York school children; this marked the beginning of her career. After completing the illustration course at the Rochester Institute of Technology, she did free lance work for a year. She went to New York City and obtained a job the very first day. Her first book was "The Shining Hours" for the Century Company. Four years later she married Sidney Wilkin. They had 4 children which kept her busy from doing too much drawing for the next 8 to 10 years. In 1944, she signed a contract with Simon & Schuster of New York which lasted until 1969. She illustrated 47 Little Golden Books for them, while at the same time doing other illustrations, altogether about 81 children's books.

Eloise Wilkin was asked to join the American Artist Group of New York City (Not N.I.A.D.A.) an honor accorded few illustrators. She is listed in Illustrators Of Children's Books-1744-1945, published by the Horn, Inc. Boston and in the Supplement 1946-56.

The book, "Baby Dear" was published in 1961. Vogue Dolls, Inc. produced "original Baby Dear," Eloise Wilkin's first doll, at the same time. It was a sensation! A 14" news article in the New York Times was devoted to it: "Doll Feels and Looks Like Child," the heading proclaimed. It then went on to sing the praises of Baby Dear, saying:

"Unlike most dolls that have a stiff, set personality, this doll called "Baby Dear" is amazing in its seeming ability to change moods and age (counted in months). This circumstance made the doll counter the scene of several controversies as sales clerks tried to convince customers that all the dolls were the same, only the clothing and their posture had been changed."

While I was trying to locate Mrs. Wilkin, one of the many letters I wrote was to Vogue Dolls. I received a very nice reply from the current president which helped me to reach her by mail. At the time Eloise Wilkin took her brown clay model of Baby Dear to the company, Mrs. Jennie Graves, the founder of Vogue, was president. They became close business friends during the years they worked together. In the 1962 Vogue catalog is a letter from Mrs. Graves which says in part, "we were joined a year or so ago, by the adorable Baby Dear, the most real-like infant baby doll in the world." The catalog advertises it as "soft, cuddly, real-live one month old baby, with delicately sculptured chubby features of soft vinyl, downy soft rooted hair, and stuffed to make me feel real. I flop like a real-life new born infant and I fold my way into your arms and heart when you hold me in your arms and love me."

The doll came in 12" and 18" sizes and was priced at $6.00 and $12.00 respectively.

Eloise Wilkin told me that she worked over a 20 year period before she was satisfied with the final design which was produced. I saw a picture of her with a table covered with baby doll heads she had modeled while trying to achieve her goal. Figure 1 shows the doll manufactured by Vogue and produced until 1964. An additional model came out with a moving mechanism and music box in it. There is also a hand puppet with the Baby Dear head.

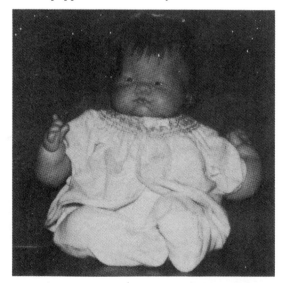

Fig. 1 "Original Baby Dear" Marked on Leg;
1960/E. Wilkin (Courtesy Adele Gioscia)

After this doll, she designed a one year old called "Baby Dear One" for Vogue (see fig. 2). It is described in the 1962 catalog as: "A bouncy, flouncy, 25" one year old darling. The all new Baby Dear One has the same delicately soft, safe,

vinyl features of a real live baby, she has sparkling moving eyes and her rooted hair is just like a one year old's, she sits up very well and is so proud of her two front teeth."

She was priced at $15.00. In 1964 Vogue advertised the third Eloise Wilkin design in the series.

Chubby "Two Dear," the cherubic, dimpled, pudgy, toddling 17" two year old likeness of the "Original Baby Dear" made of vinyl, she stands, sits and walks, has sleeping eyes and rooted hair. Too Dear and her twin brother are exquisitely outfitted at from $8.00 to $13.00. (fig. 3)

Once you are familiar with the doll designs of Eloise Wilkin, you will always recognize them. Her detailing is perfect. Each arm, hand and finger has its special little wrinkles and dimples as do the legs, feet and toes. The faces have a quality and individuality unlike that of any other doll.

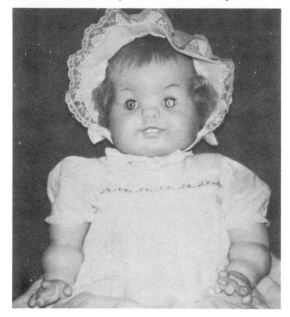

Fig. 2 Baby "Dear One."
Marked on head: 1961/E. Wilkin/Vogue Dolls

Mrs. Wilkins has also designed some dolls for another company which are on the market now but it is not their policy to give credit to any particular artist's work. A few of her dolls are shown in modern doll books. Currently there is an ad on television for Bayer's Asprin which she drew; it shows a little girl looking at a book, turning the pages, ending with a bottle of Children's Bayer Asprin. Many of her books are available now; some are new and some are reprints.

Collecting Eloise Wilkin could be a hobby all in itself; there are individual items which I have not mentioned, while 81 books almost comprise a full library. I feel especially fortunate to have corresponded so much with her from 1968 until the present with the highlight in April 1971. I flew back east and spent two wonderful days as her guest. I met some of her family, including her sister Esther, who has written quite a few of the books I love. I saw places and people she has drawn in her books, sketches she is doing for a coming books AND a partially finished doll sculpture on which she is working. It was a truly thrilling experience to become involved personally in two days in the life of my favorite illustrator of children's books. I shall never forget it."

In addition to the above article by Pat Stewart, I would

Fig. 3 "Too Dear."
Marked on head: 1963/E. Wlkin/Vogue Dolls
(Courtesy Adele Gioscia)

Eloise Wilkin shown in her apartment with the President
of her fan club..Pat Stewart. November 1972.

like to point out that not only are the Eloise Wilkin dolls
highly collectable, but all her illustrations in books are
beautiful additions to a doll collection. Her personality and
beauty of spirit are reflected in her drawings which are born
to capture the hearts of the children she draws for.

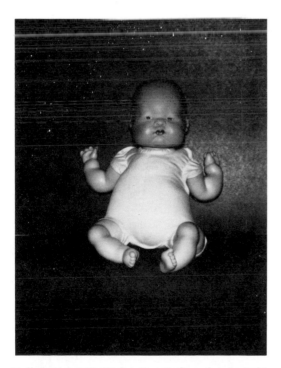

Doll Artist--12" "Baby Dear" Completely bald.
Marks: E. Wilkins on left upper leg. (Courtesy
Adele Gioscia)

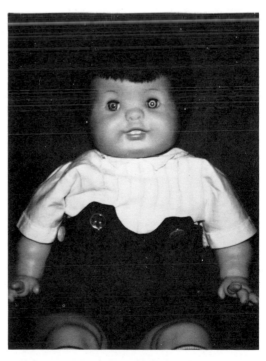

Doll Artist--24" "Bobby Dear One" Boy version
of Baby Dear One. Marks: 1961/E. Wilkins/
Vogue Dolls/Incorporated. (Courtesy Adele
Gioscia)

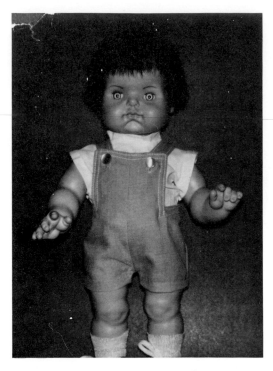

Doll Artist--17" "Too Dear" Dark hair and eye-brows. Vivid blue eyes. Marks: 1963/E. Wilkins/Vogue Dolls. This is the boy and there was also a matching girl. (Courtesy Adele Gioscia)

Doll Artist--25" "Bobby Dear One & Baby Dear One" Cloth bodies. Vinyl head and limbs. Two lower teeth.

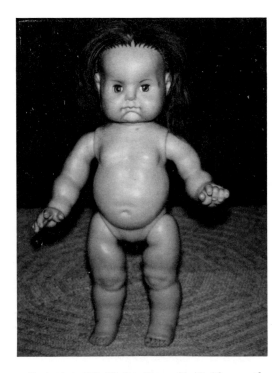

Doll Artist--17" "Baby Dear Too" Shows the body style. Marks: 1963/E. Wilkin/Vogue Doll

Vogue--17" "Baby Dear Too" Rigid plastic body and legs. Vinyl arms and head. Closed mouth with protruding upper lip. Blue sleep eyes/slashes. Original clothes. Marks: 1963 E. Wilkin/Vogue Dolls, on head.

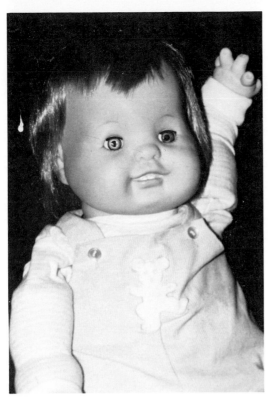

Vogue--23" "Baby Dear One" Cloth body with vinyl arms, legs and head. Blue sleep eyes/lashes. Open/closed mouth with two lower teeth. Marks: E. Wilkin/1961 high on right leg. 1961/E. Wilkin/Vogue Dolls/Incorporated, on head. Original clothes.

Vogue--Shows Baby Dear One and Baby Dear Too to show the comparative sizes of the heads.

List of Books Illustrated by
Eloise Wilkin

1927: The Shining Hours
1928: Adventures in Health (Moulton)
1930: The Reckless Seven
1932: The Choosing Book (Dalgliesh)
1936: Robin & Angus (Robinson)
  ? Robin & Tito (Robinson)
  ? Rusty Ruston (McNeely)
1938: Mrs. Peregoin & The Yak (Burns)
1939: Mrs. Peregoin at the Fair (Burns)
1939: Going on Nine
1940: A Good House for a Mouse (Eberle)
1941: Sheep Wagon Family
1944: The Great Gold Piece Mystery
1948: Rainbow For Me (Kiser)
1949: Seatmates (Reely)
1949: Apple Tree Cottage
1949: A Baby is Born (Levine & Seligmann)
1949: Sunshine for Merrily (Kiser)
1950: The Tune is in the Tree
1953: Birthday Story (Buntain)
1967: Thank You Book (Zens)
1968: Evening Prayer (Wilkin)
1970: Song of Praise

Illustrated by E. Wilkin 1960

List of "Little Golden Books" Illustrated by Eloise Wilkin

1946: New House in the Forest
1947: Fit It Please
1947: Noises and Mr. Fibberty Jib
1948: Busy Timmy
1948: The New Baby
1948: Come Play House
1949: Good Morning, Good Night
1949: Guess Who Lives Here?
1951: Holiday Book
1951: A Day at the Playground
1952: Prayers For Children
1952: My Toy Box
1952: The Christmas Story
1953: Wiggles
1953: My Kitten
1954: Hi Ho, 3 in a Row
1954: Georgie Finds a Granpa
1954: Linda & Her Little Sister
1954: Hansel & Gretel
1954: The Twins
1954: My Baby Brother
1954: My Puppy
1954: First Bible Stories
1955: The Night Before Christmas
1955: My Snuggly Bunny
1956: My Little Golden Book About God
1956: A Catholic Child's Book About God
1957: The Story of Baby Jesus
1957: Child's Garden of Verses
1957: Lord's Prayer
1958: Baby's Mother Goose
1959: Baby's First Christmas
1959: This World of Ours

1959: We Help Mommy
1960: Baby Looks
1960: Baby Listens
1960: My Dolly & Me
1961: Baby Dear
1962: We Help Daddy
1962: Christmas A B C
1963: My Teddy Bear
1963: Jamie Looks
1965: We Like Kindergarten
1965: Good Little, Bad Little Girl
1967: Play With Me
1969: So Big
1969: The Little Book
1969: Little Boy With a Drum
1970: Eloise Wilkin's Mother Goose
1973: Baby's Birthday

Other Than "Little Golden" Books

1949: Make Believe Parade (Wonder Books)
1950: Busy A B C
1961: The Lord's Prayer
1965: Mother Goose Rhymes (Open Door Book)
1965: Flight Bag Book
1967: Wonders of Nature
1967: Wonders of the Season
1967: Birds
1968: The Golden Calendar
1969: The Golden Treasury
1971: The Baby Book (Golden Shape Book)
1972: I Hear (Heritage Press)
1974: Where Did Baby Go (Little Golden)
1974: Re-release: The New Baby (Little Golden Book)
1975: Book of Prayers

Illustrated by E. Wilkin 1969

Illustrated by E. Wilkin 1970

Miss Mollye,
Americas Leading Doll Designer

Mrs. Mollye Goldman is one of the outstanding women of our times. Her dolls stand out in quality and she was a genius in the clothes design department and not only designed for her own dolls but for other companies also, including Horsman, Effanbee and Ideal. She is the designer/maker of all the Shirley Temple clothes of the 1930's. Her husband is as great of Mollye, in the realm of stuffed animals and his line was called "Golden Fleece," and these animals are as collectable to toy collectors as Mollye dolls are to doll collectors. We will let Miss Mollye tell you about herself in her own words:

"The gentleman who sent you the Mollye history seems to remember more than I do and some day I hope to thank him for the sweet memories. Most of his information is correct and most of it was contained in old Toy magazines, newspaper ads which showed that we had one of the largest factories in the Country, was the largest maker of doll clothes and later had the outstanding line of the 1940 Glamour girls and I recall one ad in the Philadelphia Inquirer, with a model named Charlotta, sitting on Golden Fleece skins wearing the same dress I made for a doll. They did call me America's leading doll designer, at the Chicago Fair, in Toy and Novelties and in many other Trade news items.

I must call my career a stormy one as no women manufacturers showed dolls at the Toy Fairs and it was an uphill climb all the way but to begin my story. I loved dolls as long as I can remember and at the age of 8, I cut up straw hats and made doll clothes and hats out of scraps. I had a beloved Aunt Nettie who saved pieces of material for me to sew with. As I look back now, I see how much my mother was against my sewing for the doll, as she thought I would end up a dressmaker and she did not approve of this and you must remember the times during the turn of the Century, a woman's lot was difficult and many "working women" ended up sewing 16 hours a day for very few dollars. As I loved to sew, I made an apron for my mother and various things for the rest of the children and finally she gave in and agreed to let me continue my sewing.

It was in 1917 that my boyfriend, Meyer Goldman, who is my wonderful husband, enlisted in the Navy and was stationed at the Great Lakes Naval Station in Illinois. It was very cold so he asked me to make sweaters for the boys. I knew nothing about knitting or crocheting but I learned fast enough and night and day I made sweaters.

It was in 1919 that we were married and moved in with his parents as Meyer was still in the Service. One day a call came that he was coming home on a furlough and I wanted to surprise him so I crocheted a multi color wool sweater and hat and in my nervous energy also made an identical outfit and a dressed a 12" celluloid doll. I remember that the sweaters had many ripples.

A short time later Meyer and I were on the Boardwalk of Atlantic City and I had the doll with us when a man approached and asked where I bought the doll and I told him that I had dressed it. He wanted to know if we would sell him a few dozen just like mine and that he would pay very well for them. My answer was "No, I am married."

When we returned to Philadelphia, Meyer returned to his ship and I recalled what the man on the Boardwalk said to me and the very next day I took a trip South where all the wholesale Toy Jobbers were and purchased 6 small 8" celluloid dolls that had movable arms and legs and could stand and sit. My father-in-law laughed at me and said, "You will never stop playing with dolls!" In pink wool, I crocheted short pants, a very full skirt, jacket, muff and booties and when I sat the doll down, she looked like a pancake and that's what I named her.

As I set out to sell my creations, I decided to make my first call to Lit Bros. where a Mrs. McCormac was the buyer and Miss Reba was her assistant. After I showed them my dolls they both smiled as they looked me over. I looked much younger than I was and weighed only 82 pounds. They told me later that they thought I was playing a game but gave me an order for several dozen dolls anyway.

After returning home and working on the orders I had gotten, I recalled an incident of two precious books of yellow trading stamps which netted me a 36" very glamorous bisque head doll with large blue eyes, golden curls, a composition body and marked Germany. What a thrill and joy it was to be surprised by my family, with a gift so desired. In those days it was a great sacrifice to waste two books of stamps for a plaything and after receiving my beautiful doll, I had a guilty conscience but could not part with my doll. My mother and sisters, who were as happy as I was, named her "My Mollye" and after bestowing much love on her and many, many hours of friendship, I thought she looked tired and one day I very carefully had packed her away.

After recalling my childhood gift of love, I went looking for her and I found My Mollye waiting for me. I dressed her in light blue wool knit. A beautiful dress, large hat trimmed in ribbon, a large muff with a rose in the center, gloves and a hand bag. And of course the first one to see her was Miss McCormac as I took her along when I delivered an order for Pancake.

Both Miss Reba and Miss McCormac thought she was very good and I left with several imported dolls and an order for 12 dozen in assorted sizes and colors.

I then called on all the department stores in Philadelphia and all placed orders for this outfit. They brought the dolls to my home and we dressed them. Some of these dolls retailed with prices as high as $25.00. So it was that for two years, I worked with 5 girls in my bedroom and had many women who worked for me, working in their own homes. After two years, we moved to a second floor flat and bought a factory machine.

While at Wanamaker's Department Store, one day, I noticed a beautiful baby doll, 20" long with a composition head, arms and legs and that cried "Mama." I bought her because I thought she was in need of better clothes.

I made that doll a Smoked Pink organdy dress and bonnet with fine cotton panties and slip. I trimmed her in bows and took her back to Wanamakers to show her to Mr. McDonald. I remember the doll was marked E.I. Horsman on the back of her head.

With one look at the changed baby doll, Mr. McDonald ordered 12. He took the dolls from stock and they were all Horsman dolls. We undressed the dolls and redressed them in dresses, coats and rompers, all made of good materials. From this I received a staggering order.

It was not very long before we moved to our own home and also rented a large factory flat with 24 sewing machines and still used many "home workers." We made and designed doll clothes for the entire countries Department Stores, for their imported dolls. Price was no object.

A Miss Wheeler was the Toy Buyer for F.A.O. Schwarz and she sent me bisque By-lo babies in all sizes and I designed and made their Christening sets for $85.00 each.

It was in 1923 when Mr. Harold Bowie called to see me at the factory and we agreed to manufacture doll clothes and design exclusively for the Horsman Company and for no other doll manufacturer but that we could continue our business with the stores. Mr. Bowie deposited $10,000.00 to my account for the purchase of materials. It was the most wonderful, trusting business relationship, with the grandest people I have ever met.

Mr. Goldenberger was their designer, Mr. William Eirenfield was the President and Mr. Bowie was in charge of all sales and production. We worked with Horsman until 1932 and both became very successful with all Mollye products. In 1932, Mr. Goldenberger retired, Mr. Eirenfield passed away and Horsman was sold to another doll manufacturer. It was the end of a great era.

We made another contract much on the same basis as the one with Horsman and thinking that they were the same great caliber people as Horsman but how wrong we were! For one entire year we financed them with materials and labor on all the doll clothes they were in need of and we were never compensated at all. They declared themselves bankrupt. It broke us but we paid all their debts and with much determination we stayed in business. It was a time of Depression when the entire country was experiencing sadness and one ray of sunshine, shone during these dark days. Her name was Shirley Temple, a child that made the people forget their own problems for a short time in darkened theatres. I saw the first picture that Shirley Temple played in and fell in love with her. I asked the theater manager where I could reach Shirley Temple so I could use her name and he remarked, "Go ahead and use it, no one knows the kid and you will be doing her a favor." At home, I called on several movie houses and received the same answer, so I set about making a line of doll dresses designed like the ones she wore in the picture and sent them to the Bureau Registration of Design in New York.

It was a few days later that I received a telegram from a gentleman, whom I had always respected, wanting to know about Shirley Temple and wanted me to come to New York to see him.

Arriving in New York, I went directly to his office. He was connected with the Toy Ass'n at the time. He said, "What is this Shirley Temple you made these beautiful dresses for?" I told him about her and that she would make a beautiful doll and that everyone would love her as much as I did. These were his very words, "A child! A doll! You are crazy, no one has ever heard of such a thing." I again told him how wonderful it would be to make a doll of her. He finally agreed and said he would see about tying her up to a contract and if we did, I would make all her doll clothes and, yes, we would make the same arrangements on the same basis as our working arrangement with Mr. Bowie of Horsman's. We shook hands on that and that was our agreement, for he was a gentleman. From 1933 to 1936, I made all of the Shirley Temple clothes they sold for their dolls.

In 1936 this fine gentleman passed away and all promises were broken. I spent many days and nights in New York looking for materials and spent many hours in the factory, advising and designing without any compensation. Making close to 1000 dozen Shirley Temple outfits a week did not keep me from making new creations and in 1935 I had the Lone Ranger, Thief of Bagdad movie tied up, Hollywood Cinema Fashions and designed and made Dolls of all Nations and Beautiful Brides.

We had the most beautiful plant, with all the special pleating machines that we bought for Shirley Temple dresses and in 1940 the Government needed our building for War materials and we turned over our largest floor to them.

Mr. Goldman joined the American Tobacco Co. and became Field Sales Manager and he later joined me in the factory as manager.

Of all the dolls dressed by Mollye Creations, Perky was about the favorite, along with Little Queen and dolls of all Nations. One buyer bought 48,000 Perkys and said she didn't do anything but sell well!

We were entirely wiped out by flood water in 1965 and only stayed long enough to pay all debts and in 1970, we retired to private life." Signed Mollye Goldman (Mrs. Meyer) December 1975.

Following are photographs, stationary cuts and other items that tell the pictorial story of Mollye Creations.

PLAYTHINGS

381 FOURTH AVENUE, NEW YORK CITY

Your attention is called to the following item which appeared in the current issue of "PLAYTHINGS"

Virginia Weidler with Her Dolls

This is a photo of the Winchester's Golden Fleece Teddy Bear that used real Lamb's skins. Mollye Goldman's husband, Meyer Goldman was President of the company. 1939.

FAMOUS JUVENILE SCREEN STARS PLAY WITH "RAGGEDY ANN" DOLLS

The accompanying photograph shows pretty little Virginia Weidler, the talented Paramount child movie star, surrounded by a bevy of "Raggedy Ann" and "Raggedy Andy" dolls. Mollye, of Molly-'es Doll Outfitters, Inc., who are exclusive manufacturers of "Raggedy Ann" and "Raggedy Andy," says that these dolls are favorites among many of the little screen stars in Hollywood. She has literally dozens of photographs showing the talented youngster playing with their "Raggedy" dolls. Mollye reports that many leading stores from coast-to-coast will feature her Hollywood Cinema Fashions for dolls during the coming Holiday season. Through exclusive arrangement Molly's organization is reproducing in doll costumes the latest screen fashions worn by the little girls in their new pictures. Children can now see their favorite young movie star and, thanks to Molly's Hollywood Cinema Fashions, go home and dress their dolls in like manner. Molly-es' large plant is operating at full capacity, turning out the largest volume of business in the history of the concern.

Mollye--These little Mollye Creations are 8" tall, all cloth with pressed faces made exclusively for her, in England. These dolls are called "Little Angels" and made in the 1920's. $75.00 each.

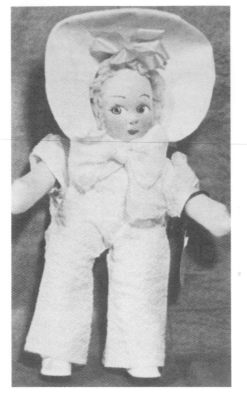

Mollye--This 12" all cloth doll was made in the late 1920's. $65.00.

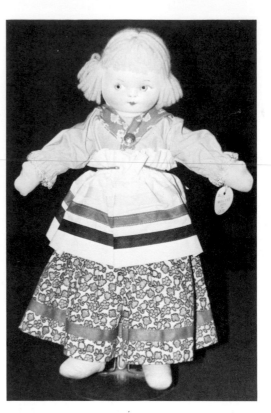

Mollye--15" "Belgium Girl" from International Series. All original. Tag: paper tag on wrist: A Mollye's Doll/T.M.Reg./App. For. Other side: Mfd. By/Mollye's/Doll Outfitters/Inc. $55.00.

Mollye--This is a beautifully dressed all cloth doll made in 1935. $75.00.

Mollye--15" "Scotland" from International Series. All original. Tag, on left hip: A Mollye's/ American Made. $55.00.

Mollye--15" Cloth Internationals. Came in 12
countries: Irish, Mexican, Swedish, Polish,
Gypsy, Czeck, English, Italian, Swiss, French,
Romanian, Dutch. $35.00 each.

Mollye--24" "Baby Criss" 1945. $75.00.

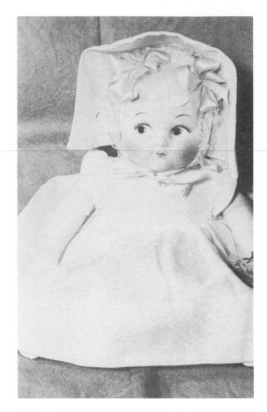

Mollye--24" All cloth "Darling" 1937. $65.00.

Mollye--24" Cloth with pressed face mask. Fur white hair. All original. Tag: A Mollye Doll. $75.00.

Mollye--21" "Royal Wedding." All composition. Blue sleep eyes with eyeshadow. Closed mouth. Doll unmarked and clothes are tagged. $125.00.

Mollye--27" "Dutch Girl" 1941. These exclusive dolls sold for as high as $80.00 in 1941. $75.00.

Mollye--18" "Debbie Deb" All high grade composition. Closed mouth and sleep eyes/eyeshadow. Stands on revolving music box. Sold for $125.00 during the 1930's.

Mollye--18" All high grade composition "Queen Elizabeth." Doll made by Effanbee and so marked. $125.00.

Mollye--22" "Lone Ranger." $125.00.

Mollye--22" "Hi-Buzzy" All cloth with pressed face mask. All original. Ideal Toy sold two dolls very similar to this as Roy Rogers with smile mouth and painted teeth and Hopalong Cassidy with white fur hair. 1949. $95.00.

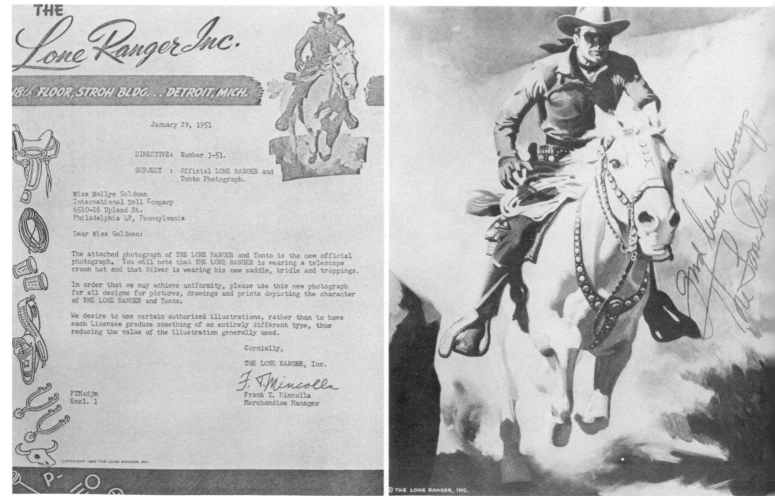

THE Lone Ranger Inc.

18th FLOOR, STROH BLDG... DETROIT, MICH.

January 29, 1951

DIRECTIVE: Number 3-51.

SUBJECT : Official LONE RANGER and Tonto Photograph.

Miss Mollye Goldman
International Doll Company
6510-16 Upland St.
Philadelphia 42, Pennsylvania

Dear Miss Goldman:

The attached photograph of THE LONE RANGER and Tonto is the new official photograph. You will note that THE LONE RANGER is wearing a telescope crown hat and that Silver is wearing his new saddle, bridle and trappings.

In order that we may achieve uniformity, please use this new photograph for all designs for pictures, drawings and prints depicting the character of THE LONE RANGER and Tonto.

We desire to use certain authorized illustrations, rather than to have each Licensee produce something of an entirely different type, thus reducing the value of the illustration generally used.

Cordially,

THE LONE RANGER, Inc.

F. T. Mincolla

FTM:djm   Frank T. Mincolla
Encl. 1   Merchandise Manager

COPYRIGHT 1949 THE LONE RANGER, INC.

© THE LONE RANGER, INC.

Mollye--30" This is the doll used for the Lone Ranger and also Cowboy Joe. All latex body filled with foam rubber. Hard plastic head. Blue sleep eyes. Open mouth/two upper teeth. 1949. Marks: 28, on head. $55.00.

Mollye--Shows Lone Ranger, Tonto, Cowboy Joe and cowgirls. Latex bodies and hard plastic heads. Two dolls center, front are all hard plastic.

Mollye--Shows a display of the exclusive rights Lone Ranger and Tonto dolls. Top row and doll on far right have hard plastic heads and magic skin bodies. Two in center are all composition. The girls were called Rangette and Tonta.

Mollye--16" "Peggy Rose" The Royal Bride. All hard plastic. Blue sleep eyes. Open mouth. Dark red fingernail polish. 1950. $65.00.

Mollye--20" "Embassy Bride" All hard plastic. Revolves on music box with wedding music. Dressed in finest laces and satins. 1949. Clothes are tagged "Mollye Creations." Doll is unmarked. $65.00.

Mollye--20" "Margaret Rose, Bride" All hard plastic. Blue sleep eyes. Open mouth. Clothes tagged "Mollye." Dolls unmarked or with 210 on head or back. $40.00.

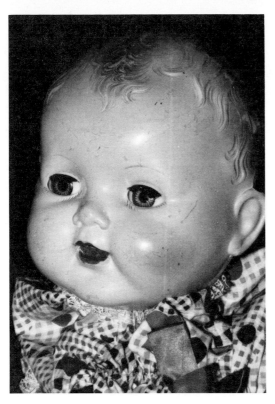

Mollye--24" "Angel Face" 1948. Cloth and composition. Cry box. Sold for $19.95 in 1948. $35.00.

Mollye--23" "Precious" Hard plastic head, cloth body with vinyl arms and legs. Called the wonder doll, she could sleep sitting up, play a tune, play patti cake, etc. without being wound up. $35.00.

Mollye--16" All composition toddlers. Came with molded hair and wigs. Sleep eyes. Top: Penny. Left: Minnie. Right: Rosalee. 1939. $35.00 each.

Mollye--24" "Baby Princess" Cloth body with composition head and limbs. Sold for $35.00 in 1935. $55.00.

Mollye--20" "Baby Fun" Shown in original outfit. $55.00.

Mollye--20" "Baby Fun" Cloth body with full cloth arms and gauntlet composition hands. Composition legs and head. Blue sleep eyes/ lashes. Marks: None. (Courtesy Joan Amundsen)

Mollye 20" "Baby Fun" All composition toddler.
Came with or without wigs over molded hair.
$55.00.

Mollye--15" "Little Girls" All old fashioned costumes. Vinyl heads with latex
bodies. Cryer. Inset eyes. Dolls not marked. Clothes are tagged. Top row,
left to right: Mary Lou, Emma Lou, Sara Lou. Bottom row, left to right:
Sally Lou, Pattie Lou. $35.00 each.

Mollye--This is also the "Baby Lov-Lee" (Bundle of Charm doll). $35.00.

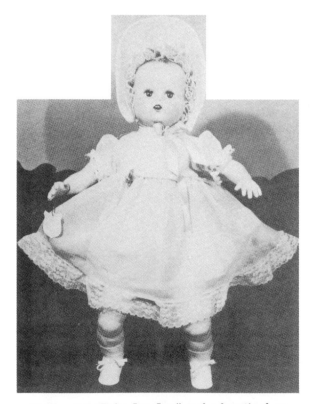

Mollye--24" "Baby Lov-Lee" and advertised as "Bundle of Charm" See page 177, Series II. Marks: A backward 650.

Mollye--This is the wigged version of "Baby Lov-Lee (Bundle of Charm). $35.00.

Mollye--8" "Holiday Girls" All hard plastic with hand painted faces. Top row left is Martha Washington. Second row is Miss Columbus and front row: Valentine Day and St. Patricks. $10.00 each.

Mollye--Shows miniature Bridal party. Bride top row center. Maid of Honor center, second row along with six Bridesmaids. All hard plastic and 8" tall. Each face is hand painted. $10.00 each.

Mollye--9" "Darling Tiny Women" See Series I, page 211 for a photo of doll. Marks: Molly E, on head. Was also used as "Darling Little Women" with mother, Meg, Jo, Beth and Amy. Also used for "Queen of the Month" and came dressed in six different outfits. Was also used for International dolls. $35.00 each.

Mollye--9" "Molly" A cute little girl. 1952. $12.00.

Mollye--9" "Italian Girl" All vinyl with sleep eyes. Dolls were mostly unmarked, some were marked "Mollye." Clothes were tagged. $18.00.

Mollye--20" "Irene Dunn" All composition. Stands on music box. Special human hair wig. All lace dress. This is one of the "Hollywood Cinema Fashions" by Mollye. She also designed stars such as Jeannette McDonald, Joan Crawford, Marilyn Monroe and many others. $125.00.

Mollye--12" "Tyrolean Girl" All vinyl. Blue sleep eyes. Closed mouth. Doll marked "Mollye" and clothes are tagged. $18.00.

Mollye--15" "Sabu" of the "Thief of Bagdad." All composition. Doll and clothes designed by Mollye. $165.00.

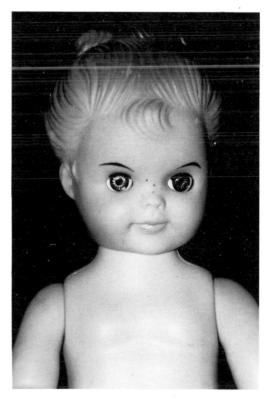

Mollye--11" "Perky" Came with and without freckles. Also came with all hair colors. Marks: back left: AE10/33, on head, Large AE/1 lower back. Back right: AE10F, on head. Large AE/1, lower back. Front: AE/9, on head. AE/1, lower back. $15.00. (Courtesy Carolyn Powers)

Mollye--11" "Perky" With molded hair. Freckles. Marks: AE/1, on lower back. $17.00. (Courtesy Alice Capps)

Mollye--12" "Perky" All vinyl, black hair and brown eyes. No freckles. $115.00.

Mollye--11" "Ida Bell" Also sold as "Lindy Sue" in different outfit. Came with or without freckles. Also sold as "Perky" and as "Darling Little Women:" Mother, Meg, Jo, Beth and Amy. $20.00.

Mollye--12" "Perky" All vinyl with white hair and blue eyes. Freckles. $15.00.

Mollye--12" "Perky-Pert" All vinyl. Blue sleep eyes. Closed smile mouth. Came with and without freckles. Clothes tagged and some dolls' heads were marked "Mollye." 1958. $15.00.

Doll Artist--19" "Court Man" and 18" "Court Lady" Portraits by Halle Blakely. 1953. Man, $495.00; Lady, $500.00. (Courtesy Kimport Dolls)

Doll Artist--26" "Marie Ann Portrait" by Halle Blakely. 1951. $575.00. (Courtesy Kimport Dolls)

Doll Artist--29" Portrait by Halle Blakely. 1958. $495.00. (Courtesy Kimport Dolls)

Doll Artist--12" "Grandpa & Grandma" by Marie Berger. Pre-1964. $300.00 pair. (Courtesy Kimport Dolls)

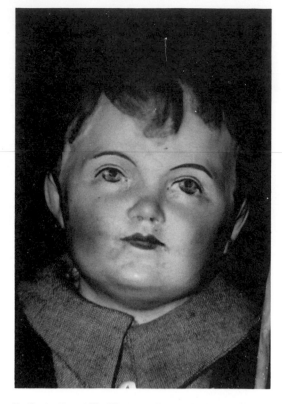

Doll Artist--16" "Danny Boy" Signed Emma Clear 1945. $300.00. (Courtesy Helen Draves)

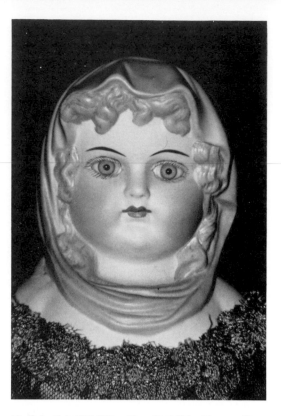

Doll Artist--20" "Blue Scarf" doll by Emma Clear in 1948. $295.00. (Courtesy Helen Draves)

Doll Artist--22" "Parian" signed by Emma Clear in 1949. $125.00. (Courtesy Helen Draves)

Doll Artist--18" "Parian" by Emma Clear in 1948. $125.00. (Courtesy Helen Draves)

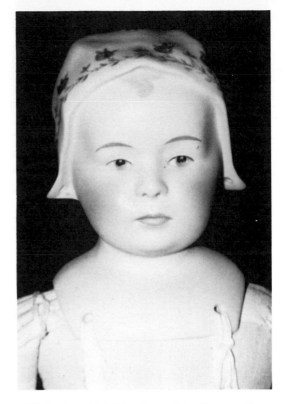

Doll Artist--18" Blonde china finish "Parian" Applied rose and pierced ears. Marks: Clear, 1946. $165.00. (Courtesy Kimport Dolls)

Doll Artist--16" "Baby Stuart" by Emma Clear. Signed 1946. $165.00. (Courtesy Kimport Dolls)

Doll Artist--19½" "George" Inset eyes. 18½" "Martha" Inset eyes, molded bonnet over molded hair. By Emma Clear. $575.00 pair. (Courtesy Kimport Dolls)

Doll Artist--18" Coronation hairdo, applied neck-lace, feather and earrings. By Emma Clear, signed 1947. $175.00. (Courtesy Kimport Dolls)

Doll Artist--16" Brown eyed Parian with grey hair. Pierced ears. Signed Anna Mae 1962. $95.00. (Courtesy Kimport Dolls)

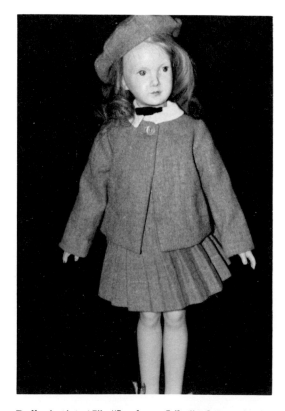

Doll Artist--15" "Look a Like" One of the children by Dewees Cockran. Original. Artist signed under left arm. $250.00. (Courtesy Barbara Coker)

Doll Artist--18" "Gibson Girl" by Emma Clear. $175.00. (Courtesy Kimport Dolls)

Doll Artist--17" Beautiful Parian with pierced ears, applied flowers and head band. Marks: Patti Jene 1964. $165.00. (Courtesy Kimport Dolls)

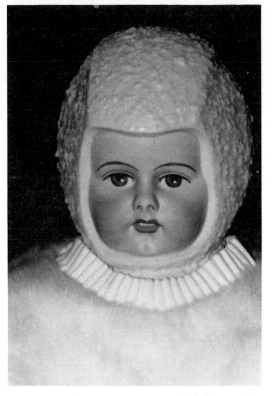

Doll Artist--18" A most beautiful Snow baby made by Gerald La Mott Pacoima. 1964. $185.00. (Courtesy Helen Draves)

Doll Artist--20" "Queen Elizabeth" Signed Rene 1959. $175.00. (Courtesy Kimport Dolls)

Doll Artist--15" Brown eyed Parian with pierced ears. Applied neck scarf. Marks: PJ '64 Patti Jene. $125.00. (Courtesy Kimport Dolls)

93

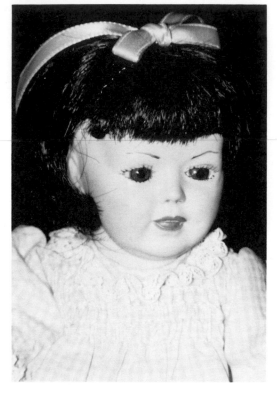

Doll Artist--9½" "Little Girl" An all bisque with open/closed mouth and painted teeth. Inset blue eyes. Dimples. Signed by Edith Gammon. 1975. $60.00. (Courtesy Kimport Dolls)

Doll Artist--23" Portrait in wax by Lewis Sorenson. (Courtesy Kimport Dolls)

Doll Artist--23" Portrait in wax by Lewis Sorenson. $200.00. (Courtesy Kimport Dolls)

Doll Artist--18" "Paul Laurence Dunbar" (1872-1906). Often known as the poet of the people, he wrote in both Negro dialect and conventional English and also authored many works of prose. Marks: Bertabels Dolls-1965. The doll was designed by Roberta Bell N.I.A.D.A. artist. $265.00. (Courtesy Maxine Heitt)

Dunbar

10 cents U.S. postage

Doll Artist--This is a picture of a U.S. Postage stamp that is currently available, commemorating Paul Laurence Dunbar. (Courtesy Maxine Heitt)

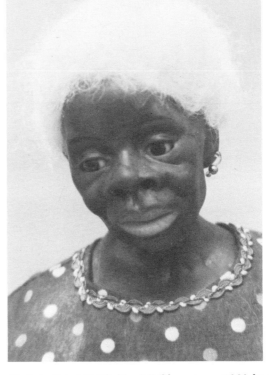

Doll Artist--14" "Caldonia" Glass eyes. 1966 by Maggie Head. First made in 1958. Still being produced. $265.00. (Courtesy Grace Ochsner)

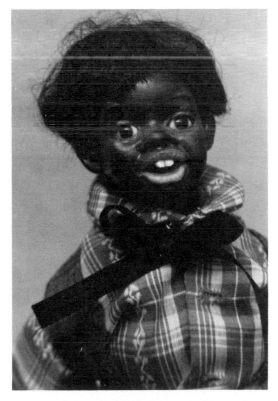

Doll Artist--15" "Nicodemus" Open/closed mouth with two upper teeth. Glass eyes. By Maggie Head. $125.00. (Courtesy Grace Ochsner)

Doll Artist--15" "Uncle Ned" Glass eyes. Maggie Head. 1966. First made in 1958. $265.00. (Courtesy Grace Ochsner)

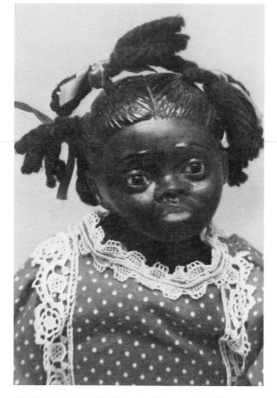

Doll Artist--14" "Peach Blossom" Glass eyes. Holes in head for hair. Signed Pattie Jean 1966. $85.00. (Courtesy Grace Ochsner)

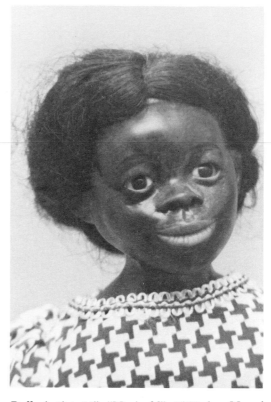

Doll Artist--14" "Marigold" 1966 by Maggie Head. Glass eyes. First made in 1959. Still being produced. $125.00. (Courtesy Grace Ochsner)

Doll Artist--20" Parian Biedermeir type by Grace Lathrop. $225.00. (Courtesy Kimport Dolls)

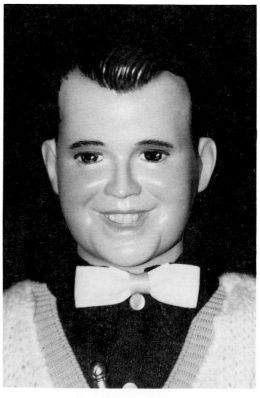

Doll Artist--22" "Dick Clark" Bisque head with cloth body. Composition hands. Marks: None. The workmanship of the doll is outstanding, it is unfortunate we do not know the artist who made him. $165.00. (Courtesy Barbara Coker)

96

Doll Artist--16½" "Miami Miss" 1961, by Fawn Zeller. $175.00. (Courtesy Kimport Dolls)

Doll Artist--"Little Howie" A modern wax portrait by Eva Bee Hill. $115.00.

Doll Artist--13½ All tanned leather. Painted eyes. Yarn hair. An Oujibbua. Artist: Margaret Chief. $35.00. (Courtesy Maxine Heitt)

Doll Artist--18" Indian by Mildred Helmuth. $60.00. (Courtesy Kimport Dolls)

97

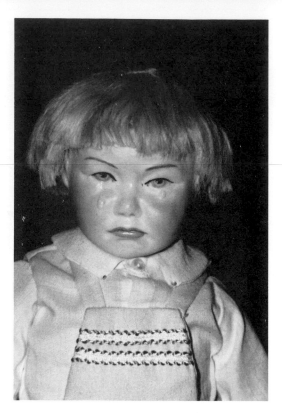

Doll Artist--16½" "Cinderella" by Lita Wilson. 1966. Made on special order for Mrs. M.A. Resch of Iowa. $200.00. (Courtesy Kimport Dolls)

Doll Artist--13" Boy with tears by Ellery Thorpe. 1970. $250.00. (Courtesy Kimport Dolls)

Doll Artist--15½" "Charlotta" Parian with applied crown and necklace. Pierced ears. Made exclusively for Kimport Dolls in 1954 by Polly Mann. $175.00.

Doll Artist--18" Girl with a dimple by Suzanne Gibson. $175.00. (Courtesy Kimport Dolls)

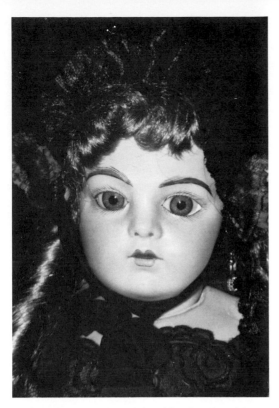

Doll Artist--18" Bisque shoulder head on bisque shoulder plate. Kid/cloth body. Marks: Jackie '71/Bru Jne/10. $85.00. (Courtesy Helen Draves)

Doll Artist--5" "Chocolate & Vanilla Fakco" Designed and made by Julia Rogers. $22.00.

Doll Artist--"Martha Gonyea" designer and originator of many cloth dolls, which are shown in this section. She also runs a doll shop and repair hospital in Roswell, N.M.

Doll Artist--25" "Little Chief" Face and clothes are originals of Martha Gonyea. This doll won a blue ribbon at Fair. $45.00.

99

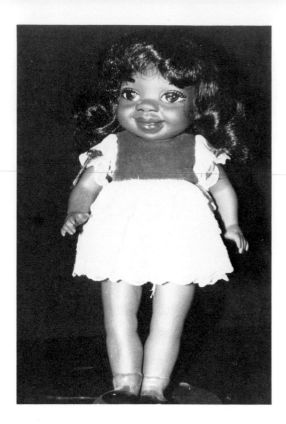

Doll Artist--33" "Miss Ping-Pong" Made during the time President Nixon went to Red China. Both face and clothes are original designs of Martha Gonyea. $65.00.

Doll Artist--8" All bisque. By Gertrude Zigler. $65.00. (Courtesy Jay Minter)

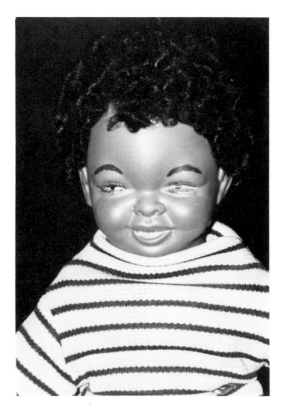

Doll Artist--12" Original by Gertrude Zigler. $65.00. (Courtesy Jay Minter)

Doll Artist--Cloth portraits of Mr. and Mrs. Houston of Richmond, Va. done by Maxine Clasen. They were made from the small photograph. (Courtesy Phyllis Houston)

Doll Artist--Original photo of Mr. and Mrs. J.C. Houston.

Doll Artist--28" "W.C. Fields" By Maxine Clasen. Composition head and hands. Wire armiture, bendable body. $165.00. (Courtesy Phyllis Houston)

Doll Artist--28" "W.C. Fields" with an unlikely friend.

These following Historic Wax Costume Dolls by Sheila Wallace of Grove City, Pa. could be best described as miniature versions of the historic figures seen in the wax museums throughout the world. Although the methods vary, as they are the result of Sheila's own training, experience and research. Sheila's background in the fields of painting, drawing anatomy and sculpture as taught in London art colleges, her visits to the doll and costume museums in Europe and her love of history are all reflected in the beauty of her work.

Each figure is a separately planned and executed project. Each head and pair of hands is individually molded, not cast, thus each is an original work. They are molded from bleached beeswax using a formula based on one used by European wax modelers of the 17th century. They are taken from portraits or death masks of famous people. The hair, eyelashes, eyebrows, beards and hair on the hands of the male characters are all implanted. Sheila's research in the field of the development of cosmetics insures that the hand painting of the faces and the dressing of the hair is correct for each period.

The basic construction of the bodies is cloth filled with polyester fiber over flexible wire armatures so each figure can be suitably posed on its own wooden stand. The lower limbs are composition with appropriate footwear, fitted to the foot and not molded on as part of the limb. Each costume is carefully researched to be as historically correct as possible and appropriately scaled, correct accessories are added to enhance the authenticity. In some cases a doll is also given a "wardrobe" of interchangeable head dresses, bonnets or wigs and a container is provided for storage of these extra accessories.

The dolls made by Sheila Wallace are extremely beautiful to see and would be fantastic to own and display in a fine collection.

Doll Artist--Family group done in wax by Sheila Wallace. This is the family of Louis XVI, Marie Antoinette, children, Maria Theresa and Louie Charles. $1,500.00 set.

DOLL ARTIST

Doll Artist--Close up of Marie Antoinette.

Doll Artist--Close up of Louis XVI.

Doll Artist--Close up of Maria Theresa and Louie Charles.

Doll Artist--Close up of the hand of Marie Antoinette which shows the vein lines and rings.

Doll Artist--Another original by Sheila Wallace. This is Elizabeth I. She is done in wax and has red hair. $695.00.

Doll Artist--A close up of Elizabeth I.

Doll Artist--A wax original by Sheila Wallace. This one is Sir Walter Raleigh. $695.00

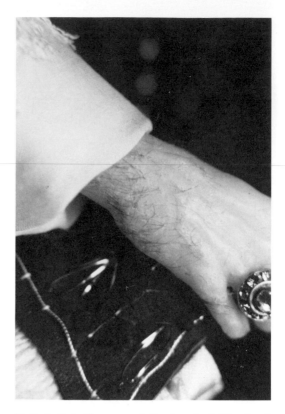

Doll Artist--Close up of the hand of Charles I. Shows embedded hair.

Doll Artist--Sheila Wallace's wax figures of Charles I and Henriette Maria. $695.00 each.

Doll Artist--Close up of Henriette Maria

The Dolls
Collectors Forgot

The following article written by Thelma C. Flack, is reprinted with permission. It appeared in the "Antique Trader" February 26, 1975. Its title is: The Dolls Collectors Forgot; W.P.A. Dolls.

A grayed building designated "Pony Express" stood on Eighth Street in Marysville, Kansas. It was almost passed by this summer, but curiosity is a magnetic leader and who knows what may exist there.

After a deep step upward one stood before a tall glass-doored case full of what appeared to be exciting little dolls about twelve to fourteen inches tall and dressed in what might be American and foreign costumes. They were well constructed and must be of some historical value.

The young lady in charge of the Express station stated that the case of the dolls was gotten for them by a retired public superintendent who had to put up a struggle to keep them from being sent West. She thought they had been made by the Public Works Administration.

There are those that remember the W.P.A. For those too young to recall the Depression, back in 1933 during the first hundred days of Franklin Roosevelt's administration, the joblessness was so bad that "made work" became necessary. Capable committees were set up to work it out. They did a splendid job, but many people considered the road work as all that was being accomplished because this was what they saw being done. Tax payers said that too many workers were just leaning on shovels and demurred at the "new deal." The dolls merit recognition and compliments from people, even today.

I read that San Diego, Cal. had such dolls. They were called "figurines" and used for visual aids in public schools and colleges. The dolls were American and Foreign historical characters.

The Visual aid man from the San Diego public schools gave me much information, but their visual aid building had burned in the Fifties, so I turned to the Kansas Historical Society and received some excellent material.

The construction of these visual aids was brought about by the need of jobs. Back in the first hundred days of Roosevelt's administration there was a haunted look in human eyes and some faces showed fear because of the scarcity of work. The larger families were already in need. Letters such as C.C.C., meaning Civilian Conservation Corps. represented camps where young men could learn to save old trees and attain health from the outdoor life. Their work was valuable to the country because we would need more wood in the future.

Fathers took hard road jobs, engineering, and building state and national buildings, while mothers and older girls met to carry out such projects as sewing for the needy. It was clearly evident that people wanted work and not a dole. W.P.A. jobs were divided into blue collar and white collar sections. Authors explored rivers and wrote historical stories about life on the river and on the shores. Photographers made documentary films of the country which are still shown on T.V. and are valuable to our education. Artists made murals and panoramas for museums and visual aid projects. Writers produced plays. Imagine all of this for approximately twenty dollars per week!

During the first hundred days in office, Roosevelt made ten speeches, sent fifteen messages to Congress, eased some laws to enactment, and talked to the press twice a week. The Federal Emergency Relief Act of May 12th appropriated $500 million and later increased to $5 billion for direct relief to the states, cities and towns. Harry Hopkins headed this, also the Civil Works Administration which grew out of it.

By January 1934, C.W.A. had over four million people on its rolls and at its height, 400,000 separate projects were underway. These included everything Hopkins could think of that would be of public benefit.

Next in importance was the N.R.A. organization. Title I of this law prescribed the drafting and application of "Codes" in every sort of industry. With multiple objectives such as recovery, reform, encouragement of collective organizing, selling, maximum hours, minimum wages and the forbidding of child labor, the N.R.A. got underway.

N.R.A. was administered by Wm. Hugh S. Johnson, a West Pointer who was in charge of the draft in World War I and had occupied a high place in army logistics. With much hard work and the alloting of the dark blue eagle clutching a cog wheel as a symbol to every store firm that adopted the system, Johnson codified about 700 industries. Businessmen in general did not like the N.R.A. They wanted to be free to cut wages and raise prices. As soon as they were "out of the woods," Title I was declared unconstitutional. In 1935, before this happened, some four million unemployed people had been reabsorbed into industry and about twenty-three million workers were under codes.

The second part of the N.R.A. was the Works Progress Administration and the Supreme Court allowed it to stand. Harry Hopkins administered it and spent billions on reforestation, water works, sewage plants, school buildings, slum clearances, and student scholarships. This is where the artists really began their best work.

A feature which caught the public eye and became named "Boondogling" was the setting up of projects to employ artists, musicians, writers and other "white collar" workers. A great many people such as librarians, catalogued the contents of state and municipal library buildings.

The Federal Theater employed over fifteen thousand workers at an average of twenty dollars a week. John Houseman directed authors who wrote and produced plays, often traveling as actor troops about the country. Orson Wells was one of the best.

On the fine arts projects, artist George Biddle, who headed the artists, says they were democratic, humane, and as intelligent as any artists the world over. The dolls seem to bear this out. They had developed through trial and error. The programs were suited to needs and one of the needs in the public schools was for visual aids which the artist could make so excellently. All of these things preceded the development of visual aids.

The foreign costume figurines show the costumes of twenty-four different nationalities. These figurines are similar in construction to the American figures. Orders were by sets made to represent such as Austria, Czechoslovakia, Denmark, Finland, France, Germany, Greece, Holland, Hungary, Ireland, Italy, Rumania, Switzerland, Wales and Yugoslavia. They ran about a dollar a pair or eighty-six cents for cloth. What would I pay to have one today!

Also available were fourteen in figurines of either men or women ready to dress for use in designing and modeling costumes as a class program. A folding wooden exhibit case would open up to exhibit the figurines and which could be made for three dollars.

The historical figurines from our country stand gravely, representing dates, costumes and important Americans. Their faces are paper-mache or hard rubber. They have mache or wooden bodies and stand fastened to a small platform with their identification printed on the base. My favorite wears a jaunty feather, my adored one in pink taffeta ruffled dress. Names one could order from included Jane Adams, Clara Barton, Steven Foster, Benjamin Franklin, Robert Fulton, Sarah Hale, Ann Hutchinson, Abe Lincoln, Paul Revere, Betsy Ross, George Washington, Frances Willard and Will Rogers.

The American figurines show development of costume for both men and women from 1600 to 1900.

The 14" figurines were hard rubber and plaster. They were authentically costumed, in proper materials, and mounted separately in a standing posture. These were dated from 1607 to 1900 and could be ordered in a twenty-four pair set or singly. The buyer ordered by date.

The figurines were offered to help give the students visual understanding of historic and nationalistic costumes that flat pictures could not portray. They were used at all ages and interest levels as teaching aids when they might correlate with learning experiences in classes such as art, music, language, dramatics, literature and social science.

There were rules to govern the visual aid dolls such as:
1. to be made in a durable and practical medium.
2. each to meet the need for which it was planned.
3. to follow specifications.
4. to be capable of being produced in quantities by workers with limited training and well-executed workmanship as an attractive visual aid article.

The object was to aid in the teaching process by supplying material which would give clearer concepts and supplement the most modern and approved classroom methods of presentation. Educators who used the models gave approval. Much research went into the production. Everything was well planned and executed. Some were made at the college in Emporia, Kansas, and some in Wichita.

The little figurines stand solemnly at the Pony Express Station in Marysville. Hundreds of little hands must have held them. Hundreds of young minds must have stored away information for the future and, thanks to an educator who cared, the little dolls were saved to represent an era, looking as attractive and authentic as they did then. Our W.P.A. era did much, much more than lean on a shovel. It helped to give our country a successful forward push. There must be many more "figurines" hidden somewhere in our country. Let us bring them out to our doll collectors and "dibs" on the first in market!

The following pictures are of the Flack collection of W.P.A. dolls and the pictures were taken by Joleen Flack. W.P.A. dolls are selling $65.00 to $85.00 per set.

Doll Artist--W.P.A. Greek

Doll Artist--W.P.A. Czechoslvakia

Doll Artist--W.P.A. Italy

Doll Artist--W.P.A. Mexico

Doll Artist--W.P.A. Switzerland

Doll Artist--W.P.A. Sweden

Doll Artist--W.P.A. Russia

Doll Artist--W.P.A. Poland

Doll Artist--W.P.A. Turkey

Doll Artist--W.P.A. Old Wales

Dream World--11" "Flower Vendor" All composition. Wig over molded hair. Original. Marks: None. Tag: Dream World Dolls/Reg. U.S./Make Dream's Come True. $25.00. (Courtesy Frances Anicello)

Dream World--11" "Florence Nightengale" All composition. Painted eyes. Original "nurse" uniform. $25.00. (Courtesy Dodie Shapiro)

Dream World--11" "Cuba" All composition. Painted features. $25.00. (Courtesy Mary Partridge)

Dream World--11" "Spanish" Molded hair under wig. All composition. Dimple in left cheek. Painted eyes. Marks: None. $25.00. (Courtesy Mary Partridge)

109

Dream World--11" "Providence" All composition. Molded hair under wig. Original. $25.00. (Courtesy Frances Annicello)

Dreamland--11" "To Market, To Market" All composition. Fully jointed. Stapled on clothes. Painted blue eyes. Original. Marks: None. $25.00. (Courtesy Mary Partridge)

Dream World--11" Close up to see the molded hair under the Dream World doll wigs.

Dream World--11" "Bride" All composition. Original. Shows wooden discs used by manufacturer for "falsies." $25.00. (Courtesy Mrs. J.C. Houston)

110

Dream World--11" "Bride" All composition with painted features. Molded hair under wig. $25.00. (Courtesy Mary Partridge)

Dream World--11" "Scotch" All composition. Wig over molded hair. Original. Marks: None. $25.00. (Courtesy Frances Anicello)

Dutchess--7½" "Mary Hartline" All hard plastic. Felt clothes. Mohair wig. Blue sleep eyes. Original. $10.00. (Courtesy Phyllis Houston)

Dutchess--7" "Roy Rogers" & "Dale Evans" All hard plastic. Roy: Blue sleep eyes. Dale: Brown sleep eyes. Both original. Marks: Dutchess Doll Corp/Design Copyright/1948, on back. $5.00 each.

111

A most popular cowboy: Roy Rogers

Roy Rogers' "Leading Lady:" Dale Evans.

Durham--8" "Wyatt Earp" All molded on clothes except hat. Button in back operates right arm to "draw." Marks: Same as Wild Bill Hicock. Still available.

Durham--6" "Young Kung Fu" Plastic with vinyl head. Button in back to make right arm "chop." Painted upper teeth. Original. Marks: Hong Kong, head. Picture of world and "I" inside "D"/ Durham Ind. Inc./New York NY 10010/Made in Hong Kong/Item No. 3010, on back. Still available.

Durham-6" "Fireman" Plastic with vinyl head. Molded ax in hand. Button in back makes ax "swing." Plastic legs are molded on pants and boots. Marks: Same as Young Kung Fu. Still available.

Durham--8" "Billy The Kid" All molded on clothes except hat. Button in back operates arm to "draw." Marks: Same as Wild Bill Hicock. Still available.

Durham--8" "Wild Bill Hicock" All molded on clothes except hat. Button in back operates right arm to "draw." Marks: D/Durham Ind. Inc./New York N.Y. 10010/Made in Hong Kong/ Item No. 3020/Design Reg. No. 965717/Durham Ind. Inc. 1975. Still available.

113

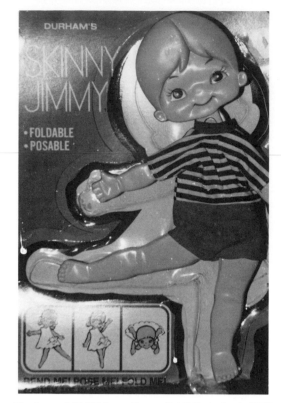

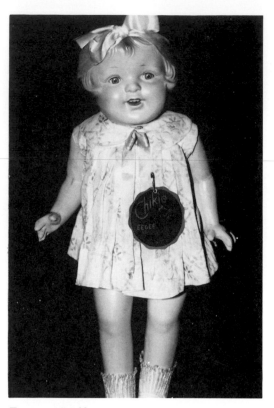

Durham--11" "Skinny Jimmy" All flat vinyl. Will fold up. Marks: Picture of world and "I" inside "D"/No 1500/Durham Industries Inc./New York NY 10010/Made in Taiwan. $3.00.

For complete information on the Eegee Doll Co. refer to Series I, page 74.

Eegee--16" "Chikie" All composition with small blue tin sleep eyes. Open mouth/3 upper teeth. Molded hair. Bangs are different than the "Patsy" doll. Bent right arm. Original. Marks: None. Tag: Chikie/Another Eegee Doll, with a picture of little girl feeding baby chicks. $60.00. (Courtesy Pat Raiden)

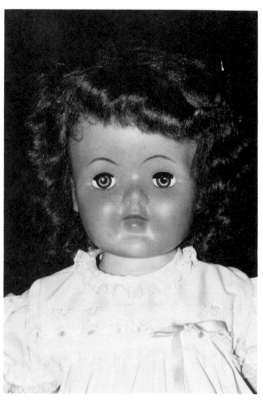

Eegee--18" "Sleepy-Time Girl" Blue sleep eyes. Molded hair. Came on a latex body (unjointed). Vinyl head. Marks: Eegee. $10.00. (Courtesy Marie Ernst)

Eegee--29" All early stuffed vinyl. Blue sleep eyes. One piece body and legs. Disc jointed arms. Marks: Eegee, on head and body. $6.00. (Courtesy Elaine Kaminsky)

Eegee--8½" "Ballerina Sherry" One piece stuffed vinyl body. Pale blue with white net overskirt. Pink slippers. Blue ribbon/pink flowers to tie ponytail. Marks: Eegee, head. Eegee/8, on body. $5.00. (Courtesy Bessie Carson)

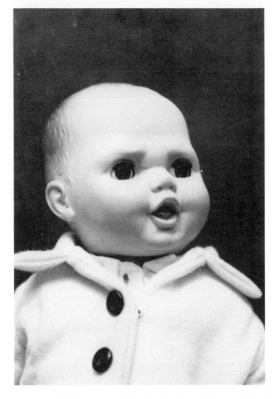

Eegee--17" "Buster" Plastic body and legs. Vinyl arms and head. Open/closed mouth. Marks: 1959/Eegee. Molded hair. Blue sleep eyes. $7.00. (Courtesy Phyliss Houston)

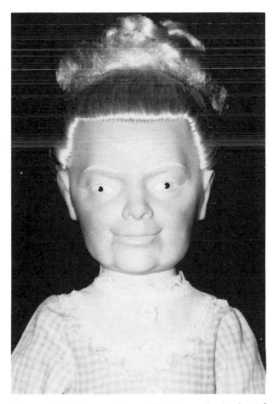

Eegee--14" Granny type. Plastic and vinyl with grey brows and eyes. Long white hair pulled up in a bun. Original. Marks: Eegee/3. $30.00. (Courtesy Linda Fox)

Eegee--15" "Luvable Baby" Also known as "Sherry Lou." All vinyl one piece body, arms and legs. Vinyl head. Blue sleep eyes. Marks: Eegee, on head. Eegee, on body. 1956. $6.00.

115

Eegee--16" "Newborn Baby Doll" Cloth with vinyl head and limbs. Sleep eyes. Open closed mouth/molded tongue. Marks: Eegee Co./173. 1963. $6.00. (Courtesy Elaine Kaminsky)

Eegee--12" "Sniffles" Plastic body. Vinyl arms, legs and head. Open mouth/nurser. Blue sleep eyes/lashes. Came with layette. Marks: 13/14 AA/Eegee Co. 1963. $4.00.

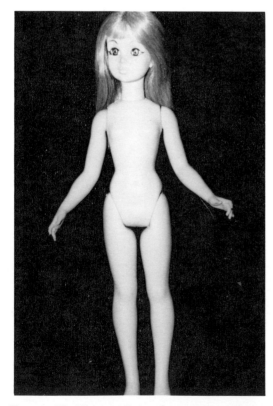

Eegee--15" "Gemette" to show body. Marks: Eegee, on head. 1963/Eegee Co., on back. This doll has been used for several personalities. $4.00.

Eegee--16" "Rose Red Flowerkin" Plastic and vinyl. Blue sleep eyes. All original. Marks: 8/F2/ Eegee, on head. Goldberger Doll/Mfg. Co. Inc./ Pat. Pend. on back. 1963. $12.00.

Eegee--17" "Kiss Me" Plastic with vinyl arms and head. Raise left arm and mouth "kisses." Blue sleep eyes. Original. Marks: 14-16/Eegee, on head. 16 inside left arm and New/16 inside right arm. Tag: Kiss Me movement protected U.S. Patent #2,988, 843. 1963. $5.00.

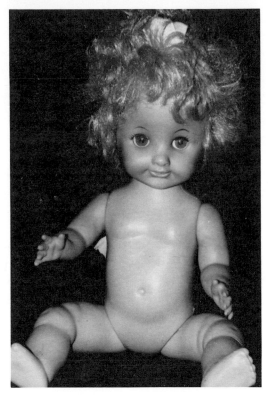

Eegee--10" "Darling Baby" Plastic and vinyl. Blue sleep eyes. Open mouth/nurser. Marks: 25/10T/Eegee Co. 1964. $3.00.

Eegee--31" "Bonnie Ballerina" Plastic and vinyl. Jointed ankles, hips, waist, shoulders and neck. Sleep eyes. Original. Marks: Eegee/5, on head. 1964. $18.00. (Courtesy Alice Capps)

Eegee--12" Plastic and vinyl. Hair rooted in ponytails. Freckles. Sleep eyes. Marks: 12 12K/Eegee. $6.00. (Courtesy Cecelia Eades)

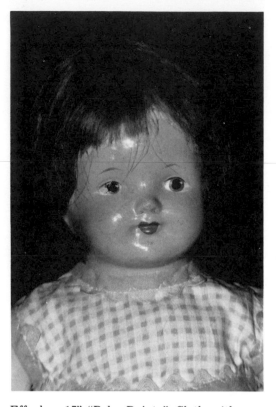

Eegee--21½" "Carol" Plastic and vinyl. Flat feet. Pre-teen body. Sleep eyes. Marks: Eegee Co./ 15 PM/1B or 8. 1968. $9.00. (Courtesy Phyllis Houston)

Effanbee--15" "Baby Dainty" Cloth with composition shoulderplate. Painted blue eyes. Mohair over molded hair. Marks: Effanbee/Baby Dainty. $50.00. (Courtesy Marie Ernst)

For complete Effanbee Company information refer to Series I, Page 83.

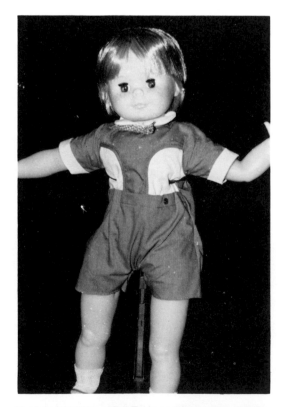

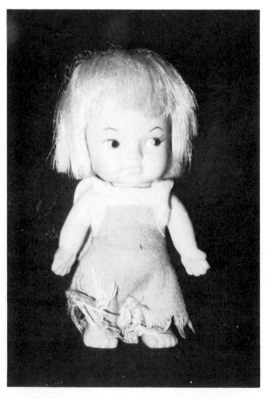

Eegee--23" "Georgie" Twin to "Georgette" Refer to Vol. II, page 86. Green sleep eyes. Freckles. Cloth body. Orange hair. Original. Marks: 17/ RNG/Eegee. 1971. $8.00. (Courtesy Marie Ernst)

Eegee--3½" All vinyl. Jointed neck only. Rooted white hair. Painted blue eyes. Marks: Eegee Co. 1966. $2.00.

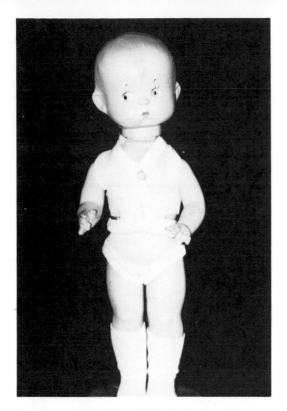

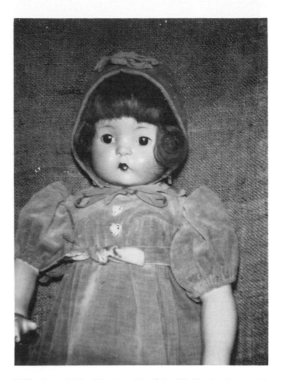

Effanbee--14" "Skippy" Cloth body with composition head and limbs. Wood block neck. Molded hair with one lock down forehead. Marks: Skippy/Effanbee. $55.00.

Effanbee--27" "Patsy Ruth" Cloth body with composition limbs and head. Brown sleep eyes. Human hair wig. All original. Marks: Effanbee/ Patsy Ruth. 1935. $150.00.

Effanbee--16" "Mary Lee" All composition. Sleep eyes/lashes. Open mouth/4 teeth and felt tongue. Marks: Mary Lee on head. Effanbee/ Patsy Joan, on back. $75.00. (Courtesy Alice Capps)

Effanbee--8" "Button Nose" All composition with painted brown eyes and molded hair. Marks: None. Button: Blue Bird/Effanbee Dolls/Finest and Best. Refer to Vol. II, page 89. 1943. $35.00.

119

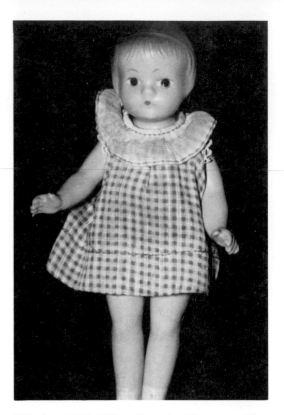

Effanbee--10" "Patsy Baby" Cloth body, legs and arms with gauntlet celluloid hands. Composition head. Sleep eyes. Original clothes minus bonnet. $45.00.

Effanbee--5½" "Wee Patsy" All composition. Molded on hair band, shoes and socks. Original. $85.00. (Courtesy Helen Draves)

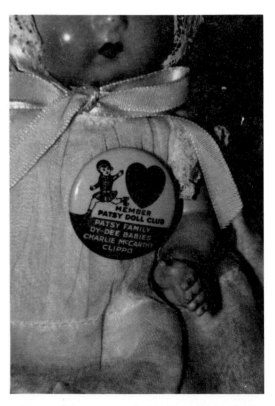

Effanbee--8" "Baby Tinyette" All composition. Came in both straight and bent baby legs. Marks: Effanbee/Baby Tinyette, on back. Effanbee, on head. Original. 1933-36. $50 each. (Courtesy Marge Meisinger)

Effanbee--Shows close up of the Patsy Doll Club pin worn by Baby Tinyette. (Courtesy Marge Meisinger)

Effanbee--18½" Hard plastic body and limbs. Vinyl head. Blue sleep eyes with molded eyelids. Smile mouth. Original. Marks: Effanbee, on head. $22.00. (Courtesy Phyllis Houston)

Effanbee--Shows interesting hairline of the 18½" girl.

Effanbee--16" "Lil Darlin" Sleep eye version. Cloth body with cry box. Sticky early vinyl head and ¾ arms and legs. Marks: Effanbee, on head. $15.00. (Courtesy Phyllis Houston)

Effanbee--12" "Baby Cup Cake" 1964 through Sears. Plastic and vinyl. Blue sleep eyes. Deep dimples. Open mouth but no wetting hole. Marks: Effanbee/1963, back and head. $5.00. (Courtesy Phyllis Houston)

121

Eugene--12" "Baby Sarah Lee" Plastic body and legs. Vinyl arms and head. Rooted black hair over molded hair. Original. Marks: Eugene, on head. 1965. $4.00.

Eugene--9½" "Baby Missey" Cloth with vinyl arms, legs and head. Blue sleep eyes. Rooted brown hair. Marks: Tag: Eugene Doll Co. 91, inside arms. 91/14, inside legs. 960/Made in Taiwan/8 Eye/5, on head. $2.00.

Eugene--Check under Lorrie for more dolls by this company. The company name is Eugene but the dolls are marked Lorrie.
12" "Bitter-Sweet" Pouty. Plastic and vinyl. Painted eyes. Also comes in white version. Marks: P/Lorrie Doll Co/1974. Eugene on box. $18.00.

Eugene--12" "Sweet-ee" Plastic and vinyl. Character face. Painted eyes. Marks: G/Lorrie Doll Co/1974, on head. Eugene on box. $18.00.

Eugene--12" "Taffy" Plastic and vinyl. Open/closed mouth with two molded and painted upper teeth. Marks: T/Lorrie Doll Co./1974, on head. Eugene on box. $18.00.

Eugene--7" "Pit & Pat" Plastic with vinyl heads. Painted features. Marks: Taiwan, on head. Made in Taiwan, on backs. $4.00.

Eugenia--6½" "Eugenia" dressed in "Goes To A Party." All composition. Jointed arms only. Painted on black shoes. Painted blue eyes. Marks: None. Box: A Touch of Paris/picture of Eiffel Tower/Copyright 1945. $12.00.

Eugenia--6½" "Friday-Eugenia Goes To The U.S.O." All composition. Jointed arms only. Painted blue eyes. Painted on black shoes. Marks: None. Box: A Touch of Paris, picture of Eiffel Tower/Copyright 1945. Friday Eugenia Goes To The U.S.O. $12.00.

Eugenia--6½" "Eugenia's Bridesmaid" All composition. Jointed at arms only. Painted blue eyes. Painted on black shoes. Marks: None. Box: A Touch of Paris/picture of Eiffel Tower/Copyright 1945/Eugenia's Bridesmaid. $12.00.

Excel--9½" "Pochahontas" Rigid plastic with vinyl head. Jointed action figure. Ball jointed waist. Molded black hair. Marks: Excel Toy Corp/Hong Kong, on head. Available in some areas.

Excel--9½" "Cochise" Action figure. Marks: Excel Toy Corp/Hong Kong, on head. Available in some areas.

Excel--9½" "Annie Oakley" Rigid plastic with vinyl head. Jointed action figure. Ball jointed waist. Molded blonde hair. Marks: Excel Toy Corp/Hong Kong, on head. Available in some areas.

Excel--9½" "Wild Bill Hickok" Action figure. Marks: Excel Toy Corp/Hong Kong, on head. Available in some areas.

Excel--9½" "Calamity Jane" Rigid plastic with vinyl head. Jointed action figure. Ball jointed waist. Molded dark blonde hair. Marks: Excel Toy Corp/Hong Kong, on head. Available in some areas.

Excel--9½" "Buffalo Bill Cody" Action figure. Marks: Excel Toy Corp/Hong Kong, on head. Available in some areas.

Excel--9½" "Deadwood Dick" Action figure. Marks: Excel Toy Corp./Hong Kong, on head. Available in some areas.

Excel--9½" "Belle Starr" Rigid plastic with vinyl head. Jointed action figure. Ball jointed waist. Molded brown hair. Marks: Excel Toy Corp/Hong Kong, on head. Men in set: Deadwood Dick, Jessie James, Buffalo Bill Cody, Cochise, Wyatt Earp, Wild Bill Cody, Davy Crockett. Available in some areas.

Excel--9½" "Davy Crockett" Action figure.
Marks: Excel Toy Corp/Hong Kong, on head.
Still available in some areas.

Excel--9½" "Jessie James" Action figure.
Marks: Excel Toy Corp/Hong Kong, on head.
Available in some areas.

Excel--9½" "Wyatt Earp" Action figure. Marks:
Excel Toy Corp/Hong Kong, on head. Available
in some areas.

Excel--12" "George Washington" 1732-1799.
Marks: Same as Gen. Lee. Available in some
areas.

Excel--12" "Ulysses S. Grant" 1822-1885. Same marks as Gen. Lee. Available in some areas.

Excel--12" "Lt. Col. Theodore Roosevelt" 1858-1919. Marks same as Gen. Lee. Available in some areas.

Excel--12" "Gen. John. J. Pershing" 1860-1948. Marks same as Gen. Lee. Available in some areas.

Excel--12" "Lt. Col. Paul Revere" 1735-1818. Marks same as Gen. Lee. Available in some areas.

Excel--12" "Gen. Robert E. Lee" Plastic and vinyl. Fully jointed action figure. Excellent modeling. Marks: Excel Toy Corp/Hong Kong. Box: 1974. Available in some areas.

Excel--12" "Gen. Joseph W. Stillwell" 1883-1946. Marked same as Gen. Lee. Available in some areas.

Excel--12" "Gen. Douglas MacArthur" 1880-1964 Marks same as Gen. Lee. Available in some areas.

Excel--12" "Admiral William F. Halsey" 1882-1959. Marks same as Gen. Lee. Available in some areas.

Excel--12" "Dwight D. Eisenhower" 1890-1969. Marks same as Gen. Lee. Available in some areas.

Excel--12" "Gen. Claire L. Chinnault" 1890-1964. Marked same as Gen. Lee. Available in some areas.

Excel--12" "Gen. George S. Patton" 1884-1945. Marked same as Gen. Lee. Available in some areas.

Flagg--6½" "Cowgirl" All vinyl and posable. Molded blonde hair in bun in back. All original. Vest removable only. Marks: None. $7.00.

Flagg--7" "Egyptian" Glued on hair. Painted features. All vinyl that is made in one piece and is bendable. $7.00. (Courtesy Marge Meisinger)

Flagg--7" "Cowboy" All bendable one piece vinyl. Molded hair and painted eyes. Original except hat. $7.00. (Courtesy Marge Meisinger)

Flagg--7" "Calypso Dancer" All posable vinyl. Molded black hair. Stapled on clothes. Marks: None. $7.00.

Flagg--7" "Flagg Dancer" Given to dance students of the Charlotte School of Dance. $7.00. (Courtesy Alice Capps)

Flagg--7" "Frenchman" ca. 1947. $7.00. (Courtesy Alice Capps)

Flagg--3" "Children" Boy and girl. All one piece vinyl that is posable. Molded hair and painted features. Girl is original. $3.00 each. (Courtesy Marge Meisinger)

Flanders, Harriet--11" All composition. Painted blue eyes. Yellow molded and glued on yarn hair. Marks: Harriet Flanders/1937. $35.00. (Courtesy Jay Minter)

131

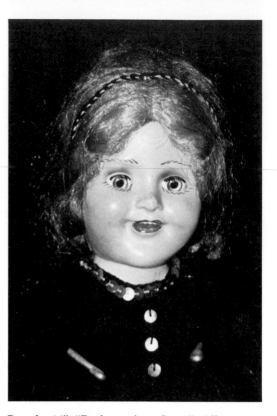

Australia--13" "Bindi" All vinyl with amber/ orange sleep eyes. Streaked hair. Painted/molded teeth. Marks: Metti/Autralia. $45.00. (Courtesy Marie Ernst)

Canada--14" "Barbara Ann Scott" All composition. Blue sleep eyes. Open mouth with six teeth. Marks: Reliable of Canada. $75.00. (Courtesy Helen Garrett)

China--9" Character doll. All composition. Molded, painted hair. Painted dark green eyes. Marks: Box: Made in the People's Republic of China. $30.00. (Courtesy Dodie Shapiro)

China--12" All composition. A beautiful quality doll. Marks: Box: Made in China. $35.00. (Courtesy Dodie Shapiro)

England--14" "Glasgon Scotland" All hard plastic with a matt finish on head. Brown sleep eyes/long lashes. Glued on red mohair. Doll is strung. Original. Marks: Politoy/35/Made in England. $15.00. (Courtesy Mary Partridge)

England--11½" "Tricia" All very good quality vinyl. Blue sleep eyes with blue eyeshadow all around eyes. Marks. Chiltern/Made in England, on back. 1961. Sold thorugh Marshall Fields. $6.00. (Courtesy Mary Partridge)

England--15" "Paulie" All hard plastic with glued on wig. Blue sleep eyes. Open/closed mouth with two painted teeth. Walker, head turns. Marks: Rosebud/Made in England/Pat. No. 667906, on back. Rosebud, on head. 1953 was used for "Baroness in Coronation Robes by L. Rees. Insert shows original clothes. $12.00.

England--7" "Twins" All hard plastic with pale blue sleep eyes/no lashes. Wide spread fingers. Painted on shoes and socks. Original velvet "dance" outfits. Marks: Pedigree, in a triangle/ Made in/England. ca. 1960. $3.00 each.

England--21" "Lucky Lisa" Plastic body, legs and right arm. Vinyl left arm and head. Blue sleep eyes. Painted teeth, "Plug in" in right hand. Battery operated. Jointed right wrist. Original. Marks: 030-00, on head. Dress Tag: Pedigree/Made in England. 1971. Holds dice cup. $8.00.

England--7½" "Chad Valley" All rubber. Painted brown eyes. Painted on black shoes. Glued on mohair. Marks: Chad Valley/Pat. 517252/Made in/England. Tag on slip: Hygienic Toys/Made in England by/Chad Valley Co. Ltd. $10.00. (Courtesy Mary Partridge)

Peggy Nisbet Dolls

The Peggy Nisbet dolls are made in the seaside town of Westonsuper-Mare in the West Country of England. Mrs. Nisbet began making dolls in 1953 (Coronation year). The dolls listed below are currently available: The numbers following them are order numbers.

THE ROYAL FAMILY
Queen Elizabeth in state robes P400
Queen Elizabeth in Garter Robes P401
Queen Elizabeth in Thistle Robes P406
Princes Charles in Garter Robes P402
Queen Elizabeth, The Queen Mother (Garter) P403
Princess Anne in Wedding Dress P405

THE PLANTAGANETS
King Henry VI P642
Margaret of Anjou P643

THE HOUSE OF TUDOR
King Henry VIII H218
Katherine of Aragon H219
Anne Boleyn H217
Jane Seymour H220
Anne of Cleves H222
Catherine Howard H221
Catherine Parr H223
Queen Elizabeth I H214
Lady Jane Grey H216
William Shakespeare P617

THE HOUSE OF STUART
King Charles I P609
Henrietta Maria H239
King Charles II P639
Catherine of Braganza H286
Nell Gwyn, Mistress of H275
King Charles II
Lady Randolph Churchill P592
Sir Winston Churchill P615
King George VI P712
Queen Elizabeth (State robes) P713
King Edward VIII P711
King George V P709
Queen Mary (State robes) P710
Queen Victoria (State robes) P708
King Edward VII P611
Queen Alexandra P612
Queen Victoria (widow) P610
Prince Albert P624

SCOTTISH KINGS & QUEENS &
HISTORICAL CHARACTERS
King James IV P559
Margaret Tudor P238
Mary Queen of Scots H209
Mary Queen of Scots (wedding) P608
Mary Seaton H247
Mary Fleming H248
Charles Edward Stuart P210
Flora MacDonald H224
King James VI P638
Anne of Denmark P249

SCOTTISH COSTUMES
Bonnie Mary BR241
Scots Lassie BR311
Scots Laddie BR312
Scottish Piper BR339
Pipper of the Royal Highlanders BR325

CRIES OF LONDON
Lavender Girl BR304
Orange Seller BR305
Cherry Ripe BR306
Flower Girl BR309
Pretty Ribbons BR378

COSTUMES OF THE WORLD
Argentine N146
Austria N108
France N101
Germany N123
Holland N109
Hungary N102
Italy N104
Japan N116
Jersy N160
Norway N114
Spain N112
Switzerland N107

COSTUMES AND UNIFORMS OF GREAT BRITAIN
England BR376
Wales BR301
Ireland BR302
Pearly King BR314
Pearly Queen BR315
Grenadier Guardsman BR317
Yeoman Warder (Beefeater) BR330

SOUVENIR RANGE
Donald (Scottish Dancer) S501
Meg (Scottish Dancer) S502
Stewart (Piper) S503
Molly S504
Blodwen S505
Susan S506
Thomas (Guardsman) S507
James (Beefeater) S508

MODELS OF YESTERYEAR
These are no longer in production
but may be reintroduced in years to come.
Elysabeth of York
Cardinal Wolsey
Pope John XXIII
Lord Darnley
James Hepburn, Earl of Bothwell
Robert Burns
Richard III
Queen Anne
William the Conqueror
Queen Matilda
Frances, Countess of Warwick
King Edward II
Queen Isabella
King Henry V
Queen Catherine

Princess Margaret
Catherine, Empress of Russia
Hengrist, Chief of the Angles
Lord Nelson
Lady Hamilton
Georgiana, Dutchess of Devonshire

BICENTENARY
Gen. George Washington P702
Martha Washington P703
Betsy Ross H226
Paul Revere P704
The Famous Minutemen H814
Minuteman's Wife H815
American Trooper H816
Indian Warrior P705
King George III (State robes) P706
British Redcoat 1776 H817
Queen Charlotte P707

THE FRENCH COURT
Marie Antoinette H215
Madame Pompadour H227
Madame DuBerry H271

CENTURY LADIES
15th Century Medieval Lady H211
16th Century Elizabethan Lady H202
18th Century Georgian Lady H204
19th Century Victorian Lady (Crinoline) H225
19th Century Victorian Lady H258
20th Century Edwardian Lady H801
Peeress of the Realm H811

SPECIAL COLLECTOR'S SETS
Each is autographed by Mrs. Peggy Nisbet. Editions are limited to 350. A set comprises 3 to 5 models. Set No. 10 was introduced March 1975 and set No. 11 was available June 1975.

King John and his Barons	Louis XIV-The Sun King
War of the Roses (Part I)	Bloody Mary-Mary Tudor
War of the Roses (Part II)	King William IV
The Spanish Armada	Regency Period
The Battle of Waterloo	The Court of King Arthur
Three Tragic Queens	

England--8" "H.M. Queen Elizabeth II" Made by Peggy Nisbet in 1971. (#1395). $25.00. (Courtesy Marie Ernst)

135

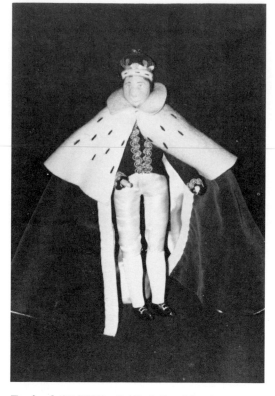

England--8½" "King" All cloth with wired arms. Original. Tag: Liberty/Made in England. $18.00. (Courtesy Barbara Coker)

England--8½" "Queen" All cloth with wired arms. Original. Tag: Liberty/Made in England. $18.00. (Courtesy Barbara Coker)

France--30" "Oriental" Plastic and vinyl with molded paper head and paper hair. Body is in two sections which allows it to "move." Original. Used in a window display. Made by G. Giroud & Cie, France. 1960. $30.00. (Courtesy Karen Penner)

France--12" All vinyl. Jointed neck, shoulders and hips. Inset eyes/lashes. Open/closed mouth. Marks: M/P, on head. ca. 1962. Original. $4.00. (Courtesy Mary Partridge)

Germany--7" All vinyl with jointed neck. No ears. Dark sun tan color with rooted white hair. Painted black eyes. 1963. Marks: Heico/H/Made in Western/Germany, seal on bottom. Necklace: Original/Western Germany. $4.00.

Germany--12" "Gucki" Rubber and felt. Tag: Mollenecht Durch/Eulan/Bayer/ Leverrisen. $8.00. (Courtesy Jay Minter)

France--16" "Edmond" Plastic body. Vinyl arms. legs and head. Golden brown sleep eyes. Bent baby legs. Individual large toes. Tiny hole in mouth/nurser. Marks: Clodrey/2018-6926, on head. Original clothes. 1972-73 and 74. $22.00.

Germany--19" "Riekchen" 1970. Cloth and rigid plastic. Painted blue eyes. Marks: Tag: Kathe Kruse/Exclusive for Neiman-Marcus. $28.00. (Courtesy Jay Minter)

137

Germany--14" "Hummel" Vinyl with open/closed mouth. Inset eyes. $8.00. (Courtesy Jay Minter)

Germany--18" Cloth over foam. Vinyl gauntlet hands. Vinyl head with inset blue eyes. Marks: None. 1968. $16.00. (Courtesy Julia Rogers)

138

Germany--5½" "Hummel" Painted green eyes. Plastic and vinyl. Marks: Bee in V 2914/2/ Charlotte Byj/1966 W. Goebel., on head. Bee in V/W. Goebel/1966/Charlotte Byj/2914/1x2/W. Germany, on back. $3.00. (Courtesy Phyllis Houston)

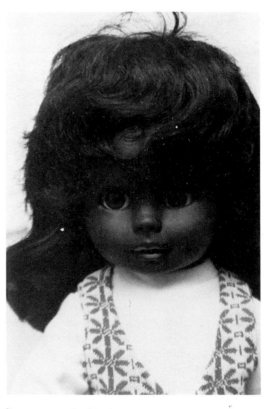

Germany--11" "Shirley Jean" Black painted eye version. Marks: 30/Made in/W. Germany, on back. Turtle mark, on head. (Courtesy Phyllis Houston)

Germany--11" "Shirley Jean" 1958-59. Plastic body, arms and legs. Vinyl head with blue sleep eyes/lashes. Open/closed mouth with two molded painted upper teeth. Deep dimples. Original sailor dress. Marks: 30/Made in/W. Germany, on back. Turtle mark, on head. $6.00. (Courtesy Mary Partridge)

Germany--11" "Shirley Jean" Plastic and vinyl. Painted very pale blue eyes. Original. Marks: Turtlemark/30/Made in/W. Germany. $6.00. (Courtesy Phyllis Houston)

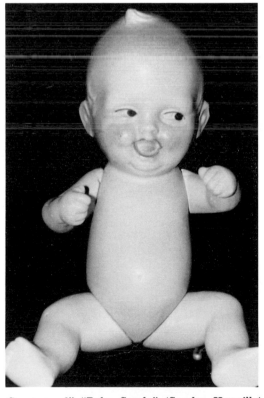

Germany--16" "Gret" All vinyl with brown sleep eyes/lashes. Original. 1968. Marks: Gotz Puppe. $12.00. (Courtesy Marie Ernst)

Germany--6" "Baby Sandy" (Sandra Henville) Painted bisque. Blue painted eyes. Open/closed mouth. Dimples. (Marks: Germany, on back. $65.00. (Courtesy Maxine Heitt)

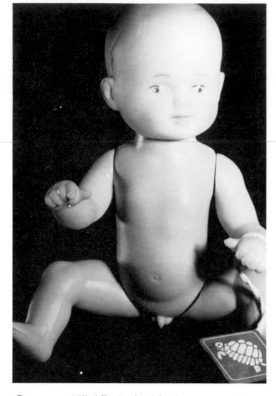

Germany--16" All vinyl with sleep eyes. Closed mouth. Marks: 36/Gotz/B. $8.00. (Courtesy Kathy Walker)

Greece--The Kehagias dolls are like most Furga's and Alexanders. The doll is the same but the outfit has name. For example this 12" doll shown is dressed as Adriadne, Sylvia, Isabella, Betty and Rania. The dolls appear to be made of above average quality materials. All I have seen have been completely unmarked. $9.00.

Greece--7" "Natalie" #7021. All vinyl with inset blue eyes. Open/closed mouth. Posable head. Original. Marks: None. Made by Kehagias, Greece. $8.00. (Courtesy Mary Partridge)

Greece--13" "Lena" Plastic and vinyl. Brown sleep eyes. Open/closed mouth, molded upper teeth unpainted. Excellent quality clothes. Marks: None. Box: Made by Kehagia and distributed by M&S Shillman Inc. Catalog shows this outfit also called: Tina, Venia, Maria and Joanna (boy: John). $9.00. (Courtesy Bessie Carson)

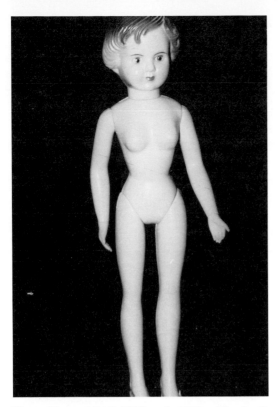

Hong Kong--14½" "Hillery" 1969. All plastic with jointed wrists. Blue sleep eyes/molded lashes. High heel feet. Marks: Evergreen/Made in/Hong Kong/9150. $3.00. (Courtesy Mary Partridge)

Hong Kong--14" Pregnant doll. Plastic and vinyl. Rooted hair. Blue sleep eyes. Original clothes. Marks: Perfekta/Made in Hong Kong, on head. $8.00. (Courtesy Sally Bethscheider)

Hong Kong--17" "Rhonda" Plastic body and legs. Vinyl arms and head. Right leg molded slightly bent at the knee. Jointed waist. Painted blue eyes. Mf'd for SS Kresge Co. Came in 5 different original outfits. Marks: Blue Girl, picture of head of girl, Hong Kong, on head. Hong Kong/Blue Girl, on back. 1974. $7.00.

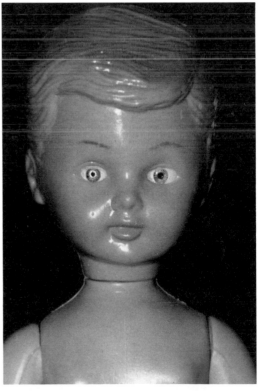

Hong Kong--20" "Robbie" All thin plastic. Inset blue eyes. Molded hair. 1967. Marks: large "M"/PF, in a circle/Made in Hong Kong. $6.00. (Courtesy Marie Ernst)

141

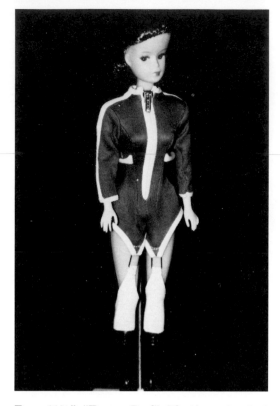

Teen--11½" "Emma Peel" Plastic and vinyl. Painted brown eyes. Brown hair. Original. Marks: Made In/Hong Kong, on back. Emma Peel, on stand. $18.00. (Courtesy B. Mongelluzzi)

Hong Kong--23" "Babs Walker" Plastic with vinyl head. Blue sleep eyes. Yellow hair. Walker. Original. Paper sticker: Made in Kong Kong. $3.00.

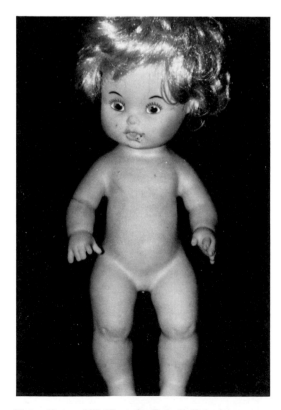

Hong Kong--11" "Lovely Baby" Poly-foam one piece body arms and legs. Vinyl head. Painted blue eyes. Open mouth/nurser. Marks: Hong Kong, picture of world in an oval, on back. Hong Kong, on head. $2.00.

Hong Kong--9" "Nancy" Plastic and vinyl. Blue sleep eyes. Posable head. Original. 1969. Marks: Hong Kong, on back. $3.00. (Courtesy Marie Ernst)

Hong Kong--3" "Vampire Troll" All vinyl.
Jointed neck only. Fangs. Marks: Made In/Hong
Kong, on head and back. 1966. $3.00. (Courtesy
Marie Ernst)

7½" "Patches" Plastic and vinyl with painted
blue eyes. Posable heads. Original. 1974. Marks:
Made in Hong Kong, on back. Sack: Made for P.
Kronow & Co. $2.00 each.

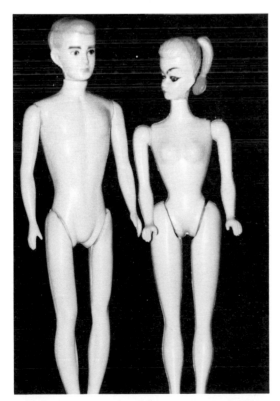

Teen--11½" "Mod Jerry & Mod Judy" All plastic. Judy: Black heavy brows. Plastic pony tail
socketed to rotate. Jerry: Molded red hair.
Painted blue eyes. Marks: Made In/Hong Kong,
lower back. Made for Australia. $4.00. (Courtesy
Marie Ernst)

Teen--"Three Generation Family" Man:12" red
molded hair. Blue painted eyes. Lady: 11½"
brown with mixed grey hair. Blue painted eyes.
Young Girl 11½" Open/closed mouth, painted
teeth, jointed like action. 4" Baby, jointed neck
only. Nurser. All have jointed waists. Marks:
Hong Kong. $25.00 set. (Courtesy Marie Ernst)

143

Teen--12" "Pool Dolls" (girl is 11½"). Plastic with vinyl heads. Man is suntanned. Reddish brown molded hair and painted teeth. Girl: Blue painted eyes to left. Came with swimming pool. Marks; Made in/Hong Kong, on back. $16.00 set. (Courtesy Marie Ernst)

Hong Kong--7½" "John Paul Jones" One of the Heroes of the American Revolution sets sold through Montgomery Wards and Kresge. This and following 6 are plastic with vinyl heads. They have jointed waists. Marks: Made in Hong Kong, on backs. RT-Hong Kong, on boxes.

Hong Kong--7½" "George Washington" Marked same as John Paul Jones.

Hong Kong--7½" "Paul Revere" Marked same as John Paul Jones.

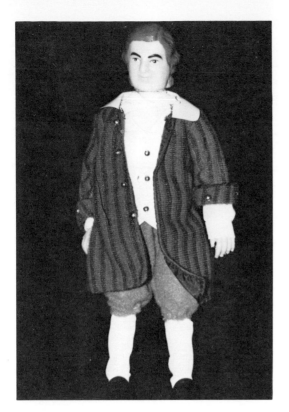

Hong Kong--7½" "Thomas Jefferson" Marked same as John Paul Jones.

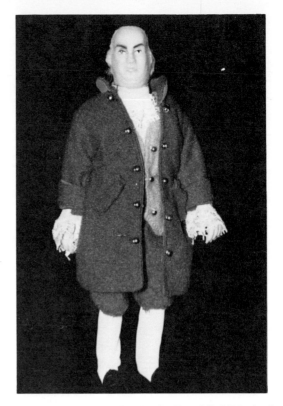

Hong Kong--7½" "Benjamin Franklin" Marked same as John Paul Jones.

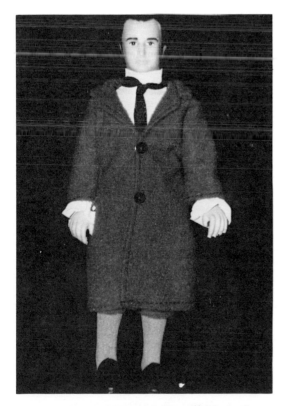

Hong Kong--7½" "Patrick Henry" Marked same as John Paul Jones.

Hong Kong--7½" "Nathan Hale" Marked same as John Paul Jones.

145

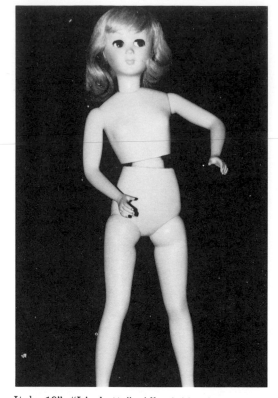

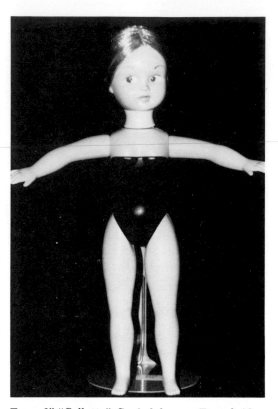

Italy--19" "Lizabetta" All rigid plastic. Ball jointed waist. Human hair wig. Flirty/sleep deep green eyes/lashes. Doll is strung. 1962. Marks: Bonomi/Italy, on head and back. Tag: Poupee/Originale/Bonomi/Fabriquee in /Italie. $30.00. (Courtesy Bessie Carson)

Teen--8" "Collette" Copied from a French idea. "Pop" apart plastic and vinyl. Came with cut out (non-sew) costumes. Sold through Sears 1961. Marks: Hong Kong, on back. $7.00.

Iran--8" "Iran" All vinyl. Blue sleep eyes. Original. Very good quality. Marks: None. $9.00. (Courtesy Marie Ernst)

Italy--12" "Little One" (translation). All painted heavy plastic. Flirty eyes/lashes. Polished nails. Original. $45.00. (Courtesy Marge Meisinger)

Italy--19" "Lizabetta" Shows one of her original outfits. Red/white check. Individual white collar.

Italy--22" "Handora" Rigid plastic. Flirty/blue sleep eyes. Ball jointed waist. Open crown with cryer box in head. Closed mouth, two painted upper teeth. Human hair black wig. Ca. 1961. Marks: Bonomi/Italy, on back. Bonomi/Italy, on head. Tag: Poupee/Originale/Bonomi/Fabriqee in/Itale. $28.00. (Courtesy Bessie Carson)

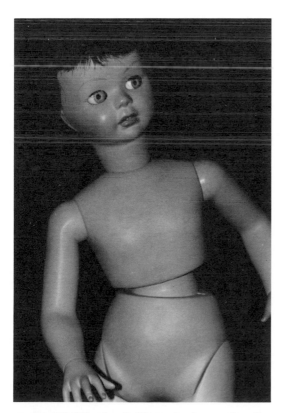

Italy--22" "Handora" Shows body construction. Same as the Vogue "Brikette."

Italy--12" "Pipi Long Stockings" Vinyl with plastic body. Blue sleep eyes. Orange rooted hair. Freckles. All original. Marks: Italy/1-C in square. $12.00. (Courtesy Marie Ernst)

147

Italy--15" "Denita" All vinyl with blue sleep eyes. Original. Marks: IC, in square/1969. $12.00. (Courtesy Marie Ernst)

Italy--5" "Nina & Nino" All vinyl. Inset plastic blue eyes. Original. Made by Italocremona. Marks: IC, in a square/1967. $25.00 set. (Courtesy Cindy Karsti)

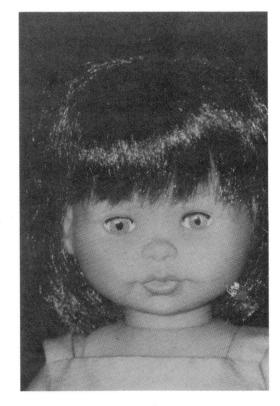

Italy--16" "Rennetta" All vinyl with set blue eyes/lashes. Marks: girl holding an "M", in a circle: Italy/Miglioratti, on head and body. $12.00. (Courtesy Marie Ernst)

Italy--12" "Sabrina" Manufactured just for SS Kresge Co. $12.00. (Courtesy Marie Ernst)

Italy--12" "Mirella" Made just for the SS Kresge Co. Marks: IC, in square. $12.00. (Courtesy Marie Ernst)

Italy--16" "Suzabette" All vinyl with sleep blue eyes. Original. Marks: IC, in square./Made in/ Italy. $12.00. (Courtesy Marie Ernst)

Italy--6½" "Twins: Lella & Lulu" All vinyl with sleep eyes. Original. Marks: 11701/Furga/Italy. $6.00 each. (Courtesy Marie Ernst)

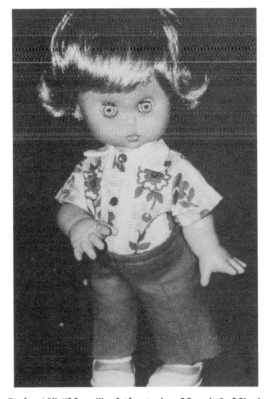

Italy--10" "Muzzi" of the twins Muzzi & Mizzi. Plastic body. Vinyl arms, legs and head. Bright blue sleep eyes/lashes. One arm bent. Original. Marks: Furga Italy, on head. $8.00. (Courtesy Bessie Carson)

149

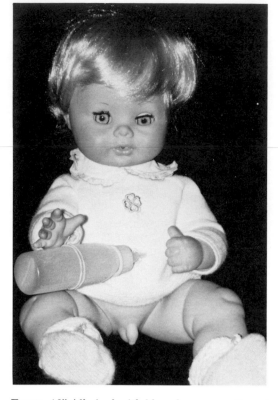

Furga--16" All vinyl with blue sleep eyes. Open/
mouth nurser. Original. Marks: 1240/Furga/
Italy, in a square. $35.00. (Courtesy Julia
Rogers)

Italy--15" "Guendalina" Plastic and vinyl. Had
feathered hat and umbrella. Dress colors are
blue/white with a touch of yellow. Marks: Furga
Italy, on head. Italy/Furga, on body. $50.00.

Italy--9" "Mary, Mary" Plastic and vinyl. Brown
hair with blue eyes. Marks: Furga/Italy. 1974.
Still available.

Italy--9" "Cinderella" Plastic and vinyl. White
hair with blue eyes. Marks: Furga/Italy. 1974.
Still available.

Italy--9" "Red Riding Hood" Plastic and vinyl.
Brown hair and blue eyes. Marks: Furga/Italy.
1974. Still available.

Italy--9" "Miss Muffet" Plastic and vinyl. White
hair and blue eyes. Marks: Furga/Italy. 1974.
Still available.

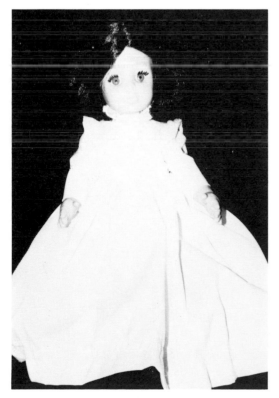

Italy--9" "Snow White" Plastic and vinyl. Brown
hair and blue eyes. All white dress. Marks:
Furga/Italy. 1974. Still available.

Italy--9" "Gretel" Plastic and vinyl. White hair
with blue eyes. Marks: Furga/Italy. 1974. Still
available.

Furga--14" "Zefirina" Flannel filled with foam. A "flat" doll. Stitched mohair. Removable clothes. Elastic in top of head for hanging. Marks: None on doll. $4.00.

Italy--21" "Titti" and son 7" "Cialdino" Baby is all vinyl with painted blue eyes. Nurser. "Titti" is plastic and vinyl with jointed waist. Key wind. Rocks baby, eyes open and close. Head lowers and raises. Marks: Baby: Made Italy/Sebino. Titti: Sebino/Made Italy, head and body. Original. Sold since 1972. $45.00.

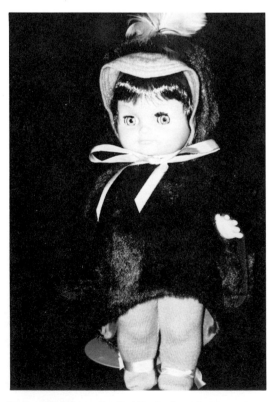

Italy--12" "Mioa, Mioa" All vinyl. Blue sleep eyes. Original clothes representing a kitten. Sebino. 1974. $25.00.

Italy--12" "Qua, Qua" All vinyl with blue sleep eyes. Original clothes representing a duck. Sebino. 1974. $25.00.

Japan--8" "Mrs. Claus" All vinyl, jointed neck and shoulders. Painted features. Marks: Made in Japan. $3.00.

Japan--7½" All vinyl with rooted black hair. Painted features. Sideward smile. Marks: Japan, on foot. 532/D/SII1DA, on head. $2.00.

Japan--7" "Patty Jean" Good quality. Excellent toe detail. Rooted orange hair. Painted blue/black eyes. Original. Marks: Japan, bottom of foot. $2.00.

Japan--10½" "Robin Good" All stuffed felt. Vinyl head. Painted features. Open/closed mouth with molded tongue. Marks: None. Tag: "Robin Good" by Sarco/Japan. $2.00. (Courtesy Mary Partridge)

153

Japan--7" "Moari" doll. New Zealand aborigine with baby. All hard plastic. Sleep eyes. Full joints: baby is one piece. Moari dolls are made in Japan. $8.00. (Courtesy Phyllis Houston)

Japan--6" "Angels Nodder" Plaster and paper mache. Painted and molded on clothes, hair and features. Marks: Paper sticker on bottom/Japan La, on cap. Angels, on shirt. Paper sticker: Anaheim, over "Los Angeles". Between 1961 and 1966. $4.00. (Courtesy Edith Goldsworthy)

Japan--Shows the end of the "Junior Margaret" box. Doll was sold in several "original" outfits.

Japan--15" "Junior Margaret" Plastic and vinyl. Posable head. An excellent quality doll. Pull string talker, with a pearl keeping the string from going in too far. She talks in Japanese. Marks: ✧ Made in Japan, on head. Same on back plus: Pat. P.O. 27057. 1972. Original including glasses. $22.00.

154

Japan--9" "Bizzy Buzz Buzz" All vinyl. Red rooted hair and painted eyes. Original clothes. Marks: King Features Synd/Gund Mfg Co., on head. A "M" in a Diamond/Japan, on back. Tag: Bizzy/Buzz Buzz/King Features Syndicate/J. Swedlin, Inc. $4.00. (Courtesy Phyllis Houston)

Japan--13" "Sucking Thumb Baby" All cloth with gauntlet vinyl hands. Vinyl head with very protruding ears. Round open/closed mouth. Freckles. Painted half closed eyes. An FAO Swartz exclusive for 1975. Marks: Tag on doll: Seikiguchi and picture of child with crown. Tag on bootie: Sakai & Co. Ltd/Japan. Box: Petite Poupee/Seki-Guchi. Original clothes. $22.00.

Cloth--9½" "Dennis the Menace" All stockinette. Original. Paper tag: Made in Japan, on foot. $6.00. (Courtesy Bev. Gardner)

Japan--5" Made in Japan and re-issued 1975. Jointed arms and neck. Red curly top knot. Unpainted wings. Still available.

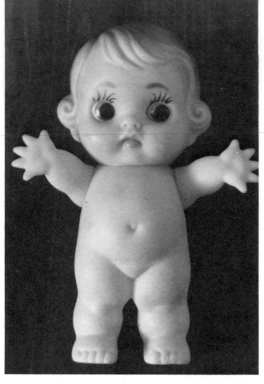

Japan--7½" All vinyl girl. Green wings. Marks: None. $3.00. (Courtesy Phyllis Houston)

Manufacturer Unknown--9½" "Artist" Silk covered wire armature. Composition type head. Original.

Foreign--5" Rooted hair, molded on clothes and brown "skin." A very small "sexed" doll. Was a gift from New Zealand. $6.00. (Courtesy Phyllis Houston)

Japan--12½" Posable silk stockinette doll. Jersey and felt clothes. Woolen hat. Painted features. Yarn hair. On self stand. Tag: Sonsco Toys/Japan. (Courtesy Phyllis Houston)

156

Korea--17" "Dance Group" Set of five fan
dancers. Sold through Military P.X.'s in 1973.
$65.00. (Courtesy Ruth Brocha)

Korea--27" Called French Type Doll. Sold
through Military P.X.'s in 1973. $20.00. (Cour-
tesy Ruch Brocha)

Korea--17" Called "Sisters" and shows the tra-
ditional carrage of children. Sold through Military P.X.'s in 1973. $22.00. (Courtesy Ruth
Brocha)

157

Poland--15" "Little Lulu" Cloth with jointed shoulders/hips. Plastic face mask. Floss type hair. Marks: Poland, stamped on back of leg. $28.00. (Courtesy B. Mongelluzzi)

Russia--21" "Takmeobckom" Excellent quality. Green sleep eyes. Glued on wig. All hand painted features (other than eyes). Has the look of wax but is vinyl. Tag: Tameobckom and other Russian characters, plus Made In USSR. $35.00. (Courtesy Dodie Shapiro)

Spain--18" All felt with felt mouth, lashes and clothes. Real fur hat (hair?). Paper eyes. $22.00. (Courtesy Virginia Jones)

Spain--16" All vinyl. Tag: Marin Chiclana/ Made in Spain. 1974. (Courtesy Louise Alonso)

Spain--16" "Nancy" Plastic and vinyl. Legs have fat calfs and very fat ankles. Pale brown sleep eyes. Came with extra hair pieces. Had many outfits available. Marks: Famosa, on head, shoes. Tag: Munecas/ Famosa/Made in Spain. $20.00. (Courtesy Bessie Carson)

158

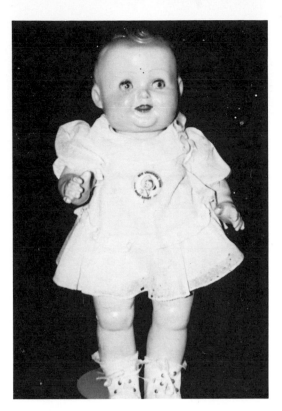

Freundlich, Ralph--16" "Sandy Henville" child movie star. All composition. Sleep eyes/lashes. Open mouth. Molded hair. All original including pin. $85.00. (Courtesy Kimport Dolls)

Fun World--6" "I Saw A Ship A-Sailing" Mother Goose Picture Book and Doll Series. Set includes: "What Are Little Girls Made Of," "Jack & Jill" & "The Queen of Hearts." Plastic and vinyl. Fully jointed. Her hair is orange and his is dark blonde. Marks: Made In/Hong Kong, on head. $4.00.

Fun World--6½" "Cissy Swinger" Bean bag style with vinyl head. Molded hair on front only. Jointed neck. Painted blue eyes. Open/closed mouth. Marks: Hong Kong, on neck. Tag: Fun World/Inc. 1975. $3.00.

Fun World--7½" "A Little Girl With a Curl" Mother Goose Storybook doll. Plastic with vinyl head. One of a series. Marks: None. $4.00.

159

Gilbert--3½" "007" played by Sean Connery, shown in Tux and with rifle. "Goldfinger," played by Gert Frobe in movie. Dolls not marked. Box: 1965 Gledrose Productions Ltd. and/Eon Production Ltd./1965 A.C. Gilbert Co. U.S. Patent Pending. Made in Portugal. $2.00 each.

Gilbert--3½" "Odd Job" played by Harold Sakata in Goldfinger. Next is "Domino" played by Claudine Auger in Thunderball. Next is "Emilio Largo" played by Adolfo Celi in Thunderball. Last is "Moneypenny" (loyal gal-Friday to 007-James Bond) played by Lois Maxwell in Goldfinger. $2.00 each.

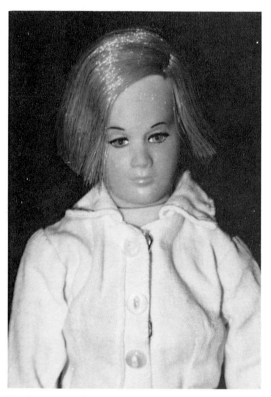

Gilbert--3½" "007-James Bond" in the scuba gear from Thunderball as played by Sean Connery. Next is "M" Bond's boss played by Bernard Lee in Goldfinger. "Dr. No" played by Joseph Wiseman. $2.00 each.

Hasbro--11" "GI Joe Nurse Jane" Green painted eyes/black lashes. Marks: Patent Pend/1967 Hasbro/Made in Hong Kong. Tag: G.I. Nurse/ By Hasbro/Hong Kong. $25.00.

G. I. Joe Series

The following information comes from Joseph L. Bourgeois who has spent many hours researching the G.I. Joe Action Figures.

"In order to show the sequence of development and changes in the G.I. Joes, I have set up my list into nine series. It isn't likely that the Hasbro company would recognize this many series as their model numbers remain the same for several of my series. A serious collector of Action Figures needs this information to catalogue his mannequins. Fortunately the Hasbro people have produced mannequins with sufficient differences, between models and series, for identification. Even with these differences there are no problems in identifying G.I. Joe Action Sailors from G.I. Joe Action Marine without their original uniforms. The same G.I. Joe is used for both categories.

The first series of G.I. Joes are identified by the letters TM (Trademark) in their mark. They are distinguished one from the other by the color of their hair and eyes, with the exception of G.I. Joe Sailor and G.I. Joe Marne that are the same mannequin.

The second series of G.I. Joes are similar to the first series. The difference is the mark. The TM has been dropped and ® has been added indicating that the name G.I. Joe has been registered. It is this second series that the first Black G.I. Joe is introduced.

In the third series we find that G.I. Joe no longer has a scar on his face. The lack of a scar is the identifying feature. The mark is the same as the second series.

The fourth series is also identified by not having the scar on the face as well as having a change in the mark. The words "Patent Pending" have been removed from the mark and the "Pat. No. 3,2777,602" has been added. It should be noted that the scarless faces of the third and fourth series have a thinner and more "nordic" appearance. It is also in this series that Hasbro introduces their first talking model

The scar returning to the face identifies the fifth series. The face is also a little rounder. The mark is the same as the fourth series. This is also the last series in which G.I. Joe is packaged with a military designation. (Soldier, sailor, etc.)

In the sixth series G.I. Joe takes on various adventures notably lacking in military flavor. For example he is now a research archeologist searching for "the secret of the mummy's tomb" or he is a deep sea diver in "Eight ropes of danger," etc. With his new adventures, G.I. Joe also takes on a new appearance. He now has flocked hair and a beard. The mark remains the same as series four and five.

The seventh series gives us a taller G.I. Joe. He is now 11¾" tall (all previous models are 11½" tall). He also has new hands called "Kung Fu grips" with which he can easily grasp things. The mark remains the same as in series four, five and six.

There is only one model in the eighth series. It is readily identifiable by its own characteristics. The mark on the right hip is the same as in series four, five, six and seven. For the first time there is a mark on the back of the head of a G.I. Joe.

The ninth series brings out an entirely new G.I. Joe. The body is now more robust and muscleman like when compared to all the previous series. Swimming trunks are molded on as part of the hip section of the body. There is also a new method of articulating the limbs. The new mark is now located in the small of the back.

I feel that the above notes and the following list give a collector sufficient information in identifying his G.I. Joes. This information has been gleaned through the examination of hundreds of G.I. Joes and their packagings. I have also had model numbers verified by the Hasbro Company. I hope I've made no errors in transcribing the information. I am still researching G.I. Joe for who designed it, etc.

	Size:	Name and Particulars	Mold mark located on lower back	
		(1st Series--4 models		
7500	11½"	G.I. Joe Action Soldier (white) Black molded hair, blue eyes		1964
7600	11½"	G.I. Joe Action Sailor (white) Brown molded hair, brown eyes	G.I. Joe TM Copyright 1964 By Hasbro® Patent Pending	1964
7700	11½"	G.I. Joe Action Marine (white) Brown molded hair, brown eyes	Made in U.S.A.	1964
7800	11½"	G.I. Joe Action Pilot (white) Blonde molded hair, brown eyes		1964

	Size	Name and Particulars	Mold mark located on lower back	
		(2nd Series--5 models)		
7500	11½"	G.I. Joe Action Soldier (white) Black molded hair, blue eyes		1965
7600	11½"	G.I. Joe Action Sailor (white) Brown molded hair, brown eyes	G.I. Joe® Copyright 1964	1965
7700	11½"	G.I. Joe Action Marine (white) Brown molded hair, brown eyes	By Hasbro® Patent Pending Made in U.S.A.	1965
7800	11½"	G.I. Joe Action Pilot (white) Blonde molded hair, brown eyes		1965
7900	11½"	G.I. Joe Action Soldier (black) Black molded hair, brown eyes		1965
		(3rd Series--5 models--no scar on face)		
7500	11½"	G.I. Joe Action Soldier (white) Black molded hair, blue eyes		1966
7600	11½"	G.I, Joe Action Sailor (white) Brown molded hair, brown eyes	G.I. Joe® Copyright 1964	1966
7700	11½"	G.I. Joe Action Marien (white) Brown molded hair, brown eyes	By Hasbro® Patent Pending Made in U.S.A.	1966
7800	11½"	G.I. Joe Action Pilot (white) Blonde molded hair, brown eyes		1966
7900	11½"	G.I. Joe Action Soldier (black) Black molded hair, brown eyes		1966
		(4th Series--6 models--no scar on face 1st Talking model)		
7500	11½"	G.I. Joe Action Soldier (white) Black molded hair, blue eyes		1967
7600	11½"	G.I. Joe Action Sailor (white) Brown molded hair, brown eyes		1967
7700	11½"	G.I. Joe Action Marine (white) Brown molded hair, brown eyes	G.I. Joe® Copyright 1964 By Hasbro®	1967
7800	11½"	G.I. Joe Action Pilot (white) Blonde molded hair, brown eyes	Pat. No. 3,277,602 Made in U.S.A.	1967
7900	11½"	G.I. Joe Action Soldier (black) Black molded hair, brown eyes		1967
7900	11½"	G.I. Joe Talking Commander (white) Blonde molded hair, brown eyes		1967

	Size	Name and Particulars	Mold mark located on lower back	
		(5th Series--6 models--Scar on face)		
7500	11½"	G.I. Joe Action Soldier (white) Black molded hair, blue eyes		1968
7600	11½"	G.I. Joe Action Sailor (white) Brown molded hair, brown eyes		1968
7700	11½"	G.I. Joe Action Marine (white) Brown molded hair, brown eyes	G.I. Joe® Copyright 1964 By Hasbro® Pat. No. 3,277,602 Made in U.S.A.	1968
7800	11½"	G.I. Joe Action Pilot (white) Blonde molded hair, brown eyes		1968
7900	11½"	G.I. Joe Action Soldier (black) Black molded hair, brown eyes		1968
7900	11½"	G.I. Joe Talking Commander (white) Blonde molded hair, brown eyes		1968
		(6th Series--9 models) **Life-like hair and/or beard Adventure team)**		
7400	11½"	G.I. Joe Adventure Team Talking Commander (white) Blonde life-like hair and beard		1970
7400	11½"	G.I. Joe Adventure Team Talking Commander (black) Black life-like hair and beard		1970
7400	11½"	G.I. Joe Adventure Team Talking Commander (white) Blonde life-like hair, no beard		1970
7401	11½"	G. I. Joe Land Adventurer (white) Brown life-like hair and beard	G.I. Joo® Copyright 1964 By Hasbro® Pat. No. 3,277,602 Made in U.S.A.	1970
7402	11½"	G.I. Joe Sea Adventurer (white Red life-like hair and beard		1970
7403	11½"	G.I. Joe Air Adventurer (white) Blonde life-like hair and beard		1970
7404	11½"	G.I. Joe Adventurer (black) Black life-like hair, no beard		1970
7405	11½"	G.I. Joe Astronaut (white) Blonde life-like hair, no beard		1970
7590	11½"	G.I. Joe Talking		1970
		(7th Series--8 models--Kung Fu Grip)		
7280	11¾"	G.I. Joe Land Adventurer (white) Black life-like hair and beard	G.I. Joe® Copyright 1964 By Hasbro® Pat. No. 3,277,602 Made in U.S.A.	1974
7281	11¾"	G.I. Joe Sea Adventurer (white) Red life-like hair and beard		1974

	Size	Name and Particulars	Mold mark located on lower back	
7282	11¾"	G.I. Joe Air Adventurer (white) Blonde life-like hair and beard		1974
7283	11¾"	G.I. Joe Adventurer (black) Black life-like hair, no beard		1974
7284	11¾"	G.I. Joe Man of Action Black life-like hair, no beard	G.I. Joe® Copyright 1964 By Hasbro®	1974
7290	11¾"	G.I. Joe Talking Adventure Team Commander (white) Brown life-like hair and beard	Pat. 3,277,602 Made in U.S.A.	1974
7291	11¾"	G.I. Joe Talking Adventure Team Commander (black) Black life-like hair and beard		1974
7292	11¾"	G.I. Joe Talking Man of Action Brown life-like hair, no beard		1975
8025	11½"	(8th Series--1 model--Atomic Man) See through right arm and left leg Mike Power, Atomic Man G.I. Joe Adventure Team (white) Brown molded hair, no beard, blue eyes	G.I. Joe® Copyright 1964 By Hasbro® Pat. No. 3,277,602 Made in U.S.A. on back of head: © Hasbro Ind. Inc. 1975 Made in Hong Kong	1975
		(9th Series--8 models New life like (Muscle man bodies		
1-7280	11¾"	G.I. Joe New Life-like Land Adventurer (white) Brown life-like hair and beard, blue eyes		1975
7281	11¾"	G.I. Joe New Life-like Sea Adventurer (white) Red life-like hair and beard, brown eyes		1975
1-7282	11¾"	G.I. Joe New Life-like Air Adventurer (white) Blonde life-like hair and beard, brown eyes		1975
7283	11¾"	G.I. Joe New Life-like Black Adventurer (black) Black life-like hair, no beard, brown eyes	Mark is now on small of back: ©1975 Hasbro® Pat. Pend. Pawt. R.I.	1975
7284	11¾"	G.I. Joe New Life-like Man of Action (white) Brown life-like hair, no beard, blue eyes		1975
1-7290	11¾"	G.I. Joe New Life-like Talking Commander (white) Brown life-like hair and beard, blue eyes		1975
7291	11¾"	G.I. Joe New Life-like Talking Black Commander (black) Black life-like hair and beard, brown eyes		1975
1-7292	11¾"	G.I. Joe New Life-like Talking Man of Action (white) Brown life-like hair, no beard, blue eyes		1975

Hasbro--3½" "Mother Hubbard" All vinyl with rooted white hair. Painted features. Original. Marks: 1967/Hasbro/Hong Kong, on head. $3.00.

Hasbro--11½" "Russian/G.I. Joe" All plastic and fully jointed. Original Russian outfit. Marks: G.I. Joe/Copyright 1964/By Hasbro/Patent Pending/Made In U.S.A. $18.00

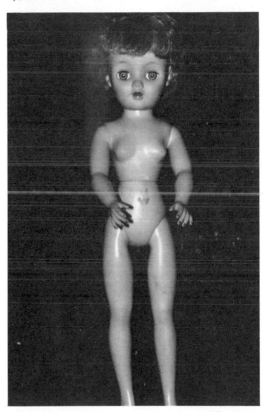

Hasbro--4½" "John" of the Dolly Darling Hat Box Series. Marks: 1965/Hasbro/Japan, on back. Tag: Dolly Darling/By Hasbro/Japan. $2.00. (Courtesy Joan Amundsen)

Hill Mfg.--21" "Movie Queen Natalie" All rigid vinyl, softer vinyl head. Sleep eyes, jointed waist. 1959. Marks: Made in U.S.A. mid back. Same doll used for several personalities. Clothes: Natalie: Pink ankle length, lace net overskirt, white "fur" stole. Felice Model: Gold/white X just below knee tight dress. Brown stole lined in dress material. Miss Julie: Long pink satin gown. Coat that is silver with pink lining and hood. Susan Prom Queen: Ankle length yellow ball gown. Flowers on each shoulder and at waist. $12.00.

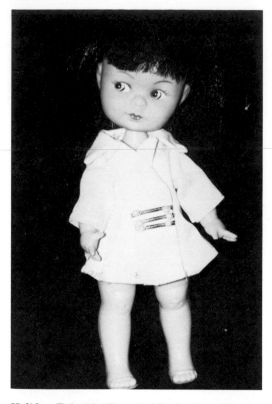

Holiday Fair--9" "Terry" All plastic with vinyl head. Black rooted hair. Painted blue eyes. Marks: Holiday Fair, Inc./Made in Hong Kong, on back. Made in Hong Kong, on head. $2.00.

Holiday Fair--6½" "Luva Girl" Plastic body. Jointed neck only. Vinyl head. Black hair. Blue painted eyes. Earrings. Original. Marks: Made in Hong Kong. $5.00.

166

For complete information on the Horsman Doll Co. refer to Series I, page 136.

Horsman--20" Composition head and limbs. Cloth body. Blue tin sleep eyes. Original. Open mouth/2 upper teeth. Marks: E.I.H. Co./Horsman. $37.00. (Courtesy Jay Minter)

Horsman--Right: Cloth with composition head, arms and legs. Swivel shoulder plate. Completely original. Blue tin sleep eyes. Marks: Rosebud, on neck. Dress tag: Horsman. Doll on left is also marked: Rosebud. Has brown sleep eyes. $45.00. (Courtesy Flacks)

Horsman--14½" Cloth body. Composition arms, legs and head. Brown tin sleep eyes. Curly molded hair. Marks. A/Horsman/Doll. $37.00. (Courtesy Maxine Heitt)

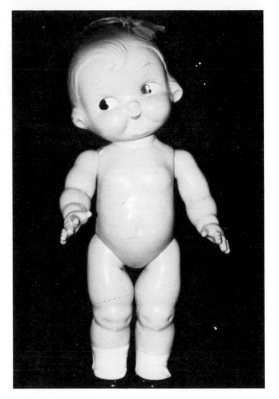

Horsman--12" Campbell Kid" All composition. Painted on shoes and socks. Stapled on ribbon. 1948. $65.00. (Courtesy Kimport Dolls)

Horsman--22" One piece stuffed vinyl body and limbs. Vinyl head. Brown sleep eyes. Marks: 96/Horsman. ca. 1955. $15.00.

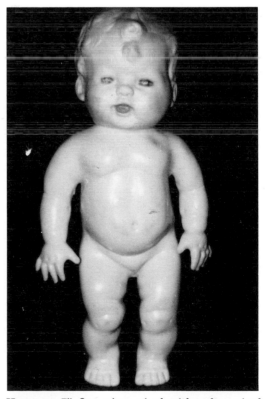

Horsman--7" One piece vinyl with softer vinyl head. Puckered crying face. Painted blue eyes. Marks: HD, on head. $3.00.

167

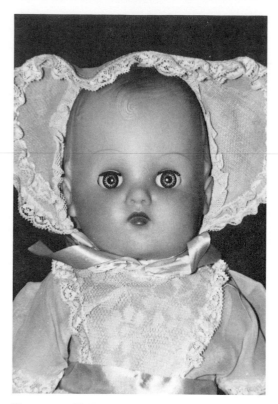

Horsman--18" "Fairy Skin Doll" One piece body and limbs. Molded hair. Sleep eyes. Marks: four dots and Horsman, on head. Tag: Horsman's/Fairy Skin/Doll/Made Entirely/Of Soft/Vinyl Plastic. $12.00. (Courtesy Alice Capps)

Horsman--13" "Polly and Pete" One piece stuffed vinyl body and limbs. Top layer on body will peel. Vinyl head with molded hair and painted features. Marks: Horsman, on head. 1957. $65.00 each. (Courtesy Alice Capps)

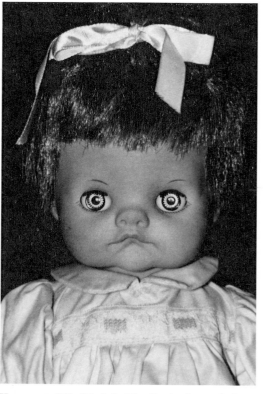

Horsman--26" "Dolly Walks" (Also the Head for Thirstee Walker when mouth is cut open) 8" Baby. Unmarked. Molded hair under rooted hair. Large one is marked: Horsman Dolls Inc./1962 CB 25. Both original. $18.00 pair. (Courtesy Tillie Kobe)

Horsman--15" "Jody" Plastic body and legs. Vinyl arms and head. Blue sleep eyes/lashes. Lower lip sucked under upper one. Marks: Horsman Dolls/1964/T13. By Irene Szors. $8.00. (Courtesy Jayn Allen)

Horsman--12" "Patty Duke" Posable arms and legs. Blue eyes to side (painted). An Irene Szor design. 1965. Marks: Horsman Doll/6211. $16.00. (Courtesy Marie Ernst)

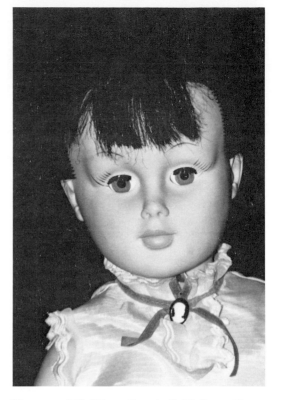

Horsman--26" "Mary Poppins" Walker. Plastic body, arms and legs. Vinyl head. Sleep eyes. Marks: 5/Horsman Dolls Inc./1966/66271. $25.00. (Courtesy Alice Capps)

Horsman--8" "Michael" from the Mary Poppins set. Plastic and vinyl. Painted blue eyes. Marks: C.T./Horsman Dolls Inc/6682. $15.00. (Courtesy Cecelia Eades)

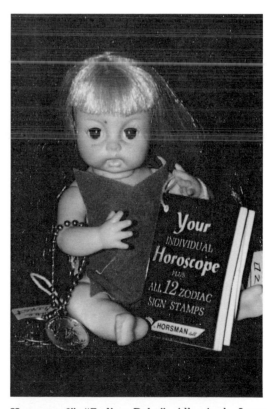

Horsman--6" "Zodiac Baby" All vinyl. Long rooted pink hair. Also came with white hair. Set black eyes. Open/closed mouth. Came with charm bracelet with signs of the Zodiac. Marks: Horsman Dolls Inc/1968, on head. $6.00. (Courtesy Marie Ernst)

169

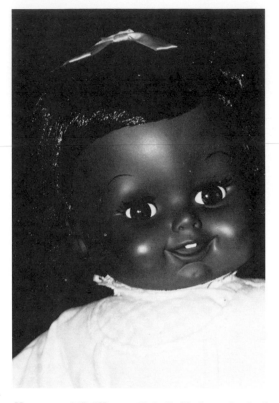

Horsman--21" "Happy Baby" Cloth and vinyl. Zipper down back to get to battery box. Throw her up in the air or bounce on knee and she laughs. Turns itself off. Cheek and chin dimples. Sleep eyes. Open/closed mouth with two upper molded painted teeth. Original. Marks: Horsman Doll Inc./1974. Still available.

Horsman--8" "Mousketeer" boy and girl. All vinyl with one piece body and legs. Blue sleep eyes. Mousketeer hats "pinned" to heads. Girl is blonde, boy is orange haired. Marks: 1273/10 Eye/33/Horsman Dolls Inc/1971, on head. 10, on back. Box: An Irene Szor design. Still available.

Horsman--13" "Betsy McCall" New for 1975. One piece green/pink jumpsuit. Doll is an earlier issue doll. Marks: Horsman Dolls Inc/Pat. Pending, on back. 1/Horsman Dolls Inc./1967, on head. Box: An Irene Szor Design.

Hoyer--15" "Margie" Plastic body and legs. Vinyl arms and head. Blue sleep eyes. Marks: AE18. Gift from Carolyn Powers.

For complete information on the Ideal Toy Corp. refer to Series I, page 153. Complete information on the Shirley Temple doll is located in Series I, page 179.

Ideal--13" "Flexy Soldier" All composition and wire. Wood feet. W.W.II doll. Marks: Ideal Doll, on head. $38.00. (Courtesy Barbara Coker)

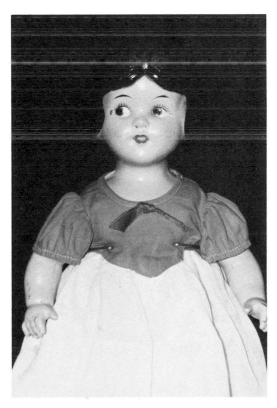

Ideal--18" "Snow White" Cloth body. Composition shoulder plate and limbs. Molded bow painted red. Marks: Ideal, on head. Original. $50.00. (Courtesy Kimport Dolls)

Ideal--18" "Mary Jane" All composition. Flirty brown sleep eyes. Blonde mohair wig. Original. Marks: Ideal 18, on head. (Courtesy Cecelia Eades)

171

Ideal--Shows end of original Ideal Shirley Temple box.

Ideal--This is the real Deanna Durbin holding one of the first issues of the doll made after her.

Shirley Temple Prices

Composition: 25" Toddler. Marks: 73/Shirley Temple. $300.00.
23" Toddler with cloth body. Marks: #1 and/or Shirley Temple. $100.00.
16" Baby. Shirley Temple, on head. $125.00.
17" Baby. Shirley Temple, on head. $125.00.
18" Baby. Shirley Temple, on head. $140.00.
22" Baby. Shirley Temple, on head. $160.00.
25" Baby. Shirley Temple, on head. $185.00.
27" Baby. Shirley Temple, on head. $195.00.
All composition dolls:
27" Marked. $200.00.
25" Marked. $110.00.
23" Marked. $95.00.
22" Marked. $85.00.
18" Marked. $85.00.
17" Marked. $85.00.
16" Marked. $85.00.
15" Marked. $85.00.
13" Marked. $75.00.
11" Marked. $140.00.
Any size Hiwaiian. $110.00.
Soap Shirley $30.00.
Plaster Shirley. $15.00.
Reliable of Canada Shirley $45.00.
Mechanical Display Shirley's $1,000.00 up.
9" all compo. molded hair. Closed mouth. Ideal Doll, on back. $60.00.
35" Vinyl and plastic. $365.00.
19" Vinyl. Flirty eyes. $65.00.
17" Vinyl $45.00.
12" Vinyl $25.00.

Ideal--This photo is from the October 1939 issue of Screen Guide and says the photo was made in December 1938. $95.00 up.

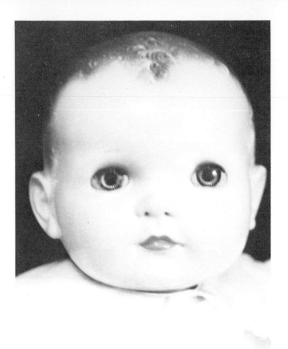

Ideal--30" "Magic Squeezums" Latex body with pin jointed arms and legs. Hard plastic head. Sleep eyes. Molded hair. Marks: Ideal Doll/ Made in USA. 1950. $22.00. (Courtesy Alice Capps)

Ideal--Shows interior of the Ideal Butterick pattern set with 12" manniken. $22.00. (Courtesy Marge Meisinger)

Ideal--Shows box top to Ideal Butterick pattern set. (Courtesy Marge Meisinger)

Ideal--18" "Judy Splinters" Latex arms and legs. Cloth body. Early vinyl head. Black yarn hair. Brown painted eyes. Open/closed mouth with molded tongue. Original. Marks: Ideal Doll, on head. 1951. $30.00.

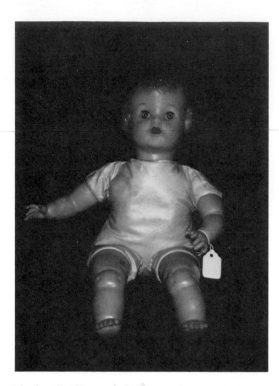

Ideal--15" "Huggee Girl" Vinyl with oil cloth body. Blue sleep eyes. Open/closed mouth. Molded curly hair. Marks: Ideal Doll/BC 16, on head. 1952. $12.00. (Courtesy Carolyn Powers)

Ideal--17" "Bonnie Walker" All hard plastic with cryer in stomach. Pin hip walker. Blue sleep eyes. Open mouth/2 upper teeth and molded tongue. Marks: Ideal Doll/W16, on head and back. $16.00. (Courtesy Joan Amundsen)

Ideal--36" "Sandy McCall" Molded hair. Sleep eyes. Marked On Head: McCall/Corp 1959. $75.00. (Courtesy Phyllis Houston)

The following is the account of Phyllis Houston and her discovery of Sandy McCall.

The standing picture of Sandy McCall is enclosed for just one reason and that is his stand. Sandy and I came together under the most unusual circumstances. I was going downtown one day for a ladylike luncheon and some shopping when I had to pause between the car park and department store for a "Don't Walk" light. Glancing idly about I met a familiar pair of eyes peering out of a 5&10 display window. It must have been the classic doubletake when I whirled and went in...Sandy McCall, no less, and I had To Have Him. After talking to several people who all giggled, said no he wasn't for sale, implying silly woman, I finally reached the store manager who also giggled and wiggled and then I told them what I would pay for Sandy. Smiles disappeared and he was mine, all 36 naked inches of him. You can imagine the looks we drew, me in white gloves and Sandy in a paper bag around his middle.

Anyway-to be used as a mannequin, they had drilled holes in his shoes, giving them first extra strength by slipping in thin pieces of plywood. The heavy block of wood which is his stand also has holes in it and screws with wing nuts at the bottom allow him to be taken loose for redressing. What a marvelous idea for all my large dolls, who will shortly all wear holey shoes.

Ideal--This shows the "Sandy McCall" on display stand just as Phyllis Houston found him.

Ideal--15" "Carol Brent" Made for Montgomery Wards in 1961. Marks: Ideal Toy Corp/M-15-L, on head. Ideal Toy Corp./M-15, on body. $20.00. (Courtesy Marie Ernst)

Ideal--15" "Twins" Other is boy. Cloth with vinyl arms, legs and head. Pouty mouth. Blue sleep eyes/lashes. Marks: Ideal Toy Corp./TW-14-2-U, on head. $20.00. (Courtesy Diana Sorenson)

Ideal--9" "Mini Monster" Plastic with vinyl arms and head. Molded eyelids, open/closed mouth and designed on same body as used on one model of Pebbles doll. Original dress. One in set of several. Marks: 1966/Ideal Toy Corp, on head. Made in Japan, on back. Dress Tag: Mini Monster/Ideal, in oval Japan. $6.00. (Courtesy Joan Amundsen)

175

Ideal--17" "Katie Kachoo" All vinyl. Raise her arm and she sneezes into hankie. Open mouth. Marks: 1968/Ideal Toy Corp/SN-17-EH-37. $20.00. (Courtesy Susan Goetz)

Ideal--Shows a Crissy with her new wig from the Crissy replacement wig set. 1970. (Courtesy Marie Ernst)

Ideal--11" "Dr. Evil" Action figure. Came with various face masks. 1965. $6.00.

Ideal--18" "Tiffany Taylor" Teen fashion model. Plastic and vinyl. Painted blue eyes/long lashes. Top of head swivels to change hair color from blonde to brunette. Original. Marks: 1974/Ideal, in an oval, Hollis, NY 11423/2M 5854-01/2, on lower back. 1973/CG-19-H-230 Hong Kong. Dress Tag: Ideal, in oval. Tiffany Taylor.

Ideal--18" Black version of "Tiffany Taylor" Hair turns from black to deep red. Still available.

Ideal--18" "Tiffany Taylor" Full length view with hair turned to brunette.

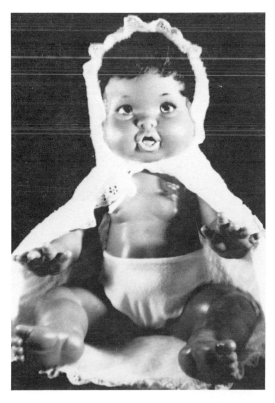

Ideal--17" "Rub A Dub Baby" Plastic body. Vinyl arms, legs and head. Open/closed mouth. Original. Marks: 1973/Ideal Toy Corp/Rad-16-H233, head. 1973/Ideal Toy Corp/HOLLIS NY 11423/RAD 17/2M-5852-01/2., on body. Still available.

Teens--"Family Rider" 10" man: woman: Plastic and vinyl. Jointed knees. Man has molded on black boots, she has molded on white shoes. Both marked: Hong Kong, that runs vertically up backs. 2½" all vinyl baby is molded in one piece in a sitting position. Battery operated. Box: An Illco Toy. Still available.

177

Imperial Crown--23" "Miss Pepsodent" All vinyl. Blue sleep eyes. Open mouth with rolling teeth. When laying down teeth are yellow, when sitting up, they rotate to white. All original.

Impco--21" "Baby Bubbles" Composition head. Cloth body. Latex arms and legs. Molded light brown hair. Blue sleep eyes. Cryer. Marks: None. Original dress. 1950. Made by Imperial Crown. $10.00.

Imperial Toy--5" "Sunny Surfers" All brown vinyl. Jointed neck only. Yellow painted under shorts. Marks: Some have Hong Kong, on foot. 1975. $2.00 each.

Imperial Toy--5" "Sunny Surfers" All brown vinyl. Jointed neck only. Yellow painted under shorts. Marks: Some have Hong Kong, on foot. 1975. $2.00 each.

Imperial Toy--5" "Sunny Surfers" All brown vinyl. Jointed neck only. Yellow painted under shorts. Marks: Some have Hong Kong, on foot. 1975. $2.00 each.

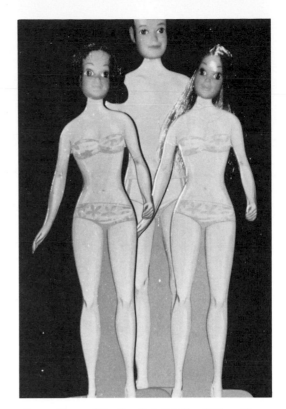

Janex Corp.--"Pretty Quix" dolls. 9" Ivy: Brown hair. 10" Glenn: brown molded hair and 8½" Holly: blonde hair. Vinyl heads with cardboard bodies. Press on fashions of fabric. Made by Janex Corp. $7.00. (Courtesy Marie Ernst)

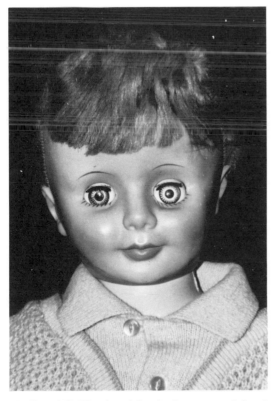

J. Cey--27" Plastic with vinyl arms and head. Smile mouth. Blue sleep eyes. Left eye hole molded larger than right. Marks: J-Cey, on head. $20.00.

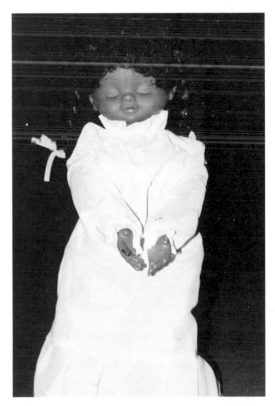

Jilmar--18" "Praying Patti" and also called "Sleepy Angel." Vinyl head with painted closed eyes. Gauntlet rigid vinyl hands. Cloth body with sewn on flannette slippers. Zipper in back for battery pack. Operation button in front. Says prayers. Sold by Niresk Industries. Marks: Tag: Sleepy Angel TM by Jilmar Co. $15.00.

179

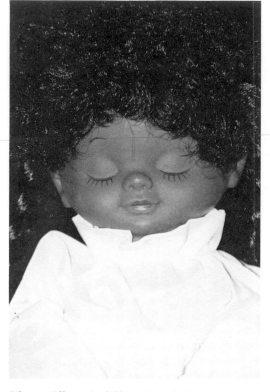

Jilmar--All original Sleep Angel. Snaps on gown hold the arms together.

Jolly Toys--16" "Baby Angel" Plastic and vinyl. Blue sleep eyes/lashes. Open mouth/nurser. Marks: Jolly Toys Inc., on head. A reversed AE on body. 1961. $2.00.

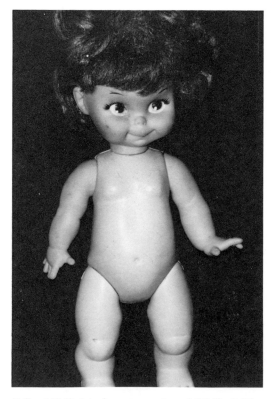

Jolly--11" Painted eyes version of "Jolly." Plastic and vinyl. Painted blue eyes. Upper lip over lower. Marks: L3. ca. mid 1960's. $3.00.

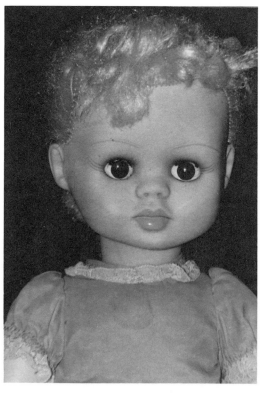

Jolly--19" "Dixie Pixie" Closed mouth version. All vinyl. Black sleep eyes/lashes. Large mouth. White rooted hair. Marks: None, except FR-18, on left arm. 1963. (Courtesy Barbara Coker)

Jolly Toy--17" "Suzanna Ballerina" Plastic and vinyl with rooted blonde hair. Blue sleep eyes. Blue eyeshadow. Marks: Jolly Toy/1965, on head.

Jolly Toys--11" "Judy Playmate" Plastic and vinyl. Blue sleep eyes/molded lashes. Open/closed mouth with molded tongue. Original dress. Hair has been cut. Marks: Jolly Toy/1968, on head. Made in Hong Kong, on back.

Jolly--7½" "Little Lil Lil" All vinyl. Painted eyes. Painted on shoes and socks. Original. Marks: None. Take off of Little Lulu. (Courtesy Cecelia Eades)

Joy Doll--14½" "Marlene Dietrich" All composition. No molded hair under wig. Blue sleep eyes. Stapled on clothes. Golden blonde mohair wig. Gold dress/white net shawl. Deep purple flower on top and in hair. 1945. $45.00. (Courtesy Mary Partridge)

Joy Doll--14½" "Colonial Lady" All composition with yellow mohair wig. Blue sleep eyes. Original. Marks: None. $18.00.

Joy Doll--14½" "Prom Queen" All composition.
Blue sleep eyes. Light red mohair. Original.
1939. $18.00.

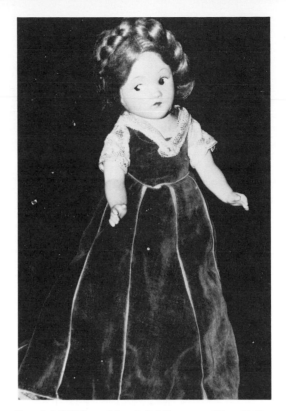

Junel--11" "Mary Lincoln" All composition. Fully
jointed. Painted blue eyes to side. Both arms
fairly straight. Original deep blue velvet dress/
gold trim. Tag: Copy of Dress worn by Mary
Lincoln 1861/Junel Novelties Inc. NY. $18.00.

Kamar, Inc.

Of the 102 letters to various companies for resumes, I received a packet and a nice letter from the Kamar company. They make only a few dolls but the quality of the dolls is good and they are character ones rather than the "dolly" kind. To future generations the Kamar dolls will be like the "novelty" dolls of the early years of this century. This company produces the FINEST of stuffed toys and it is very difficult to locate any of their animals as the quality is so good that they are kept as prize possessions and rarely are on the "used" market.

This company is so progressive for example: They developed a teddy bear, "Dear Heart" that has a heart beat, before the scientific study involving two separate groups of newborn infants in a New York hospital. Group A was presented with the sound of the human heartbeat, through a recording. Group B was monitored at the same time in the same hospital without the heartbeat. Results: The food intake was the same but Group A gained weight, while Group

B showed an overall weight loss. Group A cried less than 40 percent of the time and Group B cried about 60 percent of the time. The results of such studies show that infants need to continue the sound of heartbeats, the only sound they are familiar with (before birth). Kamar's "Dear Heart" fills this need. I will include a photo of this teddy bear in this section, along with ones of a few of the delightful, unique and original stuffed toys by Kamar.

All Kamar toys are handmade and of uncompromising quality. They produce more than 250 items that are distributed in 50 states and 32 foreign countries. These toys are produced in Japan, Portugal, Taiwan, Mexico and Korea, with the firm's home office in Gardena, California...Kamar is a privately held corporation and sells directly to the retailer. The toys range in price from $1 to $150.

The following is part of the "fact sheet" from Kamar and should be of interest to all doll/toy collectors:

Astrid Elaine Wennemark Kamar:
Wife, Mother and Super-Executive

Astrid (pronounced Ah-strid) Kamar, the attractive executive vice president of Kamar, Inc., has realized a multitude of dreams and has achieved something thousands of individuals have tried to attain--overwhelming success in a multi-million dollar business she helped develop from scratch less than 15 years ago.

At the same time she is a busy mother of three children and the wife of one of the world's most talented toy designers.

As a youngster growing up in her native California, Astrid "knew" she could never be content with a hum-drum life. "Life has always been exciting," she said. "I've always reached towards a goal--sometimes I guess my goals were more romantic than realistic, but there was always that exciting challenge to try to achieve them."

Her goal as a young woman out of business school was to use her business skills in as exciting a way as she could; so she joined the U.S. Foreign Service and worked in Washington, D.C., and Jamaica as a cryptographic clerk for 18 months.

Unfortunately, the Foreign Service did not prove to be the exciting venture she had envisioned. Several years and two jobs later, Astrid met an unusual young man, Pascal Kamar (P.K.). His life had been anything but hum-drum, having recently arrived in the United States from war-torn Jerusalem. P.K. had achieved enormous success in Jerusalem as a well-known musician; however, he was not able to become established in the music world in America. To survive and make a living, he had become a salesman in the garment industry at the time Astrid met him.

P.K. had a dream of creating something exciting and original, and Astrid shared this dream. They soon embarked on a small gift-importing business while P.K. continued his work in garment sales. The importing enterprise became a partnership when Astrid and P.K were married. They enlarged the business by importing unusual gifts from Africa and the Middle East and later became the first to import hand carved teak animals from African artisans.

The explosion into success, however, came with the "birth" of Hexter, the first doll designed by P.K. It was a wild-eyed, long-haired gangling predecessor to the troll doll; and, it was an overnight success.

Assuming at first that they had somehow run onto a wonderful, simple situation...that all dolls would sell in the same run-away manner Hexter had...the Kamars put together every scrap of cash and credit they could manage and ordered all the dolls and animals they could afford from the factories in Japan. Then, they watched them languish under dust on shelves in a rented warehouse. The truth didn't escape them for very long, however. It was soon determined that the secret of success in the business was in design...original design by P.K. He began designing more and more dolls and dropping more and more gift imports. By 1963, Kamar was solely in the stuffed doll and animal business running hard to keep up with the demand for Kamar originals.

To keep up with toy production, Astrid began a search for good plants that would produce the toys in quantity but retain the fully hand-made aspect of the toys that is so important to the Kamar quality. Her hunt for production plants took her around the world. Today Kamar has plants in Korea, Taiwan, and Japan; and Astrid established plants in Mexico and Portugal.

"One of the most interesting and rewarding experiences in my life involves establishing our plant in Portugal," recalls Astrid. In southern Portugal, there is a small remote village, Messejana, near the top of Mt. Baixo Alenjo. It is only in the last three years that Messejana has appeared on any maps of Portugal. It was a poor village which offered the villagers little hope. Food was virtually scratched from the ground and each year the supply became more meager.

The local priest, desperate to keep the villagers from near starvation the next winter, began looking into "modern" ways in which the people could earn a living. As an attempt to aid the villagers in supporting themselves, he made a small personal investment in large amounts of yarn and encouraged the local women to knit baby and children wear. Three years ago a crude "factory" was established an today the women of Messejana produce some of the finest hand-made children knit wear in the world.

At approximately the same time as the building of the "factory," Astrid met the priest and discussed her need for toy production. She was specifically looking for a plant in Portugal, for Portugal produces the finest leather in the world, a necessary item for many of the Kamar toys. Today the crude knitting factory of Messejana has expanded to include the production of Kamar leather toys, which in turn has helped assure the residents of Messejana a greater measure of security.

Not long ago, the Kamars brought the priest to the United States for a visit--the first time he had been out of his small region in Portugal--so that he might see additional toy factories and discover a broader outlook on the world. In Messejana he not only is the priest, but is the village's only teacher, doctor, and engineer.

As executive vice president of Kamar, Inc., Astrid directs marketing, shipping and internal purchasing and procedures. She has never contributed to the design of the toys. "I leave all of that to P.K.," she explained. "The design of each and every toy is his life. Besides, I'd probably end up with a five-legged cat or a bunny with no tail."

Five years ago Astrid became one of the first flying, traveling salesladies on the American business scene. At her instigation the company purchased a twin-engine Beechcraft and converted it to a flying showroom. In this manner Astrid flies into city after city meeting customers and buyers and conducting sales presentations while serving lunches and refreshments--all from 4,000 feet.

Astrid, P.K., and their children, Laurie Lynn, 4; Jenny Lynn, 10; and Christopher, 13, live in Palos Verdes (Calif.) on a cliff overlooking the Pacific.

DEAR HEART...THE WORLD'S FIRST TEDDY BEAR
WITH A HEARTBEAT. Recent scientific studies have in-
dicated that the sound of a heartbeat is soothing and
relaxing to infants. Dear Heart, available in almost every
store and shop that sells toys, is produced by Kamar, Inc.

"KAMAR'S WILD THINGS" numbering nearly 100 items
are designed by Pascal Kamar president of the firm. The line
which is changed by nearly 40 per cent twice a year is now
sold in all 50 states and 36 foreign countries.

SUPER-EXECUTIVE AND REAL-LIVE DOLL...is Mrs.
Astrid Kamar, executive vice president of Kamar, Inc., California producers of quality, handmade stuffed toys. She and
her husband, Pascal, developed their hobby into a multi-
million dollar company in less than 15 years.

Kamar--13" "John F. Kennedy" Vinyl head, hands and shoes. "Wired" so that arms and legs can be posed. Sits in rocking chair. Reads newspaper with articles about wife, Jackie and children. A music box (key wound) plays and chair rocks. $22.00. (Courtesy Virginia Jones)

Kamar--13" "Jock" Non removabale clothes. Glued tuffs of mohair. Marks: 1966 Kamar/Made in Japan, on tag. Japan, on head. $3.00.

186

Kamar--4½" "Ana" All vinyl. One piece body, legs and arms. Jointed neck. Beautiful hand detail. Two cutouts in back for original wings. Marks: Japan, on head. Tag: 1967 Kamar/Made in Japan. $2.00.

Kamar--10" "Clown" All stuffed with vinyl head. Glued on mohair. Tag: 1967 Kamar/Made in Japan. $2.00. (Courtesy Ellie Haynes)

Kamar--8" "Tia Marie" Came in brunette, blonde and red. All vinyl. Sculptured, painted brown eyes. Fully jointed. Painted on green shoes. Original. Marks: 1968 Kamar Inc./Japan. $3.00.

Kamar--9" "Mona" All vinyl with glued on vinyl hat. Also shows top of head on the second doll, without her hat. Marks: Japan. $3.00. (Courtesy Ellie Haynes)

Kamar--5" "K-Tot" All white and vinyl with "fur." Jointed neck. Tag: 1969/Kamar Ink/Japan. $2.00. (Courtesy Ellie Haynes)

Kamar--5" "April" Came in redhead, silver, blonde and brunette. All vinyl. Dimples. Sculptured, painted dark blue eyes. Molded flowers. Jointed neck only. Marks: 1968 Kamar Inc./Japan. $2.00.

187

Kamar--5" "Nobo" Jointed neck and shoulders. Glued on "fur." Excellent molding of feet and hands. Brown/black sculptured painted eyes. Marks: 1969/Kamar Inc/Japan, on bottom of foot. $3.00. (Courtesy Virginia Jones)

Kamar--6½" Wire/felt. "Red fur" dress. Vinyl head. Marks: 1968/Kamar/Japan, on head. Tag: 1968 Kamar/Made in Japan. $2.00.

Kaysam

Kaysam--There seem to be rumors that all Kaysam dolls were personalities and this seems to be in error. Kaysam, was a method of injecting molding and was the material used. Kaysam, was a part of the Jolly Toy Company.

Kaysam--15" "Red Cross Nurse" Plastic body and legs. Vinyl arms and head with rooted brown hair. Blue sleep eyes/molded lashes. Blue eyeshadow. Adult figure. High heel feet. Marks: Kaysam/1961, on head. Original clothes. $18.00.

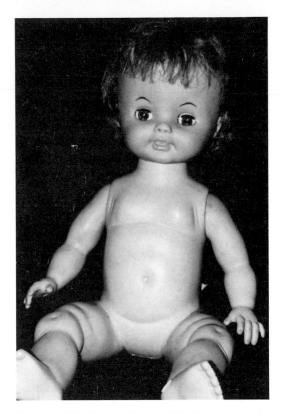

Kaysam--24" This is a Kaysam doll 1961, that is all original and bears the tag: Another Jolly Doll. Doll is marked 1961/Kaysam. This same doll sold in Alden's (1962) and 15" as June Bride, 25" as Jackie and in 16" version as Cynthia and Gerri. $22.00. (Courtesy Marie Ernst)

Kaysam--15" "Baby Judy" Plastic and vinyl. Open mouth/nurser. Blue sleep eyes/lashes. Marks: 6514/Kaysam, lower back. IID/20, on head. 1963. $4.00.

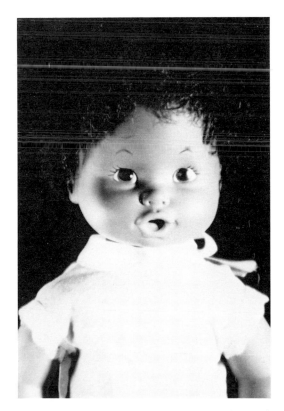

Kaysam--19" Plastic with vinyl arms and head. Black sleep eyes to side. Freckles across nose. Rooted white hair. Marks: Kaysam 4379/1966 20, on head. 6419, lower back. K24 under left arm. K33 under right arm. $10.00.

Kenner--16" "Baby Alive" One piece dublon with jointed neck only. Rooted hair in vinyl skull cap sealed over dublon head. Painted eyes. Came in white and black. Open mouth nurser and eater. Battery operated. Had special formula to feed doll. Marks: 3564/P13/Kenner Prod./1973. Still available.

189

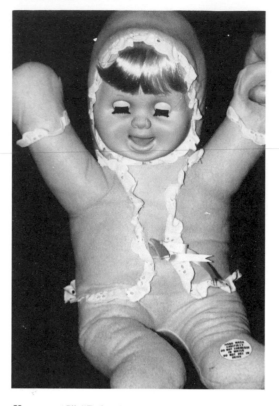

Kenner--15" "Baby Yawnie" Bellows type bulb in left hand. Squeeze and eyes close and mouth yawns. Still available.

Kenner--6" "Sippin' Sue" Plastic and vinyl with molded yellow hair. Painted blue eyes. Open mouth/not nurser. Original. Marks: 1972/General Mills/Fun Group Inc. These dolls were sold with straws/glass and could stand next to child as they sipped through their own straw. $2.00.

Keebler Co.--6½" "Keebler Elf" All vinyl jointed only at neck. Molded clothes. Painted features. Marks: 1974/Keebler Co. Premium doll. $3.00.

King--9" "Henry" All early rubber vinyl with painted features, and clothes. Marks: KF, on bottom of foot. 1950. $8.00. (Courtesy Edith Goldsworthy)

Knickerbacher--15" "Princess Glory of Lilliput" (Gulliver's Travels) All composition. Eye-shadow/sleep eyes. Bent right arm. Very long hair. Same doll with boy hair style is Prince David of Flefuscu (Gulliver's Travels). $48.00. (Courtesy Mary Partridge)

Knickerbacher--15" "Oh! Susanna" All composition with brown sleep eyes. Open mouth/three teeth. Bent right arm. Marks: Knickerbacher, on backs of some. 1937. $48.00. (Courtesy Jay Minter)

Knickerbacher--13" "Soupy Sales" Vinyl head with cloth body and non-removable clothes. Marks: 1965 Knickerbacher, on head. Tag: Soupy Sales/1966 Soupy Sales, W.M.C. $35.00. (Courtesy Barbara Coker)

Knickerbacher--14" "Theodore & Alvin (Hat)" Chipmonks. Cloth with vinyl heads. Marks: Ross Bagasarin. $10.00 each. (Courtesy B. Mongel-luzzi)

Knickerbacher--"Holly Hobbie" Comes in 9½", 16", 27" and 33" also the 7" that is put out in the purse. Still available. (Courtesy 1975 Knicker- bacher Catalog)

Knickerbacher--"Heater" Comes in 9½", 16", 27" and 33." Heater is Holly Hobbie's friend. Still available. (Courtesy 1975 Knickerbacher Catalog)

Lakeside--13" "Gumby" All green foam over wire armature. White/red foam eyes. Yellow foam mouth. Came with horse called "Pokey" and with accessories such as guns, guitar, hats, etc. Marks: Gumby/Mfg. By/Lakeside Ind. Inc/LIC. by/Newfeld Ltd./Of England. 1965, 66 and 67. $4.00.

Lakeside--"Gumby" Knight Adventure Set. Yellow/green shield. Silver helmet. Brown standard with yellow flag. Sword is silver and black. 1965, 66 and 67. $2.00.

Lakeside--6" "Lone Ranger" All vinyl and completely posable. Molded on clothes, except gun/belt. Marks: 24/1966/Lakeside/Ind. Inc, on back. Box: Wrather Corp/Lakeside Toys Division of Lakeside/Industries Inc. $2.00.

Lesney--5" "Sailor Sue" All vinyl. Rooted red hair and painted brown eyes. Marks: Lesney/1973, on head. Lesney/Products/Hong Kong, on back. $4.00. (Courtesy Marge Meisinger)

Lesney--5" "Alice in Wonderland" All vinyl with rooted blonde hair. Painted blue eyes. Marks: Lesney/1973, on head. Lesney Products/Hong Kong, on body. $4.00. (Courtesy Marge Meisinger)

Lesney--5" "Party Patty" All vinyl with red rooted hair and brown eyes. Marks: Lesney/1973, on head. Lesney/Products/Hong Kong, on back. $4.00. (Courtesy Marge Meisinger)

Lincoln International--9½" "Carl," 9" "Carol" & 3" "Baby Cutes" all of the Our Cheerful Family. Plastic with vinyl arms and heads. Inset eyes. Baby: one piece body, arms and legs. Painted eyes. Marks: Made in Hong Kong, on backs. Made by Lincoln International. Still available.

Lorrie--9" "Lucy'" Brown sleep eyes/Molded lashes. All soft vinyl. Marks: 9, on head. 9/Lorrie Doll/1971/Made in Taiwan, on back. $4.00. (Courtesy Marie Ernst)

Lorrie--12" Plastic body and legs. Vinyl head and arms. Open/closed mouth with molded tongue. Same body that was used for "Stoneage Baby." Marks: Lorrie Doll, on head and Reliable in oval on back. $3.00. (Courtesy Phyllis Houston)

Lorrie--14" "Etty Bitty" Cloth body with vinyl arms, legs and head. Rooted blonde hair. Blue sleep eyes/lashes. Marks: Lorrie Doll/1968/3, on head. Tag: Made in Taiwan/Mfg for Eugene Doll Co. Original clothes. See Eugene Section for other Lorrie Dolls. $3.00.

Lorrie--9" "Sandy" Plastic with vinyl head. Painted blue eyes. Marks: Made in/Hong Kong, on back. 26/Lorrie Doll/1969, on head. $3.00.

Lovee--23" Plastic with vinyl head. Open mouth/ nurser. Blue painted eyes. Marks: 1974/Lovee Doll, on head. $3.00. (Courtesy Carolyn Powers)

Lovee--14" Plastic with vinyl arms and head. White rooted hair. Blue sleep eyes. Open mouth with molded tongue. Marks: Lovee, Made In/ Hong Kong, on back. $2.00. (Courtesy Carolyn Powers)

Lovee--11½" "Daisy-Luv" Plastic body and limbs. Vinyl head. Blue decal eyes. Open/closed mouth with two upper and lower molded teeth. Marks: Made in Hong Kong/No. 2618, on back. 1967 Mattel Inc./Japan, on head. This mold is one of Mattel's old ones and is currently being used. Many older Mattel parts are on the market. (Courtesy Phyllis Houston)

196

Lyon--8" "Sweet Valentine" Cloth with wire through legs to make them bendable. Vinyl head with glued on white mohair. Painted features. Marks: Rene D. Lyon/Richmond Hill NY, on bottom of foot. Came with box of Whitman's Sampler candy. 1970. $2.00.

Mfg. Unknown--14" All composition. Blue sleep tin eyes. Pouty type mouth. Jointed neck, shoulders and hips. Human hair wig. Marks: None. ca. 1934. $30.00.

Mfg. Unknown--23" "Display Mannikin" All rubber. Molded hair and painted features. Painted and molded on high heel shoes with holes to be placed on a stand. Marks: None. ca. late 1930's. $28.00.

Mfg. Unknown--8" All composition. Painted brown eyes. Fully jointed. Tag: I am Sonja from Norway. $10.00. (Courtesy Maxine Heitt)

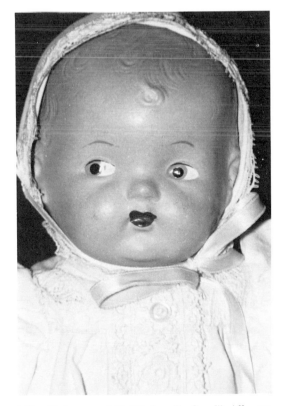

Mfg. Unknown--14" "Peter B. Good" All composition. Painted blue eyes. Orange molded hair. One piece body and head. 1941. Peter B. Good was the baby in Brother Rat & The Baby. Eddie Albert and Jane Bryan were also in the movie by Warner Bros. $12.00. (Courtesy Marie Ernst)

Mfg. Unknown--17" "Pinafore Sally" All composition. Blue sleep eyes. Open mouth/four teeth. Original. Marks: A, in a circle on head. Body: Shirley Temple/17. 1946. $30.00. (Courtesy Marie Ernst)

197

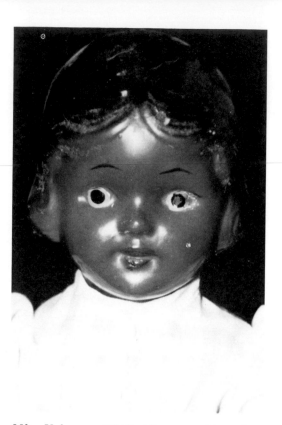

Mfg. Unknown--16" "Rosaland" All composition with brown sleep eyes. Human hair wig. All original. Sold through Wanamaker's 1947. Marks: X, in circle. $25.00.

Mfg. Unknown--13½" All composition. Came with molded as well as wigged hair. No molded ribbon. Marks: W.O.L., on head. 1939. $22.00. (Courtesy Maxine Heitt)

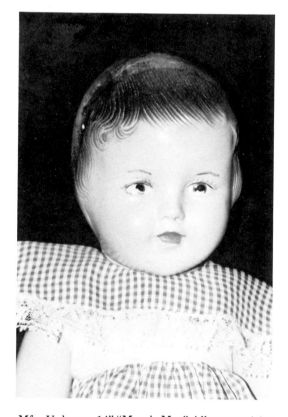

198

Mfg. Unkown--14" "Marcia Mae" All composition with straight legs. Brown decal eyes. Open/closed mouth. Sculptured black hair and had a wig over back of hair with molded bangs showing. 1941. $30.00. (Courtesy Diana Soreson)

Mfg. Unknown--13" "Maggie Ann" All composition with glued on blonde mohair. Blue sleep eyes. Open mouth/4 teeth. Marks: R, on head. Shirley Temple (very light and curved)/13, on back. Sold in catalog outlets in 1945. Original. $22.00.

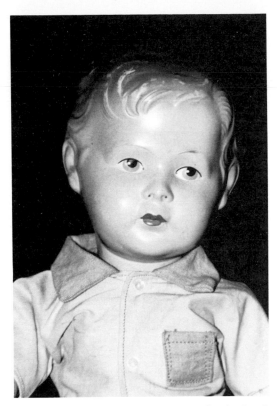

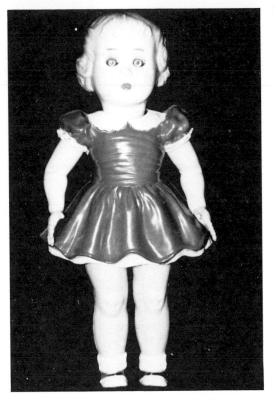

Mfg. Unknown--17" Boy of all hard plastic that is painted. Strung limbs and head. Molded hair. Painted blue eyes. Closed mouth. Original. Marks: None. ca. 1949-52. $65.00. (Courtesy Joan Amundsen)

Mfg. Unknown--9½" All plastic. Blue sleep eyes. Pin jointed walker. Head turns and arms move. Molded on clothes. Excellent quality. Marks: None. $4.00. (Courtesy B. Mongelluzzi)

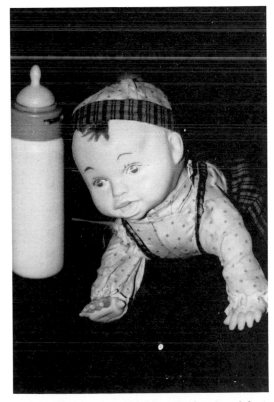

Mfg. Unknown--12" Vinyl hands, head and feet. Metal body. Bottle takes batteries, for baby to crawl. Clothing sewed on. $8.00. (Courtesy Alice Capps)

Mfg. Unknown--15" Vinyl head with large painted blue eyes. Cloth body is wired so it is posable. Gauntlet vinyl hands. Right hand cupped to hold something. Non removable clothes. Marks: None except PRR, on hat. $6.00. (Courtesy Mary Partridge)

199

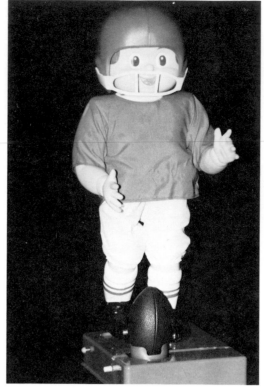

Mfg. Unknown--20" Mechanical football player. Uses batteries. Vinyl head and arms. Plastic and metal body. Plastic legs. Sold from Sears in 1973. $20.00. (Courtesy Alice Capps)

Mfg. Unknown--23" "Googly" Cloth with vinyl face mask. Inset brown eyes. Black yarn hair. Crank talker. Has record player in back. Marks: Tag Gone. ca. later 1950's. $6.00.

Mfg. Unknown--22" Bed doll. Cloth with vinyl full legs and arms. Vinyl head with molded eyelids. Painted blue eyes. Blue pastel hair. Marks: RJ/1961. $8.00. (Courtesy Barbara Coker)

Mfg. Unknown--12" "Clown" Cloth with plastic head. Chain mouth and eyes move by pulling mouth chain. Vinyl hands. Marks: A tag, I can not read. $6.00. (Courtesy Marie Ernst)

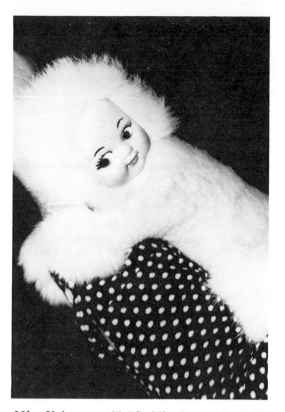

Mfg. Unknown--10" "Cuddle Bun" All stuffed plush. Vinyl face mask. Painted blue eyes. 1" wide metal bands forms arms to "hold" rabbit fur trim. Marks: None. $5.00.

Mfg. Unknown--20" Plastic and vinyl. Blue sleep eyes. Molded light brown hair. Marks: F, in a circle on head. Tag, on underwear: The Forsyth/ Pat. 1927/For Belt. $18.00. (Courtesy Marion Thuma)

Mattel, Inc.

Complete information on the Mattel Corp. is located in Series I, page 195 and Series II, page 187.

One of the funniest ladies in our nation is Erma Bombeck, who writes articles for the newspapers and I would like to quote one that she wrote in 1974:

'A small item in the newspaper the other day caught my eye. Barbie (as a doll) just celebrated her 16th birthday.

Usually I don't get too choked up about toy people's birthdays, but as I read on I realized how significant this could be to our nation.

In honor of the occasion, her manufacturer threw a "Sweet Sixteen" party for 400 grade school children and at the end of the bash gave each child a stripped-down Barbie.

Now, here's the significant part. If each of those 400 children bought Barbie just one girdle...one skating outfit... or one After 5 dress, the economy of this country could get moving again.

Sixteen years ago, naive people thought General Motors and U.S. Steel were keeping this country solvent. Actually it was the introduction of Barbie.

I first met Barbie when my daughter stood in front of a counter in a department store and pleaded, "Look, Mommy, here's a doll built just like you."

I looked at her two-inch bust, her three-inch hips and two legs that looked like two Benson & Hedges without tobacco and said, "She looks like a woman who whipped through puberty in 15 minutes."

"I want her," she sobbed clutching the doll to her bosom.

Barbie was in the house two days when it became apparent she wasn't just another doll. Barbie has needs. With the baby dolls, you could fill 'em up with water, burp them, tell them they were sleepy and sling them under a bed for a week or so.

Not Barbie. She moved, and she needed a wardrobe to do it. Barbie went skiing ($7.95 not including ski poles). Barbie was in a wedding ($10.95). Barbie needed lounging pajamas ($8.50).

We eventually bought Barbie her own car ($12.95), a house ($22.95) and two friends ($5.00 each) in the buff.

One day when my husband became entangled in Barbie's peignoir drying in the bathroom (she was spending a weekend with Ken at Ohio State) he said, "What's with this doll? When does it all stop?"

"Look at it this way," I said. "We aren't supporting just another doll, we are stabilizing the economy."

It doesn't take an economics major to figure out that if 400 Barbie dolls were outfitted for college, the stock market would soar, employment would rise, the value of the dollar would be restored, and 800 parents would start living above their means again. And that's what economy is all about.

The following is reprinted from the Los Angeles Times (c) 1973 and was written by Art Buchwald.

The Saga of Barbie and Ken

We have nothing against toy companies. They have a right to live just like everybody else. In their own way they bring happiness to the hearts of our young ones, and they give employment to thousands of people all over the country. It is only when they try to bankrupt us that we feel we should speak out. If our situation is duplicated around the country, every father who has a daughter between the ages of 4 and 12 is going to have to apply for relief.

This is what happened.

Our 7 year old daughter requested, four months ago, a Barbie doll. Now, as far as we're concerned, one doll is just like another, and since the Barbie doll cost only $3.00 we were happy to oblige.

We brought the doll home and thought nothing more of it until a week later our daughter came in and said, "Barbie needs a negligee."

"So does your mother," we replied.

"But there is one in the catalogue for only $3," she cried.

"What catalogue?"

"The one that came with the doll."

We grabbed the catalogue and much to our horror discovered what the sellers of Barbie were up to. They let you have the doll for $3 but you have to buy the clothes for her at an average of $3 a crack. They have about 200 outfits, from ice-skating skirts to mink jackets, and a girl's status in the community is based on how many Barbie clothes she has for her doll.

The first time we took our daughter to the store we spent $3 on a dress for her and $25 to outfit her Barbie doll.

A week later our daughter came in and said, "Barbie wants to be an airline stewardess."

"So let her be an airline stewardess," we said.

"She needs a uniform. It's only $3.50."

We gave her the $3.50.

Barbie didn't stay a stewardess long. She decided she wanted to be a nurse ($3), then a singer in a nightclub ($3), then a professional dancer ($3).

One day our daughter walked in and said, "Barbie's lonely."

"Let her join a sorority," we said.

"She wants Ken."

"Who is Ken?"

She showed us the catalogue. Sure enough there was a doll named Ken, the same size as Barbie, with a crew-cut hair, a vinyl plastic chest and movable arms and legs.

"If you don't get Ken," our daughter cried, "Barbie will grow up to be an old maid."

So we went out and bought Ken ($3.50). Ken needed a tuxedo ($5), a raincoat ($2.50), a terry-cloth robe and an electric razor ($1), tennis togs ($3), pajamas ($1.50), and several single-breasted suits ($27).

Pretty soon we had to put up $400 to protect our original $3 investment.

Then one evening our daughter came in with a shocker. "Barbie and Ken are getting married."

"Who's paying for the wedding?"

"They'll need a house to live in. Here's Barbie's Dream House."

"Seven ninety-five?" we shouted. "Why can't they live on a shelf like the rest of your dolls?"

The tears started to flow. "They want to live together as man and wife."

Well, Barbie and Ken are now happily married and living in their Dream House with $3,000 worth of clothes hanging in the closet. We wish we could say that all was well, but yesterday our daughter announced that Midge ($3), put out by the same toy firm, was coming to visit them. And she doesn't have a thing to wear.

The Los Angeles Times has reported the results of a special report by the Securities and Exchange Commission on the Mattel Company. The report lays the blame for Mattel's financial manipulations, falsification of sales, etc. at the feet of the founders, Ruth and Elliot Handler and their Executive Vice President Seymour Rosenberg. On Oct. 17, the Handlers resigned from the board of Mattel and since 1973 they have been figure heads with no real power. Seymour Rosenberg resigned from Mattel in the summer of 1972. The SEC began investigating Mattel in 1973.

Mattel--11½" "Lilli" Made in West Germany and known to be on the market in 1957-58. Called the "proto-type" for the Barbie doll. An excellent quality rigid plastic. Jointed at the shoulders and neck. Molded on shoes with holes to fit circular stand. Doll is not marked. $100 and up.

Mattel--First Barbie: Ponytail with curly bangs. White irises and pointed eyebrows. Holes in feet to fit prones of stand. Heavy, solid torso, marked: Barbie/Pats. Pend./MCMLVIII/By/ Mattel/Inc. Bright red lips and nails. Black and white stripe bathing suit. Gold hoop earrings. $100 and up. (Courtesy Sibyl DeWein)

Mattel--The 1960 second Barbie is basically the same doll except the holes in the feet are no longer there. This same year saw the #3 Barbie, who now has blue irises, curved eyebrows and no holes in the feet. $50.00. (Courtesy Sibyl DeWein)

Mattel--The #4 Barbie has longer eyebrows, smaller pupils and lighter lip color. $35.00. (Courtesy Marie Ernst)

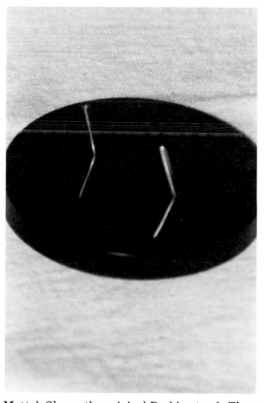

Mattel--Shows the original Barbie stand. These cylinders fit the holes in the feet of the first Barbies. $20.00. (Courtesy Marie Ernst)

203

Mattel--Barbie clock sold in 1964. Marked: Made in W. Germany. $12.00. (Courtesy Marie Ernst)

Mattel--Barbie Car. Marks: Mattel Inc. $15.00.

204   Mattel--1962 "Ken" shown in original outfit and box, and called "Dr. Ken." $18.00.

Mattel--11½" "Barbie" Shown in her Airline Stewardess outfit. 1962. $18.00. (Courtesy Marie Ernst)

Mattel--Barbie's first plane called Ken's Sports Plane. Made by Irwin Corp./Custom Designed For/Barbie & Ken & Midge/Mattel 1964. $15.00. (Courtesy Joan Ashabraner)

Mattel--Skipper & Skooter 1964 pac with the Tiny Barbie doll. $10.00.

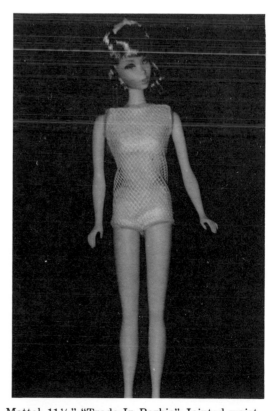

Mattel--Trade in Barbie Box, 1966. (Courtesy Bessie Carson)

Mattel--11½" "Trade In Barbie" Jointed waist. Bend knees. Pierced ears. Long lashes. Orange 2 piece suit with white/orange trim "Oversuit." Orange earrings. Marks: 1966/Mattel Inc./U.S. Patented/U.S. Pat. Pend./Made In/Japan, on hip. $15.00. (Courtesy Bessie Carson)

205

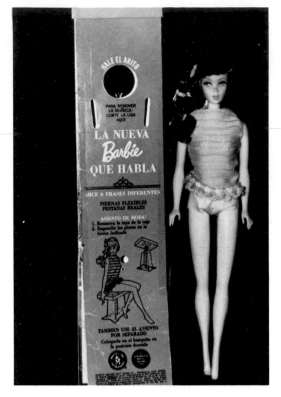

Mattel--11½" "Spanish Talking Barbie" Pink/rose and yellow. Marks: 1967/Mattel Inc/U.S. & Foreign/Pats. Pend./Mexico. $18.00.

Mattel--½" "Mini Kiddles" that go in Popups: Left to right: Soda Parlor, Fairytale, Castle and Gingerbread House.

Mattel--1967 Mini-Kiddles Popup Gingerbread House. $3.00.

Mattel--Liddle Kiddles Talking Townhouse. Plastic with built in furniture. Front comes down. Chatty ring at lower rear at side. The elevator works on elastic band. $4.00. (Courtesy Phyllis Houston)

Mattel--Liddle Kiddles Klub. Cardboard front comes down and case has molded plastic furniture. $4.00. (Courtesy Phyllis Houston)

Mattel--"Francie & Becky" #3448. "With It Whites" 3 pieces white. Red blouse/shoes/belt. Gold rings. Red top-stitched on white pieces. The Becky doll was never produced and the prototype was sold to the Shindana Toy Co. (Operation Bootstraps)

Mattel--Barbie Fan Club Membership pac of 1969. Included "Salute to Silver Dress," Family portrait, Card and certificate, "Barbie Talk" club magazine. (Courtesy Bessie Carson)

Mattel--Family portrait from the 1969 Barbie Fan Club pac. (Courtesy Bessie Carson)

207

Mattel--12" "Talking Brad" Marks: 1968/Mattel Inc/US & For. Pat'd/Other Pats. Pend/Mexico, on hip. 1969 Mattel Inc., on head. 11½" "Talking Christie" Marks: 1967/Mattel Inc/U.S. & Foreign/Pats. Pend./Mexico. $9.00 each.

Mattel--1970 "Francie" with growin' Pretty hair. Bendable knees. Gold top with rose skirt (1 pc.). $7.00.

Mattel--11½" "Francie" A rarer one with no bangs and orange head band. Brown eyes/lashes 1971. $9.00. (Courtesy Marie Ernst)

Mattel--19" "Quick Curl Casey" #8663. 1973. Marks: 1971 Mattel Inc./Hong Kong, on head. 1971 Mattel Inc/U.S.A./U.S. Patent Pending, on back. 11½" "Malibu Christie" Skin tones are darker than the regular "Christie." Twist and Turn with bendable knees. $9.00.

Mattel--4" "Teener-Doreen" #4002. Golden blonde in pink suit. Marks: 1971/Mattel/Inc./Hong/Kong, on hip. $6.00.

Mattel--4" "Teener-Coreen" #4001. White hair in yellow suit. Marks: 1971/Mattel/Inc./Hong/Kong, on hip. $6.00.

Mattel--4" "Teener-Moreen" #4004, in green suit with red hair. The Mattel 1972 catalog shows "Moreen" changed to "Maxeen" with darker skin tones than the other three. Marks: 1971/Mattel/Inc./Hong/Kong, on hip. $6.00.

Mattel--This is photograph of a photograph of the Black Skipper that was to be made and never put on the market so this one could be called a "prototype." It now belongs to Joan Ashabraner and the photo belongs to Sibyl DeWein.

Mattel--"Action Barbie" Sold in 1973 in this plastic sack. $8.00.

Mattel--"Barbie Baby Sits" 3" "Little Sweets" from the Sunshine Family. Body is unjointed rigid vinyl. Softer vinyl head. Inset blue eyes. Rooted blonde hair. Marks: 1973 Mattel Inc., on head. 1973 Mattel Inc./Taiwan, on back. $7.00.

210

Mattel--12" "Bucky Love Notes" Cloth with vinyl head. Blue decal eyes. Freckles. Press arms, legs and stomach and he plays 8 different tunes. Comes with song book. Each part of him is color coded to match song book. Marks: 1974 Mattel Inc, on head. Tag: Mattel Inc. 1974, etc. Still available.

Mattel--"Little Sweets" of the Sunshine Family #7258. This one has red hair. Still available. (Courtesy Sibyl DeWein)

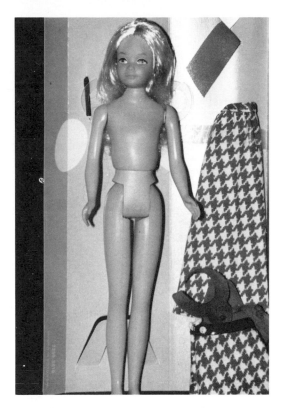

Mattel--Growing Up Skipper. Marks: 1967/Mattel Inc/Hong Kong/US & For. Pat., on hip. Issued Spring 1975. Shows original red/white outfits. Still available.

Mattel--Shows "Growing Up Skipper" as an older girl. Waist gets longer and small breasts appear, by rotating arm.

Mattel--3" "Hero's In Action" Grenade thrower. Lever moves to make and hear noise, also moves upper half of figure. Marks: Stand: Mattel Inc./Hong Kong/Patent Pending. Set of 14: Point Man, Rifleman, Company Commander, Cleanup man, Ranger, Flame Thrower, Sniper, Infantryman, Marksman, Sharpshooter, Recon Officer, Heavy Weapons and Bazookaman.

Mattel--9" and 8½" "Jazz Performers:" Mellie and Louis Harris. Other couples: Liberty Patriots: Regina and Richard Stanton and Thanksgiving Pilgrams: James and Louisa Winthrope. Still available. (Courtesy Sibyl DeWein)

211

Mattel--8½" "Colonial Girl" (Miss Alison Thompson) Hard plastic with jointed knees. Inset blue eyes. Vinyl head. Marks: 1973 Mattel Inc., on head. Still available.

Mattel-8½" "Indian Maiden" (Smiling Eyes) Hard plastic with jointed knees. Inset brown eyes. Vinyl head. Marks: 1973 Mattel Inc, on head. Still available.

Mattel--8½" "Southern Belle" (Rosa Lee Linden) Hard plastic with jointed knees. Inset blue eyes. Vinyl head. Marks: 1973 Mattel Inc., on head. Still available.

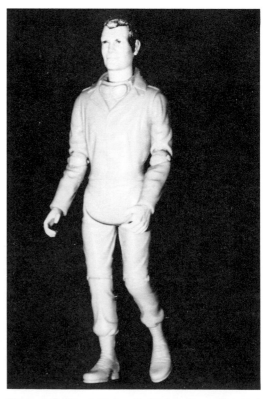

Marx--11" "Tank Driver" All heavy solid vinyl. Molded on clothes. Jointed neck, shoulders and elbows and wrists. Arms and head are strung. Soft vinyl hands. Marks: Marx/Toys, in a circle, on back. $3.00.

Marx--12" "Viking" All rigid vinyl. Marks: Louis Marx & Co/MCMLXIX/Made in U.S.A. $3.00.

Marx--11" "Stony "Stonewall" Smith" All heavy solid vinyl with molded on clothes. Arms and head are strung. Fully jointed. Marks: Marx/ Toys, in a circle. 1964. $3.00.

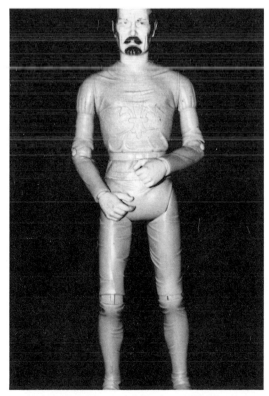

Marx--12" "Knight" All rigid vinyl Marks: Louis Marx & Co/MCMLXVII/Made in U.S.A. $3.00.

Mego--8" "Supergirl & Batgirl" Marked the same as Wonderwomen and Catwomen. Available in some areas.

213

Mego--8" "Wonderwomen & Catwomen" Marks:
NPP Inc/1973, on head. Mego Corp/MCMLXX-
II/Pat. Pending/Made in/Hong Kong, on back.
Available in some areas.

Mego--8" "Sitting Bull" Original. Marks: Mego
Corp 1973, on head. Mego Corp/Reg. US Pat.
Off./Pat. Pending/Hong Kong/MCMLXXI.
Available in some areas.

Mego--8" "Buffalo Bill Cody" Original. Marks:
Mego Corp 1973, on head. Mego Corp./Reg. U.S.
Pat. Off./Pat. Pending/Hong Kong/MCMLXXI.
Available in some areas.

Mego--8" "Wyatt Earp" Original. Marks: Mego
Corp 1973, on head. Mego Corp/Reg. U.S. Pat
Off./Pat. Pending/Hong Kong/MCMLXXI.
Available in some areas.

Mego--8" "Davey Crockett" Original. Marks: Mego Corp 1973, on head. Mego Corp./Reg. U.S. Pat. Off./Pat. Pending/Hong Kong/MCMLXXI. Available in some areas.

Mego--8" "Cochise" Original. Marks: Mego Corp 1973, on head. Mego Corp/Reg. US Pat. Off./Pat. Pending/Hong Kong/MCMLXXI. Available in some areas.

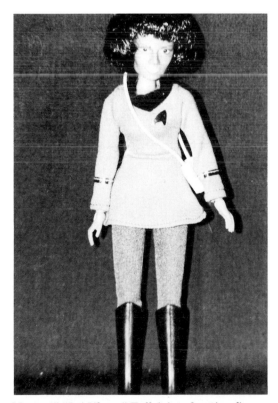

Mego--8" "Lt. Uhura" Full jointed action figure. Marks: 1974/Paramount/Pic. Corp. on head. Mego Corp/MCMLXXII/Pat. Pending/Made In/Kong Kong, on back. See color section for the other members of Star Trek. Still available in some areas.

Mego-8" "Ivanhoe" Action figure. Marks: Mego Corp/1974. Available in some areas.

Mego--8" "King Arthur" Action figure. Head marked: Mego Corp/1974. Available in some areas.

Mego--8" "Sir Lancelot" Action figure. Marks: Mego Corp/1974. Available in some areas.

Mego--8" "Long John Silver" and "Jean Lafitte" Action figures. Marks: Mego Corp/Reg. US Pat. Off./Patent Pending/Hong Kong/MCMMLXXI. 1975. Available in some areas.

Mego--8" "Captain Patch" and "Black Beard" Action figures. Marks: Mego Corp./Reg. U.S. Pat. Off./Patent Pending/Hong Kong/MCMLX-XI. 1975. Available in some areas.

Mego--8" "Friar Tuck," "Will Scarlet" and "Little John" All Action figures. All original. Marks: Mego Corp./Reg. U.S. Pat. Off./Patent Pending/Hong Kong/MCMLXXI. 1975. Available in some areas.

Mego--8" "Dorothy & Toto" and 8" "Scarecrow" Plastic and vinyl. Marks: Mego Corp/MCML-XXII/Pat. Pending/Made in Hong Kong, on back. 1974. M.G.M./Inc., on head. Toto: M.G.M. Inc. Available in some areas.

Mego--7" "Wicked Witch" All green. Plastic and vinyl. Marks: Mego Corp/MCMLXXII/Pat. Pending/Made in Hong Kong, on back. 1974. M.G.M./Inc., on head. Played by Margaret Hamilton. Available in some areas.

Mego--8" "Glenda, The Good Witch" Plastic and vinyl action figure. Hole in head for crown. Marks: 1974 Mego/Inc., on head. Played by Billie Burke. Available in some areas.

217

Mego--8" "Wizard of Oz" Same markings as the others. You can only purchase this doll when you buy the "Oz City" and the purchase price is fairly high. This head also used for Mr. Mxytpet. Available in some areas.

Mego--8" "Tin Woodsman" and "Cowardly Lion" Plastic and vinyl. Marks: Mego Corp/MCML-XXII/Pat. Pending/Made in Hong Kong, on back. 1974 M.G.M./Inc, on head. Available in some areas.

Mego--Shows the original cast of the much loved movie "Wizard of Oz" by Metro Goldwyn-Mayer.

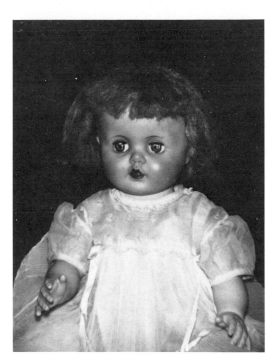

Miller Rubber--22" "Honeybunch" Dark hard plastic walker (exactly like Ideal's Saucy Walker). Vinyl rubber head with dark layer of "skin." Brown sleep eyes. Open mouth. 1956. (Courtesy Phyllis Houston)

Midwestern--24" "Darleen" (Speigels 1961) Plastic and vinyl. Blue sleep eyes. Open/closed mouth with molded tongue. Molded hair under rooted hair. Marks: Form of a flying bird, on head. 25-6/AE, lower back. $3.00. (Courtesy Carolyn Powers)

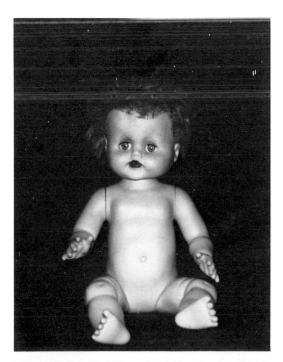

Midwestern--15" "Tiny Little" All vinyl with molded hair under rooted hair. Open mouth/nurser. Sleep eyes/lashes. Marks: PTN/18, on head. 1964. $2.00. (Courtesy Carolyn Powers)

Nancy Ann--8" "Muffie" dressed in her original Daniel Boone clothes. 1954. $15.00. (Courtesy Marge Meisinger)

219

Nancy Ann--6" Hard plastic. All original. Bride has sleep eyes. Groom has painted eyes. Marks: Nancy Ann Storybook Dolls. $12.00 each. (Courtesy Phyllis Houston)

Nancy Ann--5½" "Valentine" Painted bisque. All original. $12.00. (Courtesy Phyllis Houston)

Nancy Ann--10½" "Debbie" All hard plastic. Walker, head turns. Marks: Nancy Ann, on head. Pale blue valour coat. White rabbit head band and muff. Pale blue dress, snap shoes and socks. $10.00. (Courtesy Bessie Carson)

Nancy Ann--8" "Muffie" as Mexico. Re-issue of 1968-69. All hard plastic. $8.00. (Courtesy Marge Meisinger)

Nancy Ann--8" "Muffie" as Peru. Re-issue of 1968-69. All hard plastic. $8.00. (Courtesy Marge Meisinger)

Nancy Ann--8" "Muffie" as Poland. This is the re issue of 1968-69. Doll is hard plastic. $8.00. (Courtesy Marge Meisinger)

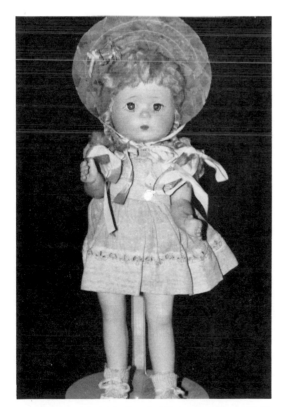

Nasco--14" "Debbie Lou" All composition. Fully jointed. Blue sleep eyes/lashes. Original. 1944. $22.00. (Courtesy Maxine Heitt)

Nasco--24" "Raggedy Ann & Andy" Rooted yarn hair in vinyl heads. Plastic bodies. Original. Marks: Nasco Doll Inc./The Hobbs-Merrill Inc./ 1973. $7.00 each. (Courtesy Marie Ernst)

221

Nasco--15" "Grow Hair Angie" Plastic and vinyl. Blue sleep eyes. Head is strung with the long hair attached to legs. Marks: Nasco, high on head. Nasco/Made in Hong Kong, on back. 1967. $4.00.

Nasco--13" "Stumbles" All cloth with vinyl head. Gauntlet vinyl hands. Painted blue eyes. Dimples. Sold as a floppy "walking" doll. Hold at back of neck and cloth legs will "walk." Marks: Nasco Doll Co Inc/Taiwan. $6.00.

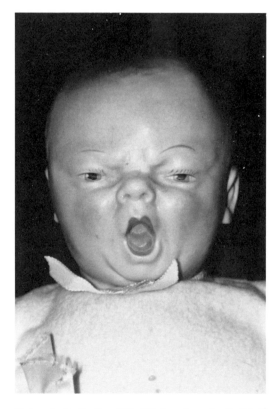

222

Natural Doll Co.--23" "Baby Jasmine" Cloth body with cryer in stomach. Vinyl head and limbs. Open/Closed mouth. Painted blue eyes. 1952. Made by Natural Doll Co. Marks: N'52. $20.00. (Courtesy Joan Amundsen)

Natural Doll Co.--17" "Miss Ritzi" All vinyl. Blue sleep eyes. Marks: A/14RA, on head. B-18, on back. Pat. Pend., on lower waist. 1959. $8.00.

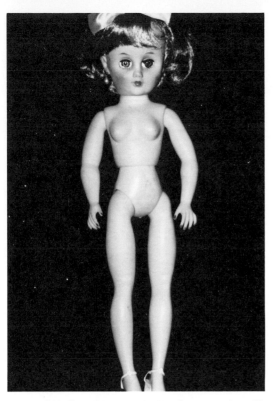

Natural Doll--17" "Miss Ritzi" (also came in 14"). To show body view of the doll.

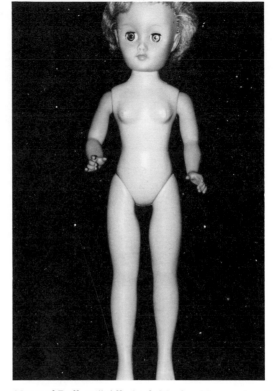

Natural Doll--14" All vinyl. Marks: None, except 15, on back of arms.

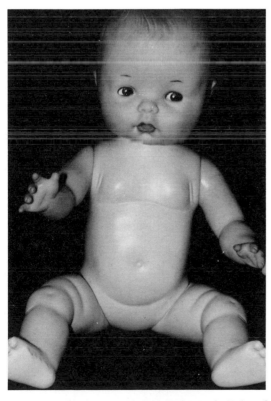

Natural--13" "Baby" Plastic and vinyl. Painted black eyes. Open/closed mouth. Marks: None. 1967.

Nilsen, Margit--7½" "Thumbs Up Victory Doll" Complete one piece construction made of Lasticoid, non flexible. Open crown under wig. Painted features. Dolls sold for the purchase of ambulances for Britain. 1940. An original outfit. Marks: None. (Courtesy Pearl Clasby)

Ocean Toys--9½" "The Happy Family" Dad: Brown inset eyes. All plastic with vinyl head. 9" Mom: Blue painted eyes. All plastic with vinyl head. 3" Baby: Painted blue eyes. All plastic one piece body. Vinyl head. Extra nice quality clothes. Marks: All: Hong Kong, on back. Box: Ocean Toys.

Plastic Molded Arts--8" "Suzy Walker" All hard plastic with blue sleep eyes. Walker head turns. Marks: None. $3.00. (Courtesy Barbara Coker)

Plastic Molded Arts--7½" "Alice in Wonderland" All hard plastic with glued on blonde hair. Blue sleep eyes. Original. $2.00.

Plastic Molded Arts--8" "Debbie Cakes" Advertising doll. All plastic with stapled on clothes. Jointed neck and shoulders. $3.00. (Courtesy Marie Ernst)

Playthings--20" "Nancy" One piece vinyl with stuffed vinyl head. Rooted blonde hair. Blue sleep eyes. Blue eyeshadow. Pierced ears and high heel feet. Marks: 25/Plaything, on head. 1954. $3.00.

Playmates--8½" "Toddler Twins" Premium for tops from two Raisin Bran and $3.50. 1974. Boy, painted brown eyes. Girl, painted blue eyes. Boy has freckles. Original. Marks: Hong Kong, on head. By Playmates, in a circle/Hong Kong/ 5092, on backs. $2.00 each.

Playmates--14" "Shelly" Plastic and vinyl. Brunette is dressed in pink and Yellow blonde is dressed in yellow. $3.00 each. (Courtesy Marie Ernst)

P&M Sales--12½" "Lotus Blossom" All vinyl with brown sleep eyes. Beauty spot on left cheek. Orange satin trousers and print cotton top original. 1966. $4.00. (Courtesy Phyllis Houston)

225

P&M Sales--14" Plastic body and legs. Vinyl arms and head. Rooted black hair. Black sleep eyes to side/lashes. Molded eyelids and brows. Large nose and ears. Original. Has two pearl necklaces and two pearl "pierced" earrings. Molded breast and high heel feet. Marks: 2040/ 10 Eye/New/1967. Backward AE, lower back. 15, inside arms. $22.00.

P&M Sales--11" "Baby Buttons" Plastic body, rest vinyl. Blue sleep eyes/molded lashes. Open mouth/nurser. Came also with painted eyes. Marks: None. 1966. $3.00.

Product People Inc--7" "Charlie The Tuna" All vinyl with molded on hat. Painted features. Marks: 1973/Star-Kist Foods Inc. on bottom of feet. $2.00.

Puppet--10" "Gene Autry" puppet. Cloth and rubber with molded on hat. Painted eyes. Marks: None on puppet. Box: National Mask &/ Puppet Corp. $18.00. (Courtesy Marge Meisinger)

Puppet--12" Cloth and composition. Marks: P. Puppet, on head. Box: Peter Puppet Playthings Inc./Designed By/Raye Copalan. $18.00. (Courtesy Joan Amundsen)

Puppet--11" "Oliver Hardy". Cloth body puppet. Vinyl head with molded on hat. Marks: Knicherbacher/1965/Japan, on head. Licensed by Harmon Pic. Corp. $5.00.

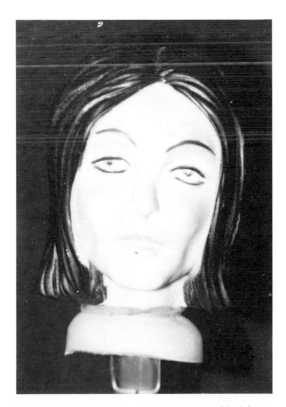

Puppet--9" "Lilly Munster" Black molded hair. Blue painted eyes with lavender eyeshadow. Marks: Filmways TV Productions Inc./1964. $4.00. (Courtesy Marie Ernst)

227

Remco Industries, Inc.

The Remco Company was founded by Sol Robbins, and was a successful company for many years and never seemed to lack in design and modeling. For example in 1968, Annuel McBurroughs, a Negro artist helped to design an "ethically correct" line of dolls for Remco. The series included: Tippy Tumbles, Polly Puff, Tiny Tumbles, Baby Laugh-a-lot, L'il Winking Winny, Growing Sally, Baby Know It All, Tina, Baby Whistle, Jumpsy, Billy, Baby Grow-A-Tooth, Bunny Baby and Tumbling Tomboy. The dolls were made all in the White versions but none became too popular and were shortly discontinued.

Many of the items for Remco were made in Canada by the Playcraft Toys Inc. With the closing of the Remco Co. doors (1974) the Miner Industries bought the "Sweet April" doll and accessories. Azrak-Hamway Int'l. purchased the name Remco, Remco Industries, Inc. and Remcraft and are sole owners of the U.S. Trademarks: 848,973; 711,485; 862,678 and corresponding Trademarks throughout the world, and is now called Remco Industries, Inc. A Division of Azark-Hamway International, Inc. The above information appeared in the January 1975 Playthings magazine, so it may be possible they will produce dolls under the Remco name at some future date.

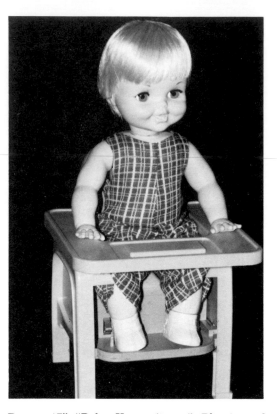

Remco--17" "Baby Know It All" Plastic and vinyl. Set blue eyes. Molded on shoes. Open/closed mouth with two lower teeth. Marks: Remco Ind. Inc./1969. $5.00. (Courtesy Ruth Clarke)

Remco--4½" "Dave Clark" and 3" "Rick, Mike, Lenny & Dennis" The small ones are all plastic. Molded hair. All have open/closed mouths. No marks: Dave Clark: has vinyl head with rooted and lacquered hair. Painted teeth. Marks: Dave Clark/5/1964 Remco Inc., on back. 22/Dave Clark/1964/Remco Ind. Inc., on head. $22.00. (Courtesy Bessie Carson)

RDF--3½" "Tiny Tim" All vinyl in sitting position. Unjointed. Very long nose. Glued on long mohair. Felt eyes. Marks: RDF '67, on foot. 1967. $8.00.

Richard Toy Co.--8" "Pilgrim-1620" Marks: Hong Kong, on head. Dress tag: Bicentennial/Fashion Friends. Other side: Made in Hong Kong/Richard Toy Co. Ltd. 1975. Available in some areas.

Richard Toy Co.--8" "Colonist-1740" Marks: Hong Kong, on back. Dress tag: Bicentennial/Fashion Friends. Other side: Made in Hong Kong/Richard Toy Co. Ltd. 1975. Available in some areas.

Richard Toy Co.--8" "Independence-1776" Marks: Hong Kong, on back. Dress tag: Bicentennia/Fashion Friends. Other side: Made in Hong Kong/Richard Toy Co. Ltd. 1975. Available in some areas.

229

Richard Toy Co.--8" "First Lady-1789" Plastic and vinyl. Blue sleep eyes. White floss hair. Marks: Hong Kong, on back. Tag: Made in Hong Kong/Richard Toy Co. Ltd. Other side: Bicentennial/Fashion Friends. TM. Available in some areas. (Courtesy Virginia Jones)

Richard Toy Co.--8" "Frontier-1848" Marks: Hong Kong, on head. Dress tag: Bicentennial/Fashion Friends. Other side: Made in Hong Kong/Richard Toy Co. Ltd. 1975. Available in some areas.

230

Richard Toy Co.--8" "Southern Belle-1861" of the Bicentennial Fashion Friends. Marks: Hong Kong, on back. Dress tag: Bicentennial/Fashion Friends. Other side: Made in Hong Kong/Richard Toy Co. Ltd. 1975. Available in some areas.

Richard Toy Co.--8" "Gibson Girl-1900" Marks: Hong Kong, on back. Dress tag: Bicentennial/Fashion Friends. Other side: Made in Hong Kong/Richard Toy Co. Ltd. 1975. Available in some areas.

Richard Toy Co.--8" "Flapper-1925" Marks: Hong Kong, on back. Dress Tag: Bicentennial/Fashion Friends. Other side: Made in Hong Kong/Richard Toy Co. Ltd. 1975. Available in some areas.

Richard Toy Co.--8" "New Look-1947" Marks: Hong Kong, on back. Dress Tag: Bicentennial/Fashion Friends. Other side: Made in Hong Kong/Richard Toy Co. Ltd. 1975. Available in some areas.

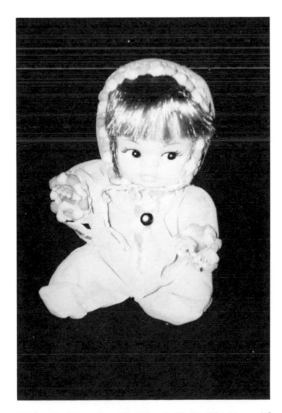

Richard Toy Co.--6" "Toni Tot" Plastic with vinyl head. Painted blue eyes. Original. Marks: Hong Kong, on head and back. Clothes Tag: Toni Tot/other side: Made in Hong Kong/Richard Toy Co. Ltd. $2.00.

Richwood Toys--Sandra Sue was created by the famous sculptor Agop Agopoff. Mr. Agopoff is known for his famous bust of Will Rogers and Anton Dvorak, the Czech composer. Sandra Sue outfits included Louisa May Alcott Little Women outfits. She also had a four poster colonial wooden bed and wardrobe.

231

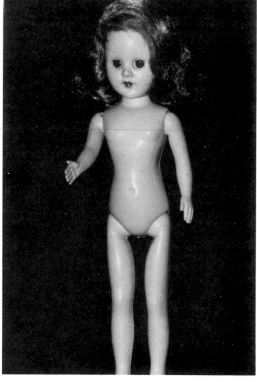

Richwood Toys--8" "Sandra Sue" All hard plastic. Walker mechanisms. (Head doesn't turn.) Blue sleep eyes, painted red lashes, red "fly away" brows. Full red mouth. Fingers straight. Looks like formed soles on plain molded feet. Clothes are excellent quality. Marks: #1, left arm. 2, right arm. (Courtesy Jeanne Niswonger)

Roberta--13" "Baby Beth" All vinyl with rooted blonde hair. Blue sleep eyes. 1961. Marks: Roberta/13, on head. $3.00.

Roberta--14" "Model" All hard plastic with glued on red mohair. Blue sleep eyes/molded lashes. Early walker with pin joints. Head turns. Marks: 14, on head. Made in USA, in circle on back. 1952. Sold with 22 piece wardrobe. $6.00.

Roberta--17" "Haleoke" From Arthur Godfrey Show. All hard plastic walker, head doesn't turn. Blue sleep eyes/lashes. Skin tones on head only are suntan. Glued on black saran hair. Marks: Made in U.S.A., on back. Clothes made in Hawaiian Islands, with Uke/shoes and hose extra. Dist. by Cast Distributing Corp. NY. $45.00. (Courtesy DeAngelo Collection)

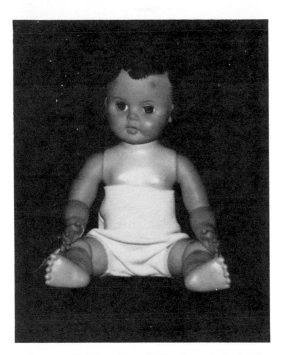

Roberta--16" "Tear Drop" Plastic and vinyl. Blue sleep eyes/lashes. Open mouth/nurser. 1966. Marks: 14-5W, on head. Backward "D", lower back. (Courtesy Carolyn Powers)

Ronald Trading Co.--6½" Plastic head. "Bean bag" (foam pellets) body. Marks: Made in/Hong Kong, on head. Bag: Ronald Trading Co. Ltd. $2.00.

Cloth--8" "Gramps" and 7½" "Granny" Vinyl heads with molded on glasses. Printed cloth bodies. Marks: Made in Hong Kong, on head. Tag: Li'l Stuffs/Made in Hong Kong for/Ronald Trading, Ltd. Still available.

Cloth--7" "Grandaughter" Vinyl head. Printed cloth body. Marks: Hong Kong, on head. Tag: Li'l Stuffs/Made in Hong Kong For/Ronald Trading Co. Ltd. Still available.

Rushton--13" "Connie" Cloth, foam stuffed. Vinyl gauntlet feet and hands. Vinyl face mask with molded blonde hair. Painted features. Yellow yarn hair glued to cloth back of head. Pants removable only. Tag: Connie. Cloth tag: A Rushton Star Creation. Top of Head: White Provision Co. $22.00. (Courtesy Mary Partridge)

Rushton--15½" "Musical Mistress Mary" Cloth body arms and legs. Felt feet. Gauntlet vinyl hands. Vinyl head with rooted orange yarn/molded hair. Side glancing blue eyes. Key wind music box in center of back. Marks: None. 1964. Set of five: Jack, Jill, Little Boy Blue, Little Bo Peep. $13.00.

Rushton--15½" "Little Bo Peep" 1964. $13.00. (Courtesy Alice Capps)

Rushton--19" "Nap Time Pal" 1961. Plush with vinyl gauntlet hands and vinyl face mask. Painted features. Marks: Rushton Co. $3.00.

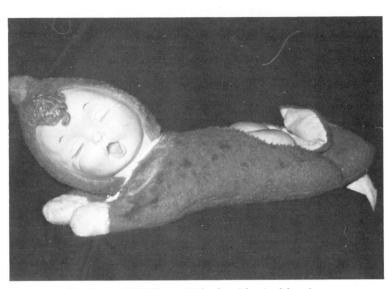

Rushton--22" "Sleepy" Plush with vinyl head on bottom. Rooted hair. Painted closed eyes. Squeeker in bottom flap. Zipper in stomach. Marks: ©, on neck. $4.00.

Sasha--"Sasha" Baby" These babies are just slightly sexed. Still available. (Courtesy Marie Ernst)

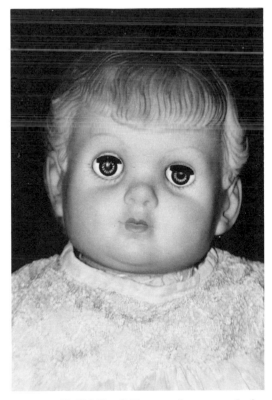

Sayco--20" "Melissa" Brown sleep eyes/lashes. Cloth body with vinyl arms, legs and head. Sculptured hair. Marks: Sayco/18-D. $40.00. (Courtesy Barbara Coker)

RUSHTON

SASHA

SAYCO

Sayco--20" "Melissa" Shows back of sculptured hair. (Courtesy Barbara Coker)

235

Sayco--17" "Laura" Hard plastic with a vinyl head. Dark brown rooted hair. Blue sleep eyes. Marks: Sayco, on head.

Sayco--14" "Bride" Rigid vinyl with softer vinyl head. High heel feet. Jointed waist. All original except bouquet. 1957. $15.00. (Courtesy Phyllis Houston)

Sayco--20" "Sherry Ann" One piece stuffed vinly body and limbs. Blue sleep eyes. Very tight outside row of hair. Was in up/back sweep. Open/closed mouth. Original. 1956. Marks: 74, on head. (Courtesy Carolyn Powers)

Shindana Toys

Shindana is a black community owned toy company, in the Watts section of Los Angeles. The President of the company is Lou Smith, who says, "It's totally unrealistic to expect black kids to play with blonde, blue eyed dolls when they, nor their children, will not grow up to look that way. Instead of making "suntanned" dolls, we use the ethnic characteristics of black people."

To give the dolls a kinky Afro hairdo, the company had to order a curling machine from Italy, as no such machine could be found that was made in the U.S. and the company's first doll, "Baby Nancy" came off the assembly line with straight black hair.

According to Herman Thompson, director of sales and marketing for Shindana, the making of a "truly black doll" came about only after a study by a black psychiatrist which showed that black children, when given a choice, preferred white dolls over black ones and stated, "We saw this as an expression of a lack of love and understanding these children held for themselves. We tackled this problem by producing and marketing 21 black dolls that black and white children can learn to relate to a very early age."

Shindana was founded without government subsidy. When Lou Smith and his partner Robert Hall, an official of the Congress of Racial Equality, started the toy company in Watts after the 1968 riots, Smith went to Mattel, Inc. for financial backing and advice. Mattel was responsive to Smith's idea and gave him $300,000 initial capital and technical advice to begin the enterprise. "There were no strings attached." Smith said. Mr. Hall, his partner died in 1973, a man in his 30's who had literally worked himself to death.

Shindana Toys is the economic arm of Operation Bootstraps, a non-profit self help business organization whose goals are to establish businesses in the riot torn Watts area.

Shindana means "complete" in Swahili and began eight years ago with one doll "Baby Nancy" and today it is a $1,300,000 a year company that makes 21 different dolls and eight educational games.

Smith did not believe the poverty programs of the '60's would work but believed that the ghettos must be changed from within. He says, "You have to establish an economic base, an educational base, a self-esteem and self-love and all this must come from within the community. Instead of going to Washington for handouts, we have to build industry to employ and train people right in the ghetto and we must manufacture products that society wants and needs."

"For example, one Shindana doll, "Wanda the Career Girl" is an off-shoot of the Mattel's white Barbie doll. But instead of just giving her a beautiful wardrobe, we use the black doll as a career woman to introduce career ideas and opportunities to black children. In the ghetto, black people aren't aware of the careers open to them."

There are three Wanda dolls on the market, the Nurse, the Ballerina and the Airline Stewardess. These careers were chosen first, as they have distinct costumes to coincide with the career but Shindana plans to introduce other professions.

Each doll (Wanda) comes with a booklet with a picture from, a successful black woman in each of the three fields. For example, Wanda the Airline Stewartess booklet has a message from Bernadette, Wanda's friend. Bernadette Gossey is a real person and actually works for TWA and she tells the youngsters about her career and why she enjoys it.

Wanda also has a Career Club. Each month, more than 5,000 career club members receive a free newsletter about careers from interior decorating to journalism.

Dolls by Shindana, a member of Operation Bootstraps, has always been of interest to the doll collector because of the beauty of the dolls themselves and for the high quality of the vinyl and of the clothes. These dolls can only enhance a collection.

Shindana--23""J.J." Talking character doll, based on J.J. Evans of the T.V. show "Good Times." Played by actor Jimmy Walker. Says ten things and is pull string operated. (Courtesy Harshe-Rotman & Druck, Inc. Public Relations firm for Shindana)

Singer--14" Pink plastic covered foam body. Vinyl head, arms and legs. Open mouth/nurser. Blue sleep eyes/long lashes. Marks: Singer Crafts/Patterson N.J./Mass T 984/Polyfoam/ Made in Hong Kong. $6.00.

Skippy--17½" "Julia" Plastic and vinyl. Blue sleep eyes. Closed mouth. Marks: A Skippy Doll/1967, on head. AE, on back and a backward AE, lower on back. $6.00. (Courtesy Carolyn Powers)

238

Squeeze Toy--9" "Annie" All vinyl with molded on underwear, shoes and socks. Molded brown hair. Inset blue eyes. Open/closed mouth. Jointed neck only. Marks: The Sun Rubber Co./ 1965, on back. $2.00.

Squeeze Toy--10" "Sweetie Pie" All vinyl, un-jointed. Molded on clothes. Doll is dressed and looks just like her. Marks(Sweetie Pie/A Stern Toy/N.E.A. 1959. $3.00.

Squeeze Toy--6" "Googly" Press stomach and eyes twirl. All vinyl. Jointed neck only. Rooted hair. Marks: U.S. Pat. No. 3451160, on head. #1012/Copyrighted 1969/Parksmith Corporation/ Japan. $2.00.

Squeeze Toy--8" "Daniel" All vinyl. Marks: Nonc. $2.00.

Squeeze Toy--6" All vinyl with molded orange hair. Has two "daisys" behind back. Marks: 1966/Ideal Toy Corp/I-D-5, on lower back legs. 1966/Ideal Toy Corp/Portugal, on bottom. $2.00. (Courtesy Virginia Jones)

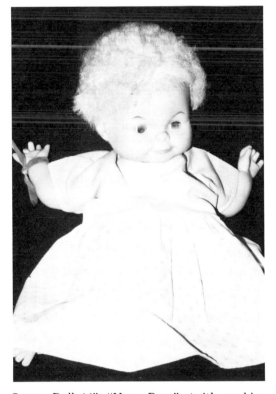

Super Doll--12" "Little Debbie Eve's Brother" Rigid vinyl body, arms and legs. Blue sleep eyes. 1960. Marks: 12-D, on lower back. $2.00.

Super Doll--14" "New Born" (with rocking plastic cradle). Cloth and vinyl with rooted white hair. Blue sleep eyes. Cryer. Marks: SD/ 18, on head. 1964. $1.00.

The Story of Terri Lee

The following article was prepared by Lula May Close. Mrs. Close is a member of the Capitol City Doll Club of Ohio. The article was written in 1968 and the author cbtained her information from Mrs. Violet Gradwohl herself.

It was a cloudy bleak December afternoon in Lincoln, Nebraska, in 1944 when a group of housewives were gathered around a huge table mending dolls for the needy. Violet Gradwohl was rather tired, having spent a busy morning at the U.S.O. and today was typical of almost every other day she had spent since the beginning of the war.

As she cemented together the jagged pieces of a broken leg, taking care not to interfer with the walking mechanism, she sighed, "Why don't they make a doll in a little girl's image, uncomplicated, with which a child can use her imagination? Dolls with eyes that can't be gouged out, without walking devices that soon stop running, with chubby legs and slightly protruding tummies, such as every little girl has?" The more she thought about it the more she felt that someone should create a doll that looked like a human being, and that did not have all the faults she felt every doll that has been manufactured so far had. For this reason Violet Gradwohl decided to enter the doll manufacturing business herself.

She began to form her own ideas of what a doll should be in order to become a durable darling of a child's heart. It was an ideal, to be sure, but Mrs. Gradwohl set out to make it a reality.

Soon after the war Mrs. Gradwohl found time hanging heavily on her hands and set about creating a model for a doll that would combine her observations, experiences and ideals; a doll with a new sytle body that would not break, durable, with an attractive appearance and plenty of pretty clothes. It was sculptured in plaster by her niece, Maxine Stevens, a California sculptress who used her own two year old daughter Adrienne as a model. For a name Mrs. Gradwohl took that of her daughter, Terri Lee.

(You will note that this contradicts with the following, which was also from Mrs. Gradwohl).

By 1946 she had accomplished several things toward making her dream a reality. From photographs of her daughter taken in childhood, she had a model and then a mold made. Because she wanted the doll to last with the child, she wanted to protect it from unsightly broken fingers and sightless eyes. She combed the market for a plastic that had a life-like appearance and selected rigid plastic for the doll parts. The head was molded so that the eyes were part of the head itself, and she selected artists to paint the eyes and all the features so that it retained humanness. There had never been a doll like Terri Lee. She was the first made of plastic which was guaranteed for life as unbreakable. Mrs. Gradwohl had seen her child in tears over a broken doll, and felt it was important for the child to have something to love, that would not break. She believed in making things beautiful, sturdy and practical for children.

Her next job was to find a wig that could be shampooed, combed and curled. Terri Lee was not only the first doll with a lifetime guarantee, but also the first doll to have a wig of this type. The finished product was so charming and beautiful, it cried out for charming and beautiful clothing. Vi Gradwohl's daughter, Terri Lee, who was also very talented, and her mother put their heads together and designed a wardrobe such as any child would like to have, and made of materials like children wear, with buttons and snaps and lovely ribbons and laces. Later, formals and Bride's dresses were added because all little girls like to play that they are grown up. Terri Lee was the first doll with a complete wardrobe and has always been America's best dressed doll.

The doll called Terri Lee suggested a brother, Jerri, which was made on the same mold, with a different wig. Next, Mrs. Gradwohl felt Negro children would like dolls made in their own likeness with the same chubby legs and pretty clothes. Vi chose a warm exotic beige brown paint and went to work with a spray gun. The result was Bonnie Lu and Benjie; then came Patty Jo, a cartoon character developed by Jackie Ormes. Next was Nanook, a slightly lighter color..an Eskimo child. The Baby Linda was brought into being, designed to be a baby's first doll, made in soft vinyl plastic 11" long. The production of Linda is a story in itself, the very first soft plastic doll completely articulated. Later on there was Tiny Terri and Tiny Jerry.

Mrs. Gradwohl, with no knowledge of the doll business, took the beautifully dressed plaster model Terri Lee to a New York doll show in March 1946, only to discover that just manufacturers could exhibit. However, Inez Holland, a manufacturer and manufacturer's representative, showed Terri Lee.

Mrs. Gradwohl spent six weeks in New York, learning about the doll business and finding out what she needed to get into business.

She encountered innumerable difficulties at the outset. With no backing other than her own determination, she walked into a large textile house and announced that she was going to manufacture a new doll and desired to purchase materials in quanity. This was in 1946, with most production was still on the war-era basis, and she was informed that no one could buy a yard of material except on quota. Manufacturers of garments, whether for humans or dolls, were being allocated materials only on the basis of past production and even that was limited. They informed her they could not supply her with raw materials since she did not have an established company, but before she left, she had somehow charmed the textile company into promising her a quota of materials if she could provide a satisfactory rating from Dun and Bradstreet. She didn't know what they were talking about, but promised anyway.

Several doll parts manufacturers refused her business, and she was told that the doll she wanted to manufacture had a funny face that nobody would buy. Finally, one consented to make parts for her, though informing her ominously that she would lose money.

Mrs. Violet Gradwohl went into the doll business in Lincoln, Nebraska in August 1946, with ten employees, working in one room. The Terri Lee doll was a success from the first.

Although Mrs. Gradwohl had planned to make the dolls of plastic (there were no plastic dolls on the market then), the first dolls were composition. Within the next year or so an Omaha firm pressed the dolls from "Unbreakable" plastic. (Lulu Cose comments that she has several Terri Lees which are made out of a whitish soft rubber, or soft plastic, probably an experimental medium in the transition from composition to hard plastic.)

Within the next several years the business had expanded so that the plant in Lincoln, with 23 employees in full production, could turn out 1,000 dolls a week, and in the peak season approximately 75 seamstresses were employed in making doll clothes. An extensive wardrobe for every season was available. Girl dolls had 20 different outfits to choose from, and boy dolls had 12. A Lincoln firm called Ben, Your Hairdresser, sub-contracted to make the wigs, and employed 7 or 8 persons making wigs during the peak season. The hair for the wigs was from Mrs. Gradwohl's own patented process from celanese yarn woven into artificial hair. This was a secret process and was never commercialized despite offers from other doll manufacturers.

By the year 1948, the Terri Lee firm had an assortment of dolls: Jerri, Bonnie, Benjie, Chiquita. They all had the same body (marked Terri Lee) but there were appropriate changes in wigs and coloring.

During an interview around the close of the second year of the venture, Mrs. Gradwohl said that Terri Lee was the first doll in the business to have real buttons, snaps and button holes in her clothes. It was attention to detail, she thought, that was partly responsible for the success of the dolls.

Besides the hairdresser wig maker, Ben, another Lincoln firm which contributed to the Terri Lee line was Dewey and Wilson, who made the motor driven merry-go-rounds which stores used to make permanent doll displays.

Terri Lee dolls were featured in newsreels, movie shorts and television programs by 1948. She was written up in Negro Digest, Ebony and other National Publications. "Jr. Magazine" for children featured Terri Lee monthly. The American Association of University Women recommended Terri Lee dolls. In the fall of 1948 Terri Lee appeared in the uniform of the Girl Scouts of America, by whom she had been adopted.

During this time the company maintained representatives in Chicago, St. Paul, Dallas, Denver, Salt Lake City, Portland (Oregon), and High Point (N.C.). During 1948 a large shipment of dolls was sent to Durbin, South Africa. Terri Lee dolls had been sold in every state in the Union and in Liberia, Norway, Switzerland, Hawaii, Nicaragua and Canada.

Within 5 years of its beginning, in 1951, Terri Lee, Inc. was one of the leading doll companies in the country, and the doll that "nobody would buy" sold at the rate of 3,000 per week, and was made in a two floor factory in Lincoln with almost 190 employees, a day and night shift, and more orders that could be filled.

At that time everything was manufactured and finished in Lincoln, except the moulding of the plastic and the production of the doll shoes, stockings, and straw hats.

Although the demand for Terri Lee dolls almost doubled every year the going for her creator was not always easy. Soon after Mrs. Gradwohl managed to acquire adequate space for efficient production, the factory was burned to the ground. The catastrophe happened just before Christmas 1951, near the end of the rush season.

Mrs. Gradwohl suffered exposure when records of the doll factory were removed from the flaming building by firemen and her husband, Dr. Harry Gradwohl. Mrs. Gradwohl went to the hospital in a state of nervous collapse.

The plant was a total loss, $75,000, and was not completely covered by insurance. Mrs. Gradwohl said that among items lost in the fire was a special luxury order doll dressed in a $250.00 mink coat.

The plant had "thousands" of small cash orders to be filled over one week-end, the plant manager said, and the plant would have shipped more than a carload of merchandise at the first of the week had they not had the fire.

However, the company received numerous letters and telegrams in regard to dolls that had been sent to the Terri Lee "hospital" for repairs, and the plant manager said these dolls were the greatest loss because of the value attached to them by their youthful owners. He said approximately 150 dolls were in the plant for repairs at the time.

Terri Lee, Inc. had scouted other business locations to house the growing doll business, and the firm was ready to build its own factory except for the current difficulties in securing construction materials.

Mrs. Gradwohl returned home from the hospital on Christmas Eve, determined to get out of business. In a corner of her living room stood two bushel baskets overflowing with letters from children, mothers and fathers, and merchants all over the country who had ordered dolls and hadn't received them because of the fire. All assured her that they would wait until she could deliver, no matter how long. She was soon in business again, filling these orders.

On May 9, 1952, Mrs. Gradwohl opened a plastic doll factory in Apple Valley in the Mojave Desert of Southern California, once the crossroads of four historic pioneer trails, with 32 persons in the assembly of her Terri Lee dolls. The business progressed and in 1953, seven years from the start of the venture in Lincoln, the company had grown to become one of something like 300 major doll manufacturing companies in the country and to hold the rank of fifth in production, more than 100,000 dolls a year.

The dolls were manufactured in Apple Valley, and the Lincoln plant which had been destroyed by fire was replaced by a plant to manufacture garments for the dolls. The Apple Valley plant also did a big business in wardrobes for the dolls and in the year 1953 sold three mink coats for them at $295 each.

From Independent Woman, November 21, 1954, was taken the following: "Alice in Wonderland never stepped into a more fantastic setting than that of the Doll House of Apple Valley. The building, which looks like a huge pink frosted birthday cake, stands in the midst of the vast golden California desert surrounded by Joshua trees. These trees, which are native to the area but which are nowhere else to be found except Palestine, add to the unreality of the scene by the incredible and amusing shapes of make-believe animals they make.

The loftiest peaks of the mountains that guard this valley of enchantment wears snow caps all year, but the valley itself is always warm with sunshine tempered by soft breezes, and the people who live there are happy. The people who work in the Doll House are probably happiest of all. The long modern building may be seen for miles around, and everyone who knows the community points it out with pride that is partly fond amusement and partly incredulity. It is difficult for them to believe that this magnificent and fantastic factory has come to stay in their midst. It is a little bit like something wonderful which has appeared by magic and might disappear just as suddenly.

But the Doll House is real and very permanent in Apple Valley. Viola Gradwohl, who called it into being, not by a wave of a fairy wand, but by good hard work, thinks there is no other place so delightful for living, and for earning a living making dolls for little girls.

Because the factory is located over a hundred miles from any large city and is the only industry in the area, the first great difficulty to be overcome was communications. "But I had fallen in love with this place on my first visit and was determined to locate here," said the Doll Lady, as she is affectionately called by everyone. She dismissed that problem with the quip, "The only thing lacking, really, was carrier pigeons."

"I have found you can't make a success of anything unless you live, eat and sleep it. In establishing a new business, there are times when all you have left is courage, and it takes a lot of courage. The manufacturing business is a man's world. A woman must learn to look at all problems as a man would, without emotion or hurt feelings. If this business were not so full of fun and challenge but it is fun to meet their faith with everything they expect of you."

Furthermore, I believe it is not necessary for a doll to have all the human attributes. In imagination children endow their playthings with every quality and function they wish. Also, I have discovered that children do not want a doll to resemble an adult. Several years ago we featured a Gene Autry doll but it was not a real success. The Gene Autry costumes which may be changed for others are much more popular.

Terri Lee wears beautiful and fashionable costumes, well made and well designed in the best available materials. Nylon, laces and nets, satin, cotton, linen of the best quality and even several kinds of fur are used to fashion her 150 varied and complete ensembles. If a capricious owner should douse Terri Lee's splendid formal gown in a basin of water, it would soon dry and be as good as new again.

Everyone who works at the Doll House radiates happiness. This work seems to have therapeutic quality. One of the girls who paints the doll's faces is a deaf mute whose personality has changed completely since she came to work at the Doll House. She is now even able to talk a little. Of the children who receive the dolls, Mrs. Gradwohl says, "The best way to teach children love and respect for possessions is to provide them with beautiful and durable things and then encourage them to care for their treasures."

This program is initiated by literature which accompanies the dolls and is maintanied by a monthly magazine sent to every owner of a Terri Lee doll as a life member of her Friendship Club. Colorful and timely, this miniature publication contains all the usual features of adult magazines slanted to juvenile readers. Terri Lee is the official Girl Scout and Campfire Girl's doll, and has her own authentic uniforms. Her philantrophies are many and varied.

Psychology is at work on a large scale in Viola Gradwohl's enterprise in exerting influence for good upon some 400 employees and the thousands of recipients of Terri Lee dolls.

During 1955, a series of fashion shows were put on by the three "City of Paris" stores in San Francisco, Vallejo and San Mateo, and proved to be a wonderful event. Thirteen nine-year-old girls were dressed exactly like the Terri Lee dolls they carried in their arms."

On November 10, 1955, forty thousand square feet of additional factory space was opened in Apple Valley by an entertainment and a conducted tour of the new plant and its facilities. The Terri Lee Sales Corporation now occupied 50,000 square feet of space. One sewing department, a molding, painting, wigging, assembling and packing units

were now housed in the addition.

Five hundred to six hundred employees were required during the busy season at Apple Valley and 300 more at the sewing plant in Lincoln, Nebraska. Terri Lee Schrepel still designed the beautifully made fashions.

In 1956, there were four basic dolls in the series: Terri Lee, a 17" all plastic doll (with Jerri Lee, a brother, like Terri in size and construction); Connie Lynn, a 20" all plastic sleeping doll with long natural eye lashes and curly soft hair; Baby Linda, 11," fully articulated vinyl baby doll; and Tiny Terri Lee (with Tiny Jerri, brother to Tiny Terri). The Tiny Terri had thirty costumes, all exactly like those of big sister Terri, and this small doll sat, walked and had movable eyes with long, sweeping eyelashes.

Somewhere along the line someone must have changed their minds about movable eyes, since both Connie Lynn and Tiny Terri and Jerri had sleeping eyes. The eyes of Connie Lynn were not guaranteed, however, and the lifetime guarantee did not cover Baby Linda nor the Tiny Terri and Jerri.

Every buyer was reportedly given a birth certificate with finger and footprints, and hospitals were maintained for sick Terri Lees. For only the bare cost of labor a practically new doll was returned to the little mother whose doll had been sent a Terri Lee Hospital.

To assure that lifetime guarantee, Mrs. Gradwohl maintained two doll hospitals during this period where for a small fee Terri Lee dolls that showed signs of aging could be rejuvenated. Repairs included new hair, repainting features or anything else necessary to restore the doll to her original perfection. One fact that pleased Terri Lee's creator is that not one Terri Lee came in with broken fingers. The hospital for dolls living east of the Rocky Mountains was located in Lincoln, Neb. and for west coast dolls in Apple Valley.

Indeed the Terri Lee, with its lifetime guarantee and hospital for sick Terri Lees would appeal to children, and the monthly magazine sent to owners, which carried patterns, stories, games and contests, together with the birthday clubs and special Terri Lee birthday cards, would keep up their interest. Note the instructions to the mother of a sick Terri Lee..."Send your dolly undressed so the doctor can put her right to bed." From the literature available you can see that there was no "talking down" to the children, but everything was in language they could understand. It has been reported that in one year alone the "mamas" of Terri Lee dolls wrote more than 300,000 letters to the "Lovely Lady." Little girls wrote, told her riddles and jokes and every letter was answered.

But misfortune struck again. Not much information can be obtained as to the demise of the Terri Lee venture in Apple Valley. It has been rumored that they had another fire there, which destroyed the Apple Valley plant; also that Terri Lee was forced into bankruptcy by the government in 1958 and all equipment and buildings in Apple Valley were sold at auction. Whatever happened to the Lincoln plant is unknown, and evidently it was closed also.

But Mrs. Gradwohl was not beaten yet. In the year 1962, Terri Lee dolls were made by I. and S. Industries in Glendale, California, and sold by Mar-fan Company of Glendale, Calif. The lifetime guarantee was still in effect and sick Terri Lees were to be sent to Mar-fan.

And something new was added. Some of the Terri Lees made by I&S had a voice. A phonograph jack was inserted in the back of the head under the hair line and a cord from the jack to the phonograph, with a Terri Lee record playing, seemed to give life to the doll. Several records by Terri Lee were available. These later dolls had softer hair, somewhat like dynel.

Although Terri Lee dolls were always in a fairly high price bracket, $12.95 and up, depending on costumes, (the dolls with voice were $8.00 more) the hospital charges were quite reasonable.

I have not been able to ascertain how long I&S Industries and Mar-fan sold Terri Lees. As said above, the hospital plan was still in effect in 1962, as well as the monthly magazine but evidently this was about the end of the Terri Lee manufacture as research reveals no further information.

It has been rumored that Terri Lees may be manufactured again, and evidently it may possibly be true as Mrs. Gradwohl wrote me the first of this year (1968)..."Am trying to get back into the manufacture of Terri Lee. If I can get the required financing, this I will do. I believe from the shabby doll clothes I see on the market that Terri Lee can again be popular, even without all the mechanical gadgets so many of the new dolls have."

The Terri Lee dolls are different and are sought after by many doll collectors, also the accessories made for the doll such as strollers that were sold for the Terri Lee dolls; Connie and Linda purses for little girls; Terri Lee lamps with a picture of Terri Lee on the shades; and Tiny Terri and Jerri kits with doll parts and dresses for children to put together and dress.

This ends Lulu Close's article and we continue with the story of Terri Lee as told in the fashion booklets that came with the dolls:

The Story of Terri Lee

"Once upon a time, not long ago, there was a Lovely Lady who had a beautiful little girl with shining curls and bright eyes like stars and oh! so many pretty clothes! This little girl's name was Terri Lee. The Lovely Lady thought, "How nice it would be if there was a doll just like my Terri Lee!" And she made a doll that looked like the real little girl. Then she thought, "How nice it would be if this pretty doll had lots of costumes!" And she made lots of costumes for the pretty doll. Then she thought, "How nice it would be if every little girl in the whole country could have a doll exactly like this one, with pretty clothes!" And that's how Terri Lee Dolls and their many beautiful costumes came to be.

The Lovely Lady thought of important things like how dolls get broken when they're loved too hard, how their clothes get mussed and soiled from being played with, and how their hair becomes all shabby after a little while. She wondered what she could do to be sure the Terri Lee Dolls would be lastingly beautiful. So she had the dolls made of fine, durable plastic that would be unbreakable. The material she selected for the hair was silky and lifelike and could be shampooed and set. And the costumes? She made them of the finest materials, with fur and lace and handwork on some, and she sewed them beautifully so they could be cleaned over and over, like a child's own garments.

Then she thought of having a real Doll Hospital and Lifetime Guarantee for the Terri Lee Dolls, where Little Mothers could send them in case anything happened to them, or where they could have new wigs put on them. That's how the Terri Lee Doll Hospital at Apple Valley, California, came to be.

And then the Lovely Lady thought, "Terri ought to have a brother!" So she made Jerri Lee, and designed all sorts of wonderful outfits for him, after that came the rest of the beautiful dolls in the Terri Lee circle, including Linda Baby. Linda Baby is the beautiful baby sister of Terri and Jerri, who is made of Rose-petal Vinyl and looks like Terri, too. There were costumes made for Linda, just like real babies wear.

And then she planned and created the monthly Terri Lee Magazines to send to all Little Mothers; the Birthday Club, the Terri Lee Thrift Club and the wonderful accessories: the Wardrobe Trunks, the Fashion Racks, the Terri Lee Records, the Bassinettes and Play Pen and Nursery Chair for Linda Baby; the Terri Lee Walker and all the rest. There were so many wonderful things to make and it seemed that every little girl wanted them, so there had to be a special place to make all these things. That's how the Terri Lee Doll House in Apple Valley came to be! If you could see the hundreds of wonderful dolls, the thousands of beautiful costumes and accessories in the Doll House, you'd think you were truly in Santa's Palace! There's a Beauty Salon, where Terri's new hair styles are designed and made; the place where each and every Terri, Jerri and Linda's face is specially, separately hand painted on; the rows and rows of Terri Lee dressed in their finest on a shelf for all to see...and everywhere you would feel the Fairyland magic that surrounds all things Terri Lee! Then, finally, she thought how nice it would be to create playmates for this little family of dolls. If you do not know the new members of the Terri Lee family, write us for information. There is Tiny Terri, available in all the costumes that Terri wears; Tiny Jerri, with a special wardrobe too; Connie Lynn...Sleepy Baby, with a very complete wardrobe all her own.

The Lovely Lady waved her magic wand and created all this from her loving thoughts...and she thought of everything, didn't she?"

The above "The Story of Terri Lee" was written for children and is conntained in some of the Terri Lee Fashion booklets with the address of Apple Valley, California. The following is a copy of the cover on one of the Fashion booklets and shows the real Terri, Connie Lynn and Linda.

A 1956 booklet has this: "This is the Story of Tiny Terri Lee"

"Terri Lee, as you know, is a real little girl, just like you. However, like all little girls, Terri Lee wished to be something else. So, Terri Lee wished to become a very tiny little girl. Princess Tinkle had given her a magic wishing stone, so Terri Lee rubs the wishing stone and Princess Tinkle appears and makes her into a tiny little doll.

Tiny Terri Lee can walk, she has closing eyes, she has hair that you may shampoo and it still will have a permanent like yours when you have a permanent. Tiny Terri Lee has many beautiful costumes, exactly the same number and kind of costumes as Terri Lee."

There is a dimensional "paper doll" that looks exactly like the 16" Terri Lee except it is about 12" tall. It was made during the early years of the doll and by a company unknown in this line. I have only seen one, and never heard of any more. No doubt there are more and will be seen in other paper doll collections in the future."

Now let us return to the begining and see what we have. Founder and designer (doll) is Mrs. Violet Lee Gradwohl of Lincoln, Nebraska, the "Lovely Lady" of the children's story of the Terri Lee doll. Terri Lee was named after Mrs. Gradwohl's first daughter by the same name. Her second daughter was Linda Lee and a trademark for this name was issued in 1951 (see below) and her third daughter was Connie Lynn.

1946: Lincoln, Nebraska...Terri Lee Doll (Composition) and not trademarked until 1948.

1948: Trademark for Jerri Lee: #528,824 on November 30. Both Terri and Jerri in composition.

1949: Dolls in hard plastic: Colored Bonnie Lu and Benjie and Eskimo Nanook.

1950: Look-a-like paper doll added to line. Patty Jo, character by Jackie Ormes.

1951: Obtained patent (trademark) #618,471 on September 19, for the use of tradename: *Linda Lee* It is not known if a doll was made but there is labeled clothing for "Linda Lee."

1951: November 10...fire destroys Lincoln operation.

1953: Reopen in Apple Valley, California Terri Lee and Jerri Lee made in early vinyl...the type that becomes "sticky" with age.

1955: Trademark #694,933 was taken out for Connie Lynn (Sept. 19)

1956: Tiny Terri and Jerri Lee were presented to the market.

1957: Trademark #28,667 for So Sleepy on April 22 but not introduced unti 1960.

1960: The factory moved to Glendale, California under the name "Mar-Fan." Introduces So Sleepy and Talking Terri Lee. Re-starts "Friendship Club." Linda Baby added.

1962: Still operating as Mar-Fan, using advertising stating "American made for American Maids." Address was 1708 Standard Street, Glendale, Calif. and Violet Lee Gradwohl is signing company letters as "Vice-President." Exchange heads to make Terri Lee "talk" are offered for $8.00. The doll could be taken to any of the Terri Lee stores and "made to talk."

The exact date that Mar-Fan closed their doors is unknown. It is known that a large California dealer bought the remaining stock.

The Terri Lee Doll Company was plagued with misfortune...some printable and others unprintable. Many rumors still abound. It is known that Mrs. Gradwohl died in 1972 in the State of Virginia.

The Terri Lee doll had a pet. It was a monkey and came as a boy or girl...dressed in boy or girl's clothing. The girl monkey's name is Penelope and the boy monkey's name is Tony. About 4" tall, fur covered except the face is all I can tell you about these pets. Terri Lee's "pet" dress is covered with umbrellas as is Jerri's one piece short suit.

Accessories for Terri Lee include: Trunks, both metal and cardboard. Hair dress kit, Wooden fashion rack/hangers with "Terri Lee" on side. Wardrobe chest, bassinete, walker...metal with rubber tires, with dolls feet placed in base and doll is strapped to stand and as walker is moved, the dolls legs move back and forth, baglets, made of imported kidskin, lamp with picture of Terri Lee, a play pen for Linda Baby, Nursery chair and baby bed...all pieces in wood.

The very early clothes tags were printed on and had a tendency to fray at the end. Late ones are embroidery. Special outfits made included: a full length mink coat, Alice in Wonderland, Scout and Brownie uniforms, Camp Fire and Blue Bird uniforms, masquerade costumes, Hula costume, Dutch girl, Dutch boy and calypso costume, Scotch costume, Nurse and Doctor uniforms, Southern Belle outfit, Engineer suit, along with cowgirl and cowboy outfits and those of

*Refer to Luella Hart's U.S. Tradmarks

cheerleaders and majorettes.

It is known that the Terri Lee Co. bought 15,000 dolls (8") from the Cosmopolitan Doll Co. (Ginger). They were dressed in the uniforms of Girl Scouts, Brownies and Blue Birds. The clothes bear the Terri Lee tag and the box information is included into this section (refer to photo) and contains the Apple Valley address.

The so called 16" "Terri Lee Walker" was actually named "Mary Jane" and has been reported to have been made by three different companies: Richwood Dolls, Cosmopolitan and Reliable of Canada. Someday one will show up that is in the original box and we will know for sure who made her. I have had 5 of them and all had black hair and very black eyebrows. A picture is included in the color section.

To sum up, the Terri Lee Company could be said to have gone out of business because of their guarantee! The doll is so indestructible as to last a life time...but some did break, many had to be restrung and repainted plus thousands of wigs had to be replaced. The only things that seemed to be left out of the guarantee was parts lost, chewed by a dog or covered with nail polish and crayons. Each doll came with an "Admission Card" to the Terri Lee Hospital. Repairs had to be taken care of because the reputation of the doll stood on the guarantee of the company.

There are reports of someone having made a mold from an original Terri Lee during the years of 1952 and 1955. This may be true as we have found Terri Lee dolls that are slightly smaller than the official ones and this would indicate a mold being taken from a doll itself. I will show the one belonging to Marge Meisinger for comparison.

Terri Lee--Mrs. Reatha Jackson reports that when her daughter was seven in 1954, she bought her a "Mary Jane" and in 1955 a friend wanted one for her daughter so Mrs. Jackson returned to the store to buy one and was told by the store manager that they were no longer being made. He said a woman who had worked at the Terri Lee factory had designed the "Mary Jane" but was made to stop production. To date we have no other information.

Terri Lee--16" "Mary Jane" All hard plastic. Flirty, blue sleep eyes. Walker, head turns. Has long plastic lashes. Marks: None. (Courtesy Marie Ernst)

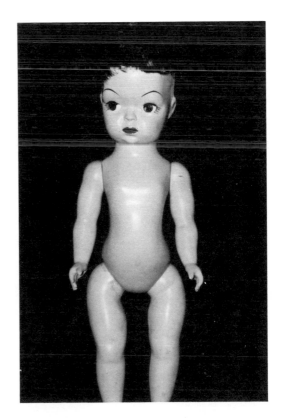

Terri Lee Family

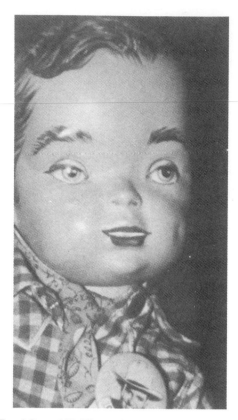

Terri Lee--16" "Gene Autry" All rigid plastic. Hand painted. Marks: Terri Lee/Pats. Pending, on back. $165.00.

Terri Lee--"Talking Terri Lee." See Series I, Terri Lee section for full description. "Jack" at base of neck in back. $50.00.

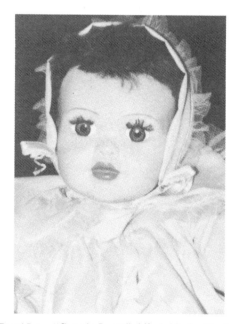

Terri Lee--"Connie Lynn" All rigid plastic. Inset eyes with long lashes. Caracul wig. $45.00. (Courtesy Jay Minter)

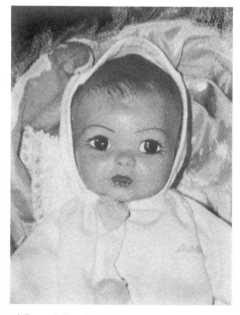

Terri Lee--All original "Linda Baby" All vinyl. $35.00. (Courtesy Jay Minter)

Terri Lee--7½" "Girl Scout" All hard plastic.
Walker, head turns. Blue sleep eyes/long
molded lashes. Tagged Terri Lee uniform. This
is "Ginger" by Cosmopolitan. (Courtesy Bessie
Carson)

Terri Lee--7½" "Brownie" Close up of "Ginger"
face.

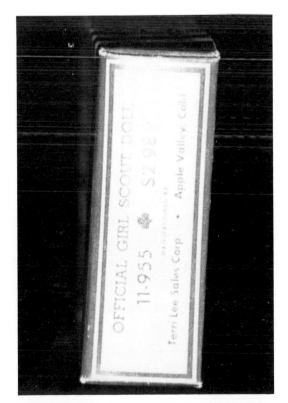

Terri Lee--Shows box end of the Terri Lee Scout
doll, made by Cosmopolitan (Ginger). (Courtesy
Bessie Carson)

Terri Lee Prices

16" Terri Lee $35.00; Compo, $45.00; Colored,
$45.00; Brown, $45.00; Oriental, $50.00
16" Jerri Lee, $50.00; Colored, $60.00; Brown,
$60.00; Oriental, $65.00
16" Early Terri Lee in vinyl. Weights in feet.
$35.00.
10" Tiny Terri Lee $25.00.
10" Tiny Jerri Lee $35.00.
12" Linda Lee. All early vinyl, $55.00.
9½" So Sleepy, $30.00.

Terri Lee--1 inch "Terri Lee Friendship Club pin." (Courtesy Bessie Carson)

59 Terri in Pet ess with Pet .95   2132 Jerri in Pet Suit with Pet 14.95

Terri Lee--Terri and Jerri Lee's Pet. The monkey dressed as a girl is "Penelope" and the one dressed as a boy is "Tony."

Terri Lee--Terri Lee shown with her pet monkey which could be either Penelope or Tony. Clothes are gone except shoes.

Terri Lee--16" "Terri Lee" shown in an original trunk. Trunk is metal and red with white boarder trim. (Courtesy Irene Gann)

Terri Lee--Box top showing Terri Lee Fashions.
(Courtesy Bessie Carson)

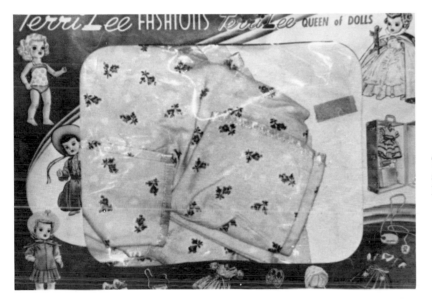

Terri Lee--Terri Lee Fashion Pac containing
sleepwear tagged "Linda Baby and Connie
Lynn"

Terri Lee--Shows top of another Terri Lee
Fashion box. (Courtesy Marie Ernst)

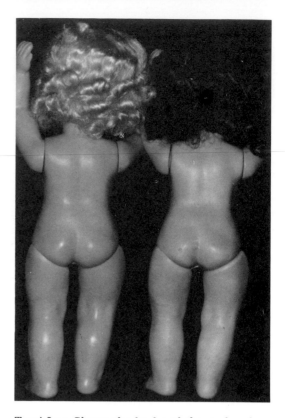

Terri Lee--Shows the Fake Terri Lee, the real 16" one and the Tiny Terri Lee, all in original Terri Lee western outfits. (Courtesy Marge Meisinger)

Terri Lee--Shows the backs of the real and reduced (by mold) Terri Lee. Blonde is the real one. Real: 9¾" at waist, 5½" at calf and is 16" tall. Fake: 9¼" at waist, 5¼" at calfs and is 15½" tall and has holes in feet. (Courtesy Marge Meisinger)

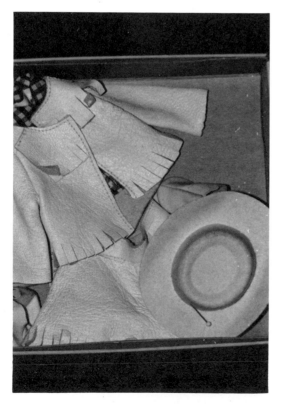

Terri Lee--Tiny Terri Lee's original boxed white cowgirl outfit. (Courtesy Marge Meisinger)

Terri Lee--Terri Lee as Cowgirl. Dark green satin shirt. White leather skirt and vest. (Courtesy Irene Gann)

Terri Lee--10" "Tiny Terri Lee" Shown in her original case. Red checkered and made of pressed carboard. (Courtesy Laura Gann)

Terri Lee--16" "Terri Lee" Shown in her real mink coat. I have heard a price tag of $300.00 for this coat but seems more reasonable that it was a lot less.

Terri Lee--Shows Terri Lee in an original full length coat of white fur and cap. (Courtesy Marge Meisinger)

Terri Lee--Shows Terri lee in her original full length blue coat. (Courtesy Marge Meisinger)

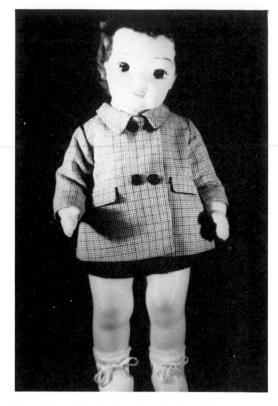

Terri Lee--Jerri Lee in Spring Coat #3590. Black/blue check on white. Black buttons. Navy lining.

Terri Lee--Early pink coat with pale blue piping.

Terri Lee--White coat and bonnet with red lamb and trim. May belong to Connie Lynn although tag is for Terri Lee.

Terri Lee--Terri Lee in red with white polka dots rain coat/hood. #1839. (Courtesy Irene Gann)

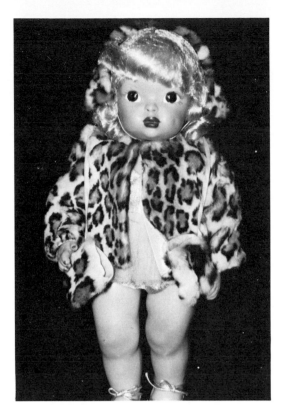

Terri Lee--This is Terri Lee's original fur jacket, cap and muff. (Courtesy Marge Meisinger)

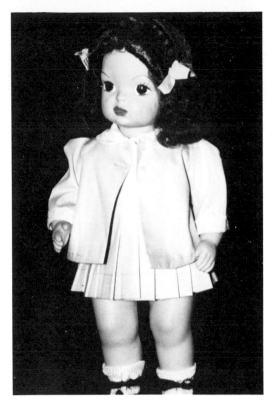

Terri Lee--#3504. Pale aqua with white cuffs. White blouse.

Terri Lee--Pale rose formal with pink overnet skirt.

Terri Lee--Pink and lavender flowers on a pink formal.

Terri Lee--#1380 Bridesmaid dress of pale pink. Pink flowers in head band. (Dress courtesy Mary Partridge)

Terri Lee--Yellow with yellow flowers and black sequin trim and ribbon tie.

Terri Lee--#3560P. White blouse with lace trim. Navy pleated skirt.

Terri Lee--Navy blue dress with white color and cuffs. White flowers on end of belt.

Terri Lee--#3520F Pique sport dress with matching panties. Navy blue/white. White plastic belt is missing.

Terri Lee--#3519D Play Dress. Blue with rose sleeves and collar. Birds on dress are rose and pale blue/white.

Terri lee--Terri Lee in #3332 and 1357 Organdy Party Dress. Hat missing. Pale blue with white collar and small flowers.

Terri Lee--Terri Lee in pinafore #3520H and 1316. Pale pink with white shoulder straps. Pink ribbon at waist.

Terri Lee--Red polka dots on top. Rest red. White/red polka dot matching panties.

Terri Lee--Terri Lee in school dress. All red with white collar. (Courtesy Irene Gann)

Terri Lee--Terri Lee in her rose-pink dress with white lace trim. "School Dress" #T-1330. (Courtesy Irene Gann)

Terri Lee--#4520F. Sport Set. White top with red dots. Navy pants.

Terri Lee--#4311. Red/white checkered shirt. Navy blue jeans. Brown belt.

Terri Lee--#4311 plus chaps and gun belt.

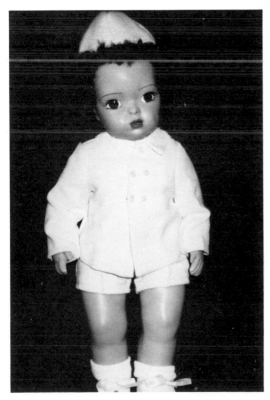

Terri Lee--Jerri Lee in white Summer Suit. #2321.

Terri Lee--Terri Lee in #35401 Brownie uniform. Belt and tam missing. Also #3351 and 1351.

Terri Lee--#3520C Pedal Pushers. Blue denim with red/white checks.

Terri Lee--White short waisted blouse (cotton) and blue jeans.

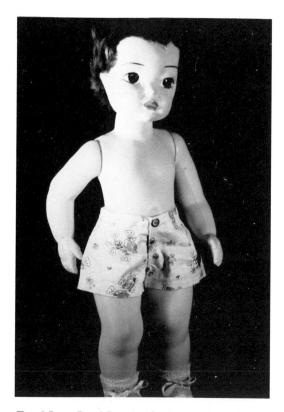

Terri Lee--Jerri Lee in shorts #4300 and 2300.

Terri Lee--Terri Lee in slip #510G. Pink.

Terri Lee--Can Can #500C. Pink.

Terri Lee--Terri Lee in red/white checkered sundress. (Courtesy Irene Gann)

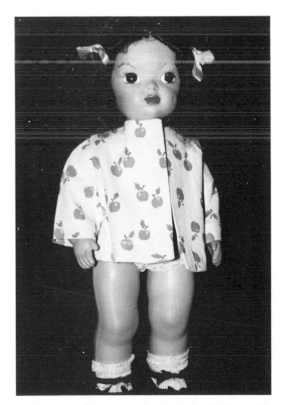

Terri Lee--#3311. Beach jacket. White with orange/blue apples.

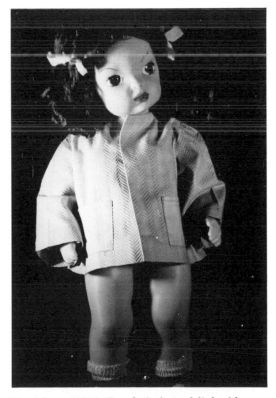

Terri Lee--#3310. Beach jacket of light blue.

Terri Lee--16" "Terri Lee" in dark green bathing suit with white trim. Green dark glasses. (Courtesy Irene Gann)

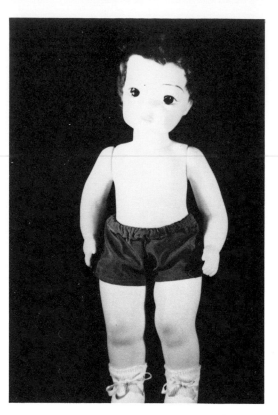

Terri Lee--#4301. Swim trunks that are royal blue.

Terri Lee--Terri Lee in pajamas with lavender roses. (Courtesy Irene Gann)

Terri Lee--Terri Lee in her pink Terry Cloth bathrobe. (Courtesy Irene Gann)

Terri Lee--Terri Lee in pedal pushers. Lavender/white checkered top and cuffs. Lavender pants. (Courtesy Irene Gann)

Terri Lee--Terri Lee in her original Hawaiian outfit. (Courtesy Marge Meisinger)

Terri Lee--16" "Jerri Lee in original Davy Crockett outfit. (Courtesy Marge Meisinger)

Terri Lee--Terri Lee has on Tea Party Dress, minus purse. #1367. Pale yellow with white insert down front. Jerri Lee has on pink pants/tam. Blue/pink/black stripe on cap bill and jacket.

Terri Lee--Terri in one piece pink chamise. Jerri in two piece shorts and T shirt of white with pink trim.

Terri Lee--Terri Lee is in pink dress with white polka dots and white insert. Jerri Lee has on an aqua #2306 suit with black stripes.

Terri Lee--Terri Lee in Birthday Dress. White with blue/white checkered top and half sleeves. Attached slip. Jerri Lee has on orange pants. Yellow shirt with orange collar. Carrots and rabbits on top are orange and grey.

Terri Lee--Tiny Terri Lee in her ballerina outfit and shows her roller skates. (Courtesy Marge Meisinger)

Terri Lee--Tiny Terri Lee in #3335 "School Dress" Red/green/blue/checkered with white trim. (Courtesy Laura Gann)

Terri Lee--Tiny Terri Lee shown in her original Majorette outfit. (Courtesy Marge Meisinger)

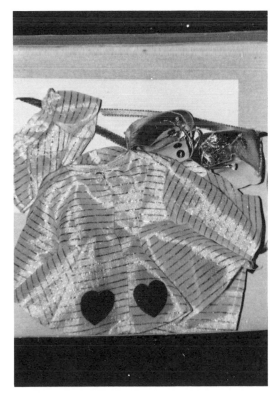

Terri Lee--Tiny Terri Lee's Ice Skating outfit shown in original box. (Courtesy Marge Meisinger)

Terri Lee--Tiny Terri Lee in one of her original Bride outfits. (Courtesy Marge Meisinger)

Terri Lee--Tiny Terri Lee in #TT3321 "Squaw Dress." Navy blue. 2 piece. (Courtesy Laura Gann)

Terri Lee--Tiny Terri Lee in Pinafore Party #3316. Pink with white top. Pink panties. (Courtesy Laura Gann)

Terri Lee--Tiny Terri Lee in her #3805 Clown pajamas. (Courtesy Laura Gann)

Terri Lee--Tiny Terri Lee in an original snow suit. (Courtesy Marge Meisinger)

Terri Lee--Tiny Terri Lee in her Cowgirl Outfit. Hat and shoes missing. Blue/white with brown plastic trim. (Courtesy Laura Gann)

Togs and Dolls--12" "Penny Walker" All hard plastic with glued on brown hair. Chubby build. Blue sleep eyes. Walker, head turns. Marks: Pat. Pend., on head. Tag: Penny Walker. Box: Togs & Dolls Corp/New York 1, NY/Factory at Greensboro N.C. 1951. $8.00. (Courtesy Virginia Jones)

Togs and Dolls--17" "Mary Jane" Hard plastic walker, head turns. Arms only raise to shoulder high. Vinyl head. Blue sleep eyes/lashes. Marks: None. Tag: My Name is/Mary Jane. I am made of Celanese/Acetate Plastic. I have 36 pretty outfits. $45.00.

Togs and Dolls--Close up of 17" "Mary Jane" head.

Tomy--12½" "Ricky" Tin body and legs. Plastic non-removable shoes. Pants glued on. Vinyl arms, holding bell. Vinyl head. Molded hair. Painted blue eyes. Walker (battery), bell rings. Marks: Box: Ricky the Walking Toddler/By Amico. Paper label on back has drawing of boy and girl/Tomy/Made in Japan. $8.00. (Courtesy Edith DeAngelo)

UFS--16" "Charlie Brown" Blow up balloon type doll. Marks: 1969 United Feature Syndicate Inc. $2.00.

Uneeda--21" "Toddles" Hard plastic walker. Original clothes. Vinyl head. Blue sleep eyes. Wide open/closed mouth. Marks: Uneeda, on head. $9.00. (Courtesy Alice Capps)

Information on the Uneeda Doll Co. will be found in Series I, page 279.

Uneeda--12" "Twinkle Tears" All vinyl. Mouth designed to hold bottle without hands. After "feeding," sit doll up and slightly forward and squeeze body and tears will start. Original. Same doll as "Yummy" but without "sucking" mechanism. 1961. Marks: None. $3.00. (Courtesy Edith DeAngelo)

Uneeda--11" "Twins" Came as boy or girl. Plastic and vinyl. Molded hair. Bright blue sleep eyes/molded lashes. Open mouth/nurser. Bent baby legs. Marks:11/Uneeda/1965. $4.00. (Courtesy Bessie Carson)

Uneeda--2½" "Nurse Keywee" Sold in pocket purse with key chain. 1968. Marks: None. $2.00.

Uneeda--3" "Troll" All vinyl with red mohair. Inset yellow eyes. Dressed in Pee Wee outfit called Gardentime. 1966. $2.00.

Uneeda--6" "Troll Wishnik" Lavender hair. Jointed neck only. All vinyl. Marks: Uneeda/Wish-Nik TM/Pat. #. $2.00.

Uneeda--8½" "Georgia" Blue eyes. White hair. Marks: U.D.Co. Inc./MCMLXXI/Made in Hong Kong, head and body. Box: MCMLXIV/Dist. 1975. American Gem Collection. Available in some areas.

Uneeda--8½" "Carolina" Blue eyes. White hair. American Gem Collection. Available in some areas.

Uneeda--8½" "Patience" Blue eyes. Brown hair. American Gem Collection. Available in some areas.

Uneeda--8½" "Prudence" Blue eyes. Red hair. American Gem Collection. Available in some areas.

Uneeda--8½" "Priscilla" Blue eyes. Brown hair. American Gem Collection. Available in some areas.

Uneeda--8½" "Virginia" Blue eyes. Blonde hair. American Gem Collection. Available in some areas.

Uneeda--6" "Tiny Penelope" Vinyl head with freckles and orange rooted hair. Soft filled body. Removable dress. Marks: UD Co. Inc./MCML-XXIV/Hong Kong, on head. Tag: Undeeda. $2.00.

Uneeda--10" "Clover" Plastic with vinyl head. Head sockets into body. Original. Marks: Hong Kong, on back. Available in some areas. (Courtesy Marie Ernst)

269

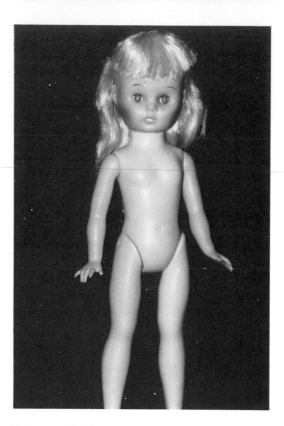

Uneeda--6" "Grannykins" Plastic with vinyl arms and head. Black/grey hair. Painted blue eyes with painted on glasses. Original. Marks: U.D. Co. Inc./MCMLXXIV/Hong Kong, on head. Available in some areas. (Courtesy Marie Ernst)

Unique--15" "Margie" Plastic and vinyl with rooted blonde hair. Blue sleep eyes/molded lashes. Marks: Unique/19. This is the same doll as the late and last Mary Hoyer dolls. $2.00.

Unique--16" "Flying Nun" Plastic and vinyl. One row of rooted hair in front. Blue sleep eyes/ molded lashes. Original. Marks: Unique/11, on head. $6.00. (Courtesy Virginia Jones)

Universal--"Springtime Family" 9" man, 8½" woman and 3" baby. Man: brown eyes, with or without mustache (painted) plastic and vinyl. Marks: Hong Kong, head and Universal Associated Co. Ltd. vertically down back. Baby has jointed neck only, blue eyes and is smiling. Baby is marked: H.K. in square/Hong Kong, on back. Made for S.S. Kresge. 1975. Still available.

Valentine--14" "Margie Ann" Hard plastic head with glued on blonde wig. Blue sleep eyes. Open/closed mouth. 1949. Marks: 128, on back. $7.00.

Valentine--11½" All hard plastic. Blue sleep eyes/long molded lashes. This doll was used in the "Mona Lisa" series and they were dressed in long gowns. Marks: 12, on head. 12/Made in USA, on back. $6.00. (Courtesy Marie Ernst)

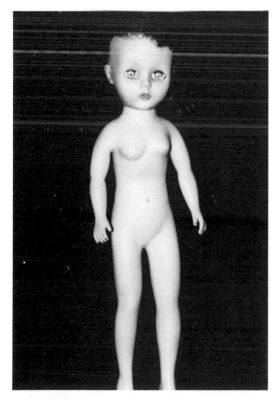

Valentine--13" One piece stuffed vinyl. Marks: AE1406/46, on head. V, on lower back. V-15, back of arms. $5.00.

Valentine--19" "Debbie Reynolds" As grown up "Tammy." All hard plastic. Open mouth/5 teeth. Blue sleep eyes. Red lips/nails. Walker, head turns. Mid high heel feet. Jointed knees/ankles. Pale golden blonde hair glued on. Marks: Made in U.S.A., back. Medium blue on pale blue/white lace trim. (Courtesy Mary Partridge)

Valentine--18" "Bride" A Mona Lisa Doll. Hard plastic with vinyl head. Blue sleep eyes. Pin jointed hips with rivets. Walker, head turns. Left arm socketed to raise shoulder height only. Original. Marks: Made in USA, on back. 17 VW, on head. Tag: I'll Love You/Valentine Dolls, Inc. $8.00. (Courtesy Edith DeAngelo)

Valentine--15½" "Connie" Plastic with vinyl arms and head. Molded curls with molded hair bow. Manufactured by Eegee for Natural Doll Co. 1963. (Courtesy Carolyn Powers)

Valentine--14" "Ballerina" Hard plastic with vinyl head. Rooted ash blonde hair. Blue sleep eyes. Jointed ankles. Original. Marks: AE, on head. Made in USA/Pat. Pending, on back. 1955.

Valentine--15" "Patient" All vinyl. Blue sleep eyes. Open/closed mouth. Same head used for "Dondi" with hair painted black and teeth painted in. This issue was put out with "hospital" items and sold as "Perfect Patient." 1957.

Valentine--15" "Bonnnie" Plastic and vinyl. White rooted hair. Blue sleep eyes. 1964. "Bonnie" was issued as a baby, toddler and teen. $6.00.

Valentine--30" "Susy Walker" Sold through Speigel's in 1960. Plastic and vinyl. Blue sleep eyes. Widespread legs. Marks: AE/3006/16, on head. $18.00. (Courtesy Phyllis Houston)

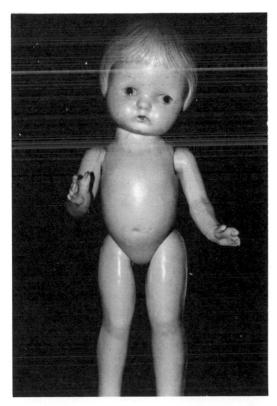

Vanity Doll--11" "Paula" All composition. Bent right arm. Second and third fingers molded together. Blonde molded hair. Painted blue eyes. Marks: None. (Courtesy Mary Partridge)

Vanity Doll--13½" "Peggy Ann" (also came in 15" size). All composition. Bent right arm. Brown sleep tin eyes. 1941. Marks: None. (Courtesy Maxine Heitt)

273

Wood--6" "Girl Scout" and "Brownie" All wood. Nodder type heads. Marks: Japanese, in script on bottom. $3.00. (Courtesy Ellie Haynes)

Wood--2" "Seattle Pioneer Woman/Man, Early 1850's." Carve/painted wood. These miniatures were designed/produced by Mrs. John R. Bringloe, member of the Research Committee of the Seattle Historical Society. Funds from sales further work of the Committee. $15.00 pair. (Courtesy Frances and Mary Jane Anicello)

Wood--3" "Dutch Boy & Girl" All wood. Springs for necks and part of arms. Metal buckets. Braids are stiffened string. Marks: Made/Goula/In Spain, on feet. $6.00. (Courtesy Frances and Mary Jane Anicello)

Wood--2¾" All wood. Carved from one piece. Unjointed. All painted. Marks: None. $12.00. (Courtesy Frances and Mary Jane Anicello)

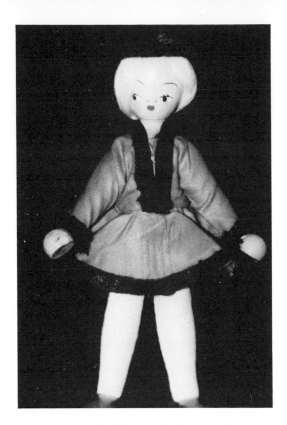

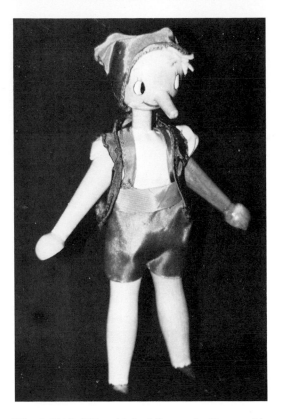

Wood--7¼" "Miski Dancer" All wood. One piece body and head. Painted features. Glued on hair. Non removable clothes. Marks: Paper tag: Made/In/Poland. (Courtesy Mary Partridge)

Wood--7½" "Pinochio" All wood. Removable clothes. Yellow yarn hair. Jointed shoulder and hips only. Original. Marks: Pinochio, one foot and Poland, other foot. (Courtesy Mary Partridge)

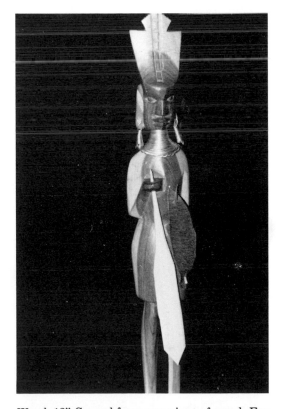

Wood--9" "Skater" All wood. Jointed shoulders and hips. Non-removable clothes. Marks: None. Sticker: Made in Poland. (Courtesy Ellie Haynes)

Wood--12" Carved from one piece of wood. Earrings and neck piece are wire. Hide shield and wood spear. From Kenya. (Courtesy Ellie Haynes)

Wood--11" "Koheshi Doll" All wood. Painted features and scene. Dip painted on swirl area. Marks: Made in Japan, on back. (Courtesy Ellie Haynes)

Wood--8" "Ragman" All wood. Jointed shoulders and hips. ca. 1950, although these basic dolls are still available. Marks: sticker: Made in Poland. (Courtesy Mary Partridge)

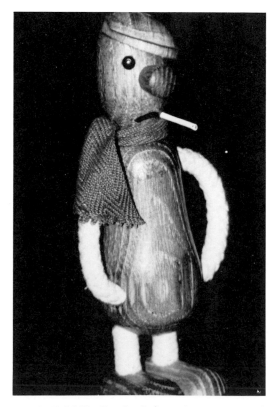

Wood--5" "Alfie Smoker" One piece wood with separate wood hat and shoes. Legs and arms are tightly woven rope. Smokes tiny cigarettes. Made in Denmark. 1963. Marks: None. $4.00. (Courtesy Ellie Haynes)

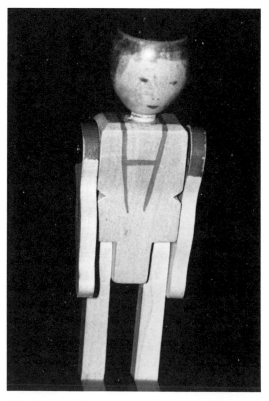

Wood--5½" All wood. Nail pegged shoulders and hips. One piece body, head. Painted features. Marks: None. $3.00. (Courtesy Mary Partridge)

Wood--8" "Pioneer Lady" All wood with one piece body and head. Jointed shoulders and hips. Original. Marks: Tag: Copyright Shackman/ 119591 Japanese Patent No. 208916. Still available. (Courtesy Frances and Mary Jane Anicello)

Wood--12" "Spanish Lady" All wood with floss hair. Marks: None. $12.00. (Courtesy Elaine Kaminsky)

Wood--3½" All one piece. Made in 1963 and carved by Kay Archer, an 80 year old Indian lady of the Hesqwit tribe, Canada. Hand painted. $2.00. (Courtesy Ellie Haynes)

Picture Index

278

281

Numbers, Letters and Symbol Index

MODERN COLLECTOR'S DOLLS
REVISED PRICES FOR SERIES 1 & 2

The following are the revised prices for Series I and Series II. It was designed to be easily used with these books.

It is important to repeat that these prices are based on COMPLETELY ORIGINAL AND IN MINT CONDITION dolls. If your doll is any less than perfect DEDUCT accordingly.

With the tapering off of the doll market by collectors be-coming more selective and upgrading their collections and by many collectors "specializing" doll prices have dropped in many areas and have only increased in two areas, those dolls by Alexander and personality dolls. A word about the Madame Alexander area...ALL the 8" dolls shown in these books have BEND KNEES and prices are based on that fact.

A "S.A." behind a price means that the doll is STILL AVAILABLE in some areas.

14..7" Dionne Quints ...200.00 set	28..Little Huggums ...9.00 (S.A.)	41..Butterball 30.00
15..14" Dionne Quints ..85.00 each	28..Big Huggums ....22.00 (S.A.)	41..Talking Marie.........25.00
15..McGuffy Ana 55.00	28..Sugar Darlin' 35.00	42..Tressy 12.00
15..Princess Alexandria 55.00	29..Sweet Tears .....13.00 (S.A.)	42..New Tiny Tears........4.00
15..Butch 35.00	29..Bo Peep ....18.00 (S.A.)	43..Nancy 32.00
16..Snow White 75.00	29..Pussy Cat ......16.00 (S.A.)	43..Debu-teen 35.00
16..13" Snow White.......65.00	29..Sugar Darlin' 35.00	44..Little Angel 20.00
16..Princess Elizabeth.....70.00	30..Alice In	44..Sonja Henie 45.00
16..McGuffy Ana 55.00	Wonderland...16.00 (S.A.)	44..Snuggle Doll 20.00
17..Flora McFlimsey 95.00	30..Leslie 65.00	45..Snuggle Bun 6.00
17..Kate Greenway 85.00	30..Scarlet O'Hara 24.00	45..Peachy 4.00
17..Sonja Henie 75.00	30..Storybook Doll........35.00	45..Judy.................35.00
17..McGuffy Ana 35.00	31..Hansel & Gretel 40.00	46..Angeline 35.00
18..Sonja Henie 75.00	31..Hungarian ....18.00 (S.A.)	46..Nanette 35.00
18..W.A.A.C. 55.00	31..India ....18.00 (S.A.)	46..17" Nanette..........35.00
19..Scarlett O'Hara......100.00	31..Spanish Friend ...18.00 (S.A.)	46..Dream Bride..........35.00
19..Margaret O'Brien 185.00	32..Elise ....22.00 (S.A.)	47..Taffy 40.00
19..Baby Genius 25.00	32..Rebecca ....18.00 (S.A.)	47..New Happytot 8.00
20..Kathy 55.00	32..Betsy Ross.......18.00 (S.A.)	47..Nanette 35.00
20..Alice 55.00	32..Degas ....18.00 (S.A.)	48..Francine 35.00
20..Maggie Mixup 55.00	33..Happy 45.00	48..Littlest Angel.........6.00
20..Annabelle 50.00	33..Grandma Jane 40.00	48..Prom Queen 35.00
21..McGuffy Ana 65.00	33..Blue Boy .....15.00 (S.A.)	48..Littlest Angel.........6.00
21..Cissette 35.00	33..Red Boy .....10.00 (S.A.)	49..My Angel 22.00
21..Dumplin Baby 35.00	33..Cinderella ......13.00 (S.A.)	49..Littlest Angel.........8.00
22..Rosebud 40.00	35..Dandy 10.00	50..21" Skookum 42.00
22..Cry Dolly 40.00	35..Little Love 25.00	50..14" Skookum 32.00
22..Bonnie..............40.00	35..Miss Chicadee 15.00	50..Playful..............5.00
22..Cissy 35.00	35..Tiny Tears 12.00	50..Bye-Bye Baby........10.00
23..Marme..............45.00	36..Baby Lou...........4.00	51..Baby Doo 2.00
23..Kathy Cry Dolly 25.00	36..Sweet Susanne 35.00	51..Candy 2.00
23..Princess Ann 45.00	36..Sweet Sue...........35.00	51..Pretty Lady 12.00
23..Bonnie Prince Charles ..45.00	36..Tiny Tears 12.00	51..Pouty 10.00
24..Elise 45.00	37..Bride 35.00	52..Cindy 4.00
24..Shari Lewis 85.00	37..American Beauty 40.00	52..Master..............2.00
24..Kathy 25.00	37..Sweet Sue 45.00	52..My Friend 2.00
24..Little Genius 35.00	37..Sweet Susanne........25.00	52..Little Miss Gadabout ...25.00
25..Little Shaver 35.00	38..Peek a Boo Toodles 20.00	53..Raving Beauty 25.00
25..Marybel 40.00	38..Toodles 22.00	53..Lov You.............12.00
25..Edith 40.00	38..Sweet Sue...........20.00	53..Miss B 1.00
25..Kathy Tears 25.00	38..Betsy McCall 25.00	53..Ballerina Belle 4.00
26..Genius Baby 30.00	39..New Born Baby 18.00	54..Belle-Lee.............2.00
26..Little Cherub 30.00	39..Tiny Tears 12.00	54..Jimmy 2.00
26..Queen 60.00	39..Astronaut 35.00	54..Timmy 2.00
26..Melanie 125.00	39..Graduate............35.00	54..Babies First Doll 3.00
27..Godey 125.00	40..Whimmsie 35.00	55..Rock A Bye Baby 2.00
27..Chatterbox 45.00	40..Hedda Get Bedda.......35.00	55..Perky Bright 7.00
27..Melinda 45.00	41..Betsy McCall 15.00	55..Poor Pitiful Pearl......18.00
284 27..Laurie ....17.00 (S.A.)	41..Toodle-Loo 30.00	55..Rusty 16.00

56..Liza ...3.00	75..Grace ...12.00	94..New Dy Dee Baby ...5.00
56..Tim ...3.00	76..Luvable Susan ...5.00	94..Honey Bun ...9.00
57..Plum ...40.00	76..Little Debutante ...25.00	95..Lil Sweetie ...12.00
57..Miss Peep ...16.00	76..Baby Susan ...3.00	95..Tiny Tubber ...7.00
58..New Born Miss Peep ...16.00	76..Tina ...5.00	95..Baby Face ...4.00
58..Scootles ...65.00	77..Lil Susan ...2.00	95..Button Nose ...16.00
58..Ragsy ...6.00	77..Tandy Talks ...18.00	96..Butterball ...6.00
58..Kewpie ...4.00	77..Andy ...5.00	96..Little Luv ...7.00
59..Kewpie Gal ...6.00	77..Little Miss ...5.00	97..Color Me ...3.00
59..Kewpie ...18.00	78..Gemette ...4.00	97..Personality Playmate ...35.00
59..Sad Eyes ...3.00	78..Daisy Darlin ...12.00	97..Sandra ...30.00
59..Cleaning Day ...2.00	78..Flowerkin ...12.00	97..Precious ...12.00
60..Bride ...2.00	78..Sandi ...5.00	98..Curly ...4.00
60..Gloria ...15.00	79..Bundle of Joy ...4.00	98..Winkin' ...2.00
60..Emily ...20.00	79..Pix-i-Posie ...4.00	98..Sissy ...3.00
60..Pam ...20.00	79..Annette ...6.00	99..Fredel ...10.00
61..Paula Marie ...16.00	79..Musical Baby ...4.00	99..Trudila ...10.00
61..Baby Brite ...8.00	80..Susan ...4.00	99..Bettina ...10.00
62..Penny Brite ...4.00	80..Bundle of Joy ...2.00	99..Jamie ...30.00
62..Bonnie Bride ...4.00	80..Adorable ...3.00	100..Dee Dee ...8.00
62..Susie Cute ...4.00	80..Baby Sniffles ...3.00	100..Nantoc ...16.00
62..Baby Boo ...6.00	81..Sleepy ...10.00	100..Eskimo ...12.00
63..Baby Magic ...7.00	81..Posi-Playmate ...5.00	100..Col. Sanders ...7.00
63..Cool Cat ...5.00	81..Softina ...3.00	101..Swimmer ...40.00
63..Baby Tickle Tears ...7.00	81..Baby Softina ...3.00	101..Janie ...10.00
64..Susie Homemaker ...6.00	82..Cuddlekins ...2.00	101..Rosette ...20.00
64..Party Time ...5.00	85..Patricia ...65.00	102..Mariann ...9.00
64..Lil Miss Fussy ...5.00	85..Anne of Green Gables ...55.00	102..Flirty ...9.00
65..Tickles ...5.00	85..Ann Shirley ...60.00	102..Cindy ...16.00
65..Bikey ...7.00	86..Suzanne ...40.00	102..Rose ...12.00
65..Baby Catch A Ball ...18.00	86..Little Lady ...45.00	103..Beatles ...35.00
65..Baby Peek 'n Play ...8.00	86..Candy Kid ...45.00	103..Sonja ...15.00
66..Baby Bunny ...5.00	86..Patsy Joan ...50.00	104..Andra ...10.00
66..Dawn ...4.00	87..DyDee Baby ...12.00	104..Jumeau ...225.00
66..Smarty Pants ...5.00	87..Lil Darlin' ...15.00	105..Lorraine ...80.00
67..Sunny ...125.00	87..Honey Girl ...18.00	105..Bella Bee ...25.00
67..Prince Ranier ...150.00	87..Tintair ...35.00	105..Lynette ...10.00
67..Liz Taylor ...165.00	88..Mommy's Baby ...12.00	105..GeGe ...20.00
68..Gypsy Mother&Child ...365.00	88..Baby Cuddle Up ...20.00	106..Polly ...10.00
68..Uncle Sam ...115.00	88..Fluffy ...6.00	106..Soupee ...18.00
68..Little Women ...95.00 set	88..Polka Dottie ...32.00	106..El Poupee ...12.00
69..Little Women ...95.00 set	89..Candy Twins ...35.00 set	106..Soupee Bella ...20.00
69..Boy ...35.00	89..Mickey ...5.00	107..Rosemund ...30.00
70..John Kennedy ...35.00	89..Fluffy ...6.00	107..Michella ...20.00
70..Good Luck Troll ...2.00	89..Katie ...16.00	107..Claudette ...32.00
70..May ...1.00	90..My Fair Baby ...9.00	107..Pretty ...12.00
70..Cinderella ...2.00	90..Twinkie ...5.00	108..Pauline ...85.00
71..Scotch Miss ...1.00	90..Patsy Ann ...18.00	109..Crawler ...8.00
71..Martha Washington ...1.00	91..My Precious Baby ...5.00	109..Katinka ...18.00
71..Scarlet ...2.00	91..Suzie Sunshine ...20.00	109..Peasant Family ...5.00
71..Carmen ...1.00	91..Gumdrop ...20.00	109..Gura ...10.00
72..Tinker Bell ...3.00	91..Precious New Born ...9.00	110..Gretchen ...9.00
72..Peter Pan ...3.00	92..Baby Butterball ...3.00	110..Barbel ...7.00
72..Miss Hollywood ...1.00	92..Baby Sweetie ...3.00	110..Pride ...80.00
72..Danny Groom ...2.00	92..Babykin ...2.00	111..Lonee ...4.00
73..Miss Tastee Freeze ...2.00	92..My Fair Baby ...3.00	111..Freckles ...3.00
73..Miss North America ...2.00	93..Miss Chips ...15.00	111..BeeBee ...2.00
74..Miss Charming ...45.00	93..Peaches ...16.00	111..Lovely ...3.00
74..Gigi Perreaux ...45.00	93..Thumpkin' ...4.00	112..Eggie ...2.00
75..Bobby ...25.00	93..Chipper ...15.00	112..Jane ...1.00
75..Robert ...32.00	94..Pum'kin ...4.00	112..Lily ...4.00
75..Lil Susan ...5.00	94..Half Pint ...5.00	112..Clown ...2.00

113 . . Junie 4.00	128 . . Dress Me Doll 2.00	147 . . Teensie Baby 2.00
113 . . My Little Girl 2.00	129 . . Buddy Lee, hard plastic . 55.00	147 . . Ruthie 10.00
113 . . Mod 4.00	129 . . Buddy Lee, composition .75.00	147 . . Tuffie 12.00
113 . . Lil Bit 2.00	130 . . Doll House Mother 1.00	148 . . Mommy's Darling 8.00
114 . . Little Guy 2.00	130 . . Poodle-oodle 2.00	148 . . Ruthie 4.00
114 . . Baby Jane 2.00	130 . . G.I. Joe . . . . 5.00 (S.A.)	148 . . Ruthie Baby 6.00
114 . . Liza 2.00	131 . . Sunday 2.00	148 . . Walker Ruth 2.00
114 . . Picture This 3.00	131 . . Little Miss No Name 26.00	149 . . Baby Tweaks 10.00
115 . . Miss India 18.00	131 . . Flying Nun 12.00	149 . . Lullabye Baby 4.00
115 . . Red Riding Hood 4.00	132 . . Sleeping Beauty 6.00	149 . . Songster 10.00
115 . . Carolina 18.00	132 . . Rumpelstilskin 6.00	149 . . Twistie 2.00
115 . . Angelica 16.00	132 . . Goldilocks 6.00	150 . . Athlete 2.00
116 . . Betta 6.00	132 . . Snow White/Dwarfs 9.00	150 . . My Baby 2.00
116 . . Sweet Adraina 35.00	133 . . Prince Charming 6.00	150 . . Lil Softee 2.00
116 . . Bride 35.00	133 . . Michelle 8.00	150 . . Softee Baby 3.00
116 . . Valentina 15.00	133 . . World of Love 5.00	151 . . Love Me Baby 2.00
117 . . Anita 35.00	133 . . Baby Ruth 4.00	151 . . Pooty Tat 1.00
117 . . Guilietta 20.00	134 . . Little Miss Muffet 8.00	151 . . Bootsie 6.00
117 . . Alicia 65.00	135 . . Masquerade 8.00	151 . . Cindy 2.00
117 . . Gabriella 50.00	135 . . Bonnie Blue Bell 8.00	152 . . Buttercup 1.00
118 . . Florenza 50.00	135 . . Red Riding Hood 8.00	152 . . Bi Lo . . . . .9.00 (S.A.)
118 . . Bonomi 10.00	135 . . Sweet Janice 6.00	154 . . Deanna Durbin . . . . . .95.00 up
118 . . Vanessa 9.00	137 . . JoJo 40.00	154 . . 21" Deanna Durbin . .95.00 up
119 . . Nina 12.00	137 . . Baby Chubby 22.00	155 . . Judy Garland 85.00
119 . . Lizza 9.00	137 . . Shadow Wave Baby 25.00	155 . . Magic Skin Baby 5.00
119 . . Mariella 10.00	137 . . Cindy Kay 20.00	155 . . Georgous 16.00
119 . . Christina 20.00	138 . . Betty Ann 16.00	156 . . Magic Skin Doll 8.00
120 . . Dama 30.00	138 . . Little Sister 9.00	156 . . Miss Deb 22.00
120 . . Mia 5.00	138 . . Dolly 20.00	156 . . Flexy Soldier 38.00
120 . . Kitten 7.00	138 . . Gold Medal Doll 85.00	156 . . Sparkle Plenty 22.00
120 . . Christina 28.00	139 . . Pretty Betty 10.00	157 . . Baby Coos 25.00
121 . . Bed Doll 30.00	139 . . Chubby Baby 8.00	157 . . Tickletoes 9.00
121 . . Kewpie 12.00	139 . . Betty 6.00	157 . . Tickletoes 12.00
121 . . Playmate 7.00	140 . . Cindy Kay 25.00	157 . . Plassie 16.00
121 . . Sailor 12.00	140 . . Little Miss Betty 4.00	158 . . Magic Skin Baby 5.00
122 . . Monkey 12.00	140 . . Baby Precious 8.00	158 . . Toni 22.00
122 . . Baby 15.00	140 . . Peggy 35.00	158 . . 15" Toni 22.00
122 . . Kewpie Type 18.00	141 . . Ruthie 6.00	159 . . Toni Walker 26.00
122 . . Indy 1.00	141 . . Cindy 9.00	159 . . Tiny Girl 2.00
123 . . Santa Claus 12.00	141 . . Fair Skin Doll 6.00	159 . . Pete 2.00
123 . . Eskimo & Patty 1.00	141 . . Ruth's Sister 22.00	159 . . Saucy Walker 18.00
123 . . Kutie 11.00	142 . . Flopsie 10.00	160 . . Kiss Me 22.00
123 . . Edy 1.00	142 . . Little Happy Fella 22.00	160 . . Bonnie Braids 18.00
124 . . Swimmer 4.00	142 . . Kathy 6.00	160 . . Miss Curity 25.00
124 . . Doris 1.00	142 . . Betty Jo 10.00	160 . . Betsy McCall 24.00
124 . . Mary Mary 1.00	143 . . Grown Up Miss 6.00	161 . . Saucy Walker 18.00
124 . . Crawler 15.00	143 . . Gloria Jean 3.00	161 . . Harriet Hubbard Ayers .35.00
125 . . Tiny 1.00	143 . . Princess 30.00	161 . . 18" H.H. Ayers 40.00
125 . . Brat 2.00	143 . . Poor Pitiful Pearl 16.00	161 . . Baby Big Eyes 25.00
125 . . Charleen 25.00	144 . . Buttercup 3.00	162 . . Princess Mary 12.00
125 . . Wind Song 28.00	144 . . Thirstee Baby 3.00	162 . . Saucy Walker 18.00
126 . . Cisco Kid 12.00	144 . . Tynie Toddler 2.00	162 . . Betsy Wetsy 12.00
126 . . Romona 6.00	144 . . Lullabye Baby 2.00	162 . . Magic Lips 40.00
126 . . Americana 4.00	145 . . Baby Buttercup 1.00	163 . . Miss Revlon 22.00
126 . . Juanita 4.00	145 . . Betty 2.00	163 . . Baby June 25.00
127 . . Pam 5.00	145 . . Mary Poppins 18.00	163 . . Betsy Wetsy 5.00
127 . . Cowgirl Pam 7.00	145 . . My Ruthie 4.00	164 . . Little Miss Revlon 14.00
127 . . Sleepy Head 2.00	146 . . Softie Baby 2.00	164 . . Miss Revlon 18.00
127 . . Soul Sister 2.00	146 . . Toddler Baby 2.00	164 . . 19" Miss Revlon 18.00
128 . . Huggles 1.00	146 . . Sleepy Baby 18.00	164 . . Mrs. Revlon 22.00
128 . . Chubby Kid 32.00	146 . . Answer Doll 3.00	165 . . Betsy Wetsy 4.00
128 . . Emerald 20.00	147 . . Baby Darling 2.00	165 . . Penny Playpal 50.00

165..Betsy Wetsy 16.00	183..Hawaiian Shirley Temple...110.00	201..Bunson Bernie 8.00
165..Miss Ideal 32.00	183..12" Shirley Temple 25.00	202..Lola Liddle 8.00
166..Pattie Playpal 26.00	183..15" Shirley Temple 35.00	202..Cinderella 8.00
166..Cream Puff.............18.00	184..17" Shirley Temple 45.00	202..Liddle Diddle 8.00
166..Betsy Wetsy 8.00	184..1972 17" Shirley Temple...25.00	202..Florence Niddle 8.00
166..Dew Drop 4.00	186..Love Me 6.00	203..Casey..................5.00
167..Tiny Kissey 22.00	186..Dolly 2.00	203..Francie 5.00
167..Thumblina 16.00	186..Tiny Bubbles 9.00	203..New Barbie.............5.00
167..Tammy 5.00	186..Bashful Boy 2.00	203..Julia 10.00
167..Betsy Wetsy 5.00	187..Sherri 4.00	204..Tiny Cheerful-Tearful....6.00
168..Ted 8.00	187..Trudy 4.00	204..Drowsy ....6.00 (S.A.)
168..Pepper 5.00	187..Pretty Girl 3.00	204..Baby See N Say 9.00
168..Pebbles 8.00	187..Twistee 2.00	205..Baby's Hungry 9.00
168..BamBam 9.00	188..Nikki 5.00	205..Buffie.................10.00
169..Pebbles 9.00	188..Jolly 6.00	205..Randy Reader 12.00
169..Cuddly Kissey 22.00	188..Cuties 8.00	205..Sleeping Beauty 8.00
169..Baby Betsy Wetsy 4.00	188..Judy 3.00	206..Sister Small Talk 5.00
169..James Bond 25.00	189..Playpen Doll...........2.00	206..Small Talk.............5.00
170..Illya Kuryakin 25.00	189..Cutie Pie 2.00	206..Doctor Doolittle 12.00
170..Miss Clairol...........8.00	189..Timmy 6.00	206..22½" Dr. Doolittle 25.00
170..Honeymoon 22.00	189..Linda 9.00	207..Shelia Skediddle 3.00
170..Goody Two Shoes 25.00	190..Lil Lil 2.00	207..Tippy Toes 8.00
171..Betsy Wetsy 20.00	190..Catherine 22.00	207..Busy Ken 8.00
171..Baby Snoozie 16.00	190..Miss Sweet 2.00	207..Dancerina 12.00
171..Pebbles 5.00	190..Pumpkin 2.00	208..Bouncy Baby 3.00
171..Tabatha...............40.00	191..Snow White 48.00	208..Baby Tenderlove 3.00
172..Honeyball 2.00	191..Raggedy Ann & Andy....4.00	208..Chatty Tell 16.00
172..Tearful Thumblina 18.00	191..My Baby 4.00	208..Baby Sing A Song 16.00
172..Baby Giggles 26.00	191..Cuddly Infant..........2.00	209..Beany 22.00
172..Tiny Baby Kissy 8.00	192..Baby 2.00	209..Charlie Brown Skediddle .3.00
173..Tubsy 12.00	192..Louise 4.00	209..Breezy Bridgit 1.00
173..Giggles, White 25.00	192..Pastel Miss 2.00	209..Dressy 3.00
173..Giggles, Colored 30.00	192..Delightful 4.00	210..Big Jack ....4.00 (S.A.)
173..Daisy 4.00	193..Lorrie 2.00	210..Kretor & Zark 12.00
174..Pixie 5.00	193..Marsha 3.00	211..Haddie Mod 4.00
174..Newborn Thumblina, Colored 7.00	193..Little Linda 3.00	211..Joe Namath 8.00
174..Newborn Thumblina, White....5.00	193..Miss Toddler 20.00	211..Nun Nurse 3.00
174..Tearie Betsy 4.00	194..Twinkie 6.00	211..Molly 12.00
175..Toddler Thumblina 6.00	194..Jamie West ......3.00 (S.A.)	212..Monica.................60.00
175..April Showers 12.00	194..Mary Hoyer 25.00	212..Christening Baby........5.00
175..Little Lost Baby........25.00	196..Barbie 5.00	212..Claudette 4.00
176..Crissy, White ...:.....6.00	196..Mattie 22.00	212..Topsy-Turvy 22.00
176..Crissy, Colored 9.00	197..Sister Belle 22.00	213..Happy Toddler 20.00
176..Velvet 6.00	197..Charming Chatty 25.00	213..Walker 65.00
176..Dale 3.00	197..Chatty Cathy 18.00	213..Lone Ranger...........145.00
177..Lissing Thumblina 4.00	197..Midge 7.00	214..Eva 20.00
177..Tiny Thumblina 4.00	198..Shrinking Violet 45.00	214..American Child 65.00
177..In a Minute Thumblina ...5.00	198..Rickey 7.00	214..Lois Jane..............42.00
177..Patti Playful 20.00	198..Skooter 9.00	215..Dutch Girls 6.00
178..Baby Belly Button......2.00	198..Skipper 5.00	215..Betty Grable...........65.00
178..Play N Jane 9.00	199..Baby Pattaburp 12.00	216..False Snow White 10.00
178..Dina 30.00	199..Singing Chatty.........12.00	216..Happy Baby 6.00
178..Lazy Dazy.............3.00	199..Baby First Step 15.00	216..Air Force 35.00
181..13" Shirley Temple 75.00	199..Talking Baby First Step .15.00	216..Henry 25.00
181..17" Shirley Temple 75.00	200..Scooba Doo 25.00	217..Henrette 25.00
182..16" Shirley Temple 85.00	200..Baby Cheryl 8.00	217..Topsy 15.00
182..22" Shirley Temple 85.00	200..Casper The Ghost 22.00	217..Big Boy 8.00
182..27" Shirley Temple 200.00	200..Baby Teenie Talk 6.00	217..Gingham Gal 16.00
183..17" Shirley Temple Baby...125.00	201..Cheerful-Tearful 6.00	218..Lollypop Kid 3.00
	201..Baby Secret 12.00	218..Abbi-Gail 35.00
		218..Dream Doll 12.00
		219..Pauline 10.00

287

219 . Crying Baby 15.00	235 . Dillar A Dollar 8.00	251 . Ling Toy 6.00
219 . Pretty Baby 6.00	235 . Muffie 10.00	251 . Chi-Lu 4.00
219 . Baby Benny 5.00	236 . Christening Baby 12.00	251 . Snow White 60.00
220 . Bendee 12.00	236 . Valentine 8.00	252 . Polish Girl 4.00
220 . Johnny 3.00	236 . Nancy Ann 6.00	252 . Mammy's Baby 4.00
220 . Dimply Baby 4.00	236 . Linda Williams 12.00	252 . Dutch Girl 3.00
220 . Polly 15.00	237 . Dolly Ann 10.00	252 . Mammy 7.00
221 . Little Traveler 6.00	237 . JoAnn 6.00	253 . Marie 6.00
221 . Janie 2.00	237 . Belinda 7.00	253 . Abby 2.00
221 . Teena 4.00	237 . Baby Princess 6.00	253 . Norah Sue 32.00
221 . Miss Curity 10.00	238 . Royal Princess 3.00	253 . Miss Smith 18.00
222 . Little Sister 6.00	238 . Poppin Fresh 1.00	254 . Tak-Uki 48.00
222 . Nun 2.00	238 . Flowergirl 1.00	254 . Soo Ming 3.00
222 . World Traveler 16.00	238 . Bride 1.00	254 . Dutch Boy & Girl . . . 2.00
222 . Mary Lou 10.00	239 . Captain Hook 3.00	254 . Girl & Doll 9.00
223 . Ninette 5.00	239 . Nun 3.00	255 . Dancing Partner 9.00
223 . Rosy Walker 22.00	239 . Graduate 2.00	255 . Santa Claus 35.00
223 . Amy Louise 40.00	239 . Bride 2.00	255 . Little Lulu 35.00
223 . Pansy 8.00	240 . Miss America 1.00	255 . Sweet Pea 12.00
224 . Sweet Lou 12.00	240 . Lady Ravencroft 1.00	256 . Popeye 18.00
224 . Cuddly Kathy 6.00	240 . Miss Valentine 1.00	256 . Baby's Doll 2.00
224 . My Baby 6.00	240 . Crusader 2.00	256 . Daisy 7.00
224 . Pert & Sassy 4.00	241 . Polish Girl 1.00	256 . Flip 4.00
225 . Miss Glamour Ann 6.00	241 . Lady Hampshire 2.00	257 . Candy Striper 2.00
225 . Kleenex Baby 2.00	241 . Miss 1953 . . . . 2.00	257 . Cindy 1.00
225 . Baby Bunting 16.00	241 . Priscilla Alden 2.00	257 . Mickey Mouse 6.00
225 . Dream Doll 4.00	242 . Bride 1.00	257 . Mr. Magoo 5.00
226 . Yuletide 6.00	242 . Greenbrier Maid 3.00	258 . Eskimo Pie 2.00
226 . Angel 9.00	242 . Dress Me 1.00	258 . Multi-Face 5.00
226 . Pert Teenager 7.00	242 . Scotch Groom 2.00	258 . Sleepyhead 2.00
226 . Bed Doll 20.00	243 . Nelly 2.00	258 . Pinocchio 5.00
227 . Stunning 30.00	243 . New Baby 3.00	259 . Little Bo Peep 13.00
227 . Baby Beth 2.00	243 . Glorious Gold Princess . . 3.00	259 . Clown 4.00
227 . Sugar & Spice 2.00	243 . Flowergirl 3.00	259 . Mickey Mouse 7.00
227 . Trousseau Bride 6.00	244 . Bride 3.00	259 . Scarecrow 8.00
228 . Peggy Ann 2.00	244 . Polish Girl 3.00	260 . Ronald McDonald 1.00
228 . BeeBee 1.00	244 . Pert Pierrette 1.00	260 . Oh My 2.00
228 . Campbell Kid 4.00	244 . Red Riding Hood 2.00	260 . Little Orphan Annie 15.00
228 . Bonny 2.00	246 . Emily Ann 55.00	260 . Hansel 1.00
229 . Mattie Mame 2.00	246 . Marie 2.00	261 . Lil Soul 2.00
229 . Pretty Girl 3.00	246 . Tomas 2.00	261 . Talk A Little 4.00
229 . Pixie 3.00	246 . Howdy Doody . . . . 16.00 (S.A.)	261 . Holly 2.00
229 . Pixie Haircut Baby 3.00	246 . Poodle 10.00	262 . Gramma 12.00
230 . Imp 2.00	246 . Dick & Sally 6.00	262 . Doughboy 2.00
230 . Suzy Smart 7.00	246 . Woody Woodpecker 2.00	262 . Jolly Green Giant 3.00
230 . Valerie 7.00	247 . Teto 1.00	262 . Mr. Peanut 3.00
230 . Amish Boy & Girl 4.00	247 . Puppetrina 35.00	263 . Eskimo 1.00
231 . Jockey & Fox Hunter . . . 10.00	247 . Jiminy Cricket 1.00	263 . Louise 2.00
231 . African Native 3.00	247 . Donald Duck 2.00	263 . Jan 4.00
231 . Sexed Caveman 5.00	248 . Yogi Bear 1.00	263 . Heidi 3.00
232 . Little Joan 12.00	248 . Pluto 1.00	264 . Baby Stroll Along 3.00
232 . Flowergirl 12.00	248 . Donald Duck 1.00	264 . Baby Sad N Glad 6.00
233 . Queen of Hearts 12.00	248 . Sylvester 1.00	264 . Snugglebun 5.00
233 . Elsie Marley 12.00	249 . Tom 2.00	265 . Tippy Tumbles 4.00
233 . Winter 12.00	249 . Baby 1.00	265 . Heidi 4.00
233 . Daffidown Dilly 12.00	249 . Charlie McCarthy . 50.00 (S.A.)	265 . Bottle Baby 2.00
234 . Miss Muffett 8.00	249 . Betty Ballerina 1.00	265 . Baby Crawalong 7.00
234 . Bride 8.00	250 . Popeye 3.00	266 . Linda Lee 5.00
234 . Doll of Day 8.00	250 . Dr. Doolittle 4.00	266 . Baby Grow A Tooth 6.00
234 . Bride 8.00	250 . Happy Me 2.00	266 . Tumbling Tomboy 5.00
235 . Commencement 8.00	250 . ByeLo 95.00	266 . Baby Laugh A Lot 6.00
235 . Little Sister 12.00	251 . Charlie Chaplin 75.00	267 . Jumpsy 4.00

288

267..Whistler 2.00	278..Mannequin 12.00	291..Debteen 2.00
267..Sweet April 1.00	278..Dawk 4.00	291..New Born Yummy 1.00
267..Funny 1.00	279..Carmen 75.00	292..Tiny Trix.............1.00
268..Rosa 1.00	280..Sweetum 6.00	292..Kim 2.00
268..Elmer Fudd 4.00	280..Surprise Doll 18.00	292..Baby Sleep Amber 4.00
268..First Date 1.00	281..Princess Bride 6.00	292..Jennifer..............4.00
268..Lonely Liza 18.00	281..Country Girl 12.00	293..New Gerber Baby 5.00
269..Joy 15.00	281..Dollikins 8.00	293..Happy Pee Wee 2.00
269..Valentine Bonnet	281..Pri-thilla 9.00	293..Toe Dancing Ballerina ..18.00
Toddler...4.00	282..Baby Dollikins 16.00	293..Ballerina 9.00
269..St. Pat's Day Toddler 4.00	282..Wiggles 45.00	294..Big Girl..............22.00
269..Easter Bonnet Toddler ...4.00	282..Betsy McCall 26.00	295..Ginny 16.00
270..Billy Joe 25.00	283..Blue Fairy 4.00	295..Ginny 16.00
270..New Happytime Baby....6.00	283..Freckles 16.00	296..Ginny 14.00
270..Walking Bride 5.00	283..Pollyanna 45.00	296..Ginny 14.00
270..Mommy's Baby 3.00	283..Tinyteen 5.00	296..Ginny 10.00
271..Adorable 2.00	284..Yummy 12.00	296..Ginny Baby 18.00
271..Bubble Bath Baby 2.00	284..Purty 12.00	297..Jeff.................15.00
271..Indian Troll 2.00	284..Cuddly Baby 1.00	297..Jan 15.00
271..Nurse Troll 2.00	285..Blabby 15.00	297..Jill 15.00
272..Baby Janie 10.00	285..Miss Debteen 6.00	297..Brickette.............35.00
272..Tamu ....6.00 (S.A.)	285..Debteen Toddler 12.00	298..Baby Dear............25.00
272..Flip Wilson ....9.00 (S.A.)	286..Baby Sweetums 5.00	298..Little Baby Dear 8.00
273..Muff Doll.............2.00	286..Bob.................6.00	298..Ginny 10.00
273..Amosandra............35.00	286..Coquette 6.00	298..Ginny Baby 16.00
273..Betty Bows 12.00	286..Bare Bottom Baby 8.00	299..Baby Dear............16.00
273..Tod-L-Dee & Tod-L-Tim..6.00	287..Posin Elfy 2.00	299..Baby Dear............8.00
274..Banister Baby 20.00	287..Debteen 6.00	299..Littlest Angel..........8.00
274..Babee Bee 6.00	287..Little Coquette 4.00	299..Posie Pixie 10.00
274..Chunky 2.00	287..Posable Baby Trix 2.00	300..Littlest Angel..........8.00
274..Baby 1.00	288..Needa Toodles 2.00	300..Angel Baby 8.00
275..Gerber Baby 12.00	288..Tiny Toodles..........1.00	300..Picture Girl 9.00
275..Tod-L-Tee 2.00	288..Pretty Portrait 4.00	300..Star Brite 25.00
275..So Wee 2.00	288..Baby Pee Wee 2.00	301..Little Miss Ginny 6.00
275..Gerber Baby 10.00	289..Secret Sue 0.00	301..Dearest One 22.00
276..Little Debbie Eve 4.00	289..50th Anniversary Doll ..20.00	301..Ginny Baby 8.00
276..Melody Baby Debbi.....3.00	289..Penelope 3.00	301..Pinocchio 45.00
276..Baby Debbie 6.00	289..Baby Sweetums 2.00	302..Dashful 35.00
276..Talking Terri Lee 50.00	290..First Born Baby 1.00	302..Snow White 40.00
277..Terri Lee 35.00	290..Daffi Dill 3.00	302..Tinker Bell 12.00
277..Jerri Lee 50.00	290..Dolly Walker 2.00	302..Mousketeer 16.00
277..Tiny Jerri Lee 25.00	290..Dollikins ....3.00 (S.A.)	303..Christopher Robin 12.00
277..Tiny Terri Lee 35.00	291..Bathtub Baby 1.00	303..Winnie Pooh..........8.00
278..Baby Linda 35.00	291..Adorable Cindy 1.00	303..Jiminy Cricket 2.00

REVISED PRICES FOR SERIES 2

1..Mimi 75.00	9..Scarlett O'Hara 100.00	11..Alice in Wonderland 55.00
4..Lady Hamilton.........3.00	9..Ginger Rogers 85.00	11..Nina Ballerina 50.00
4..Dainty Dolly...........7.00	9..W.A.V.E. 55.00	12..Fairy Queen 55.00
5..Musical Sweetheart 4.00	9..Margaret O'Brien 185.00	12..9" Latex 18.00
5..Lady Lettie............3.00	10..Scotch 35.00	12..Prince Charming 75.00
5..Empress Eugenie 18.00	10..Norwegian 35.00	12..Cinderella 75.00
7..Bobby Q & Susie Q 85.00	10..Swiss 35.00	12..Violet................45.00
8..China 35.00	10..Jeannie Walker 85.00	13..Alice in Wonderland 55.00
8..Jane Withers 185.00	11..Bride 50.00	13..Sonja Henie 65.00
8..Little Shaver 60.00	11..Babs................65.00	13..Kathy 55.00

13 . . Madeline 45.00	33 . . Mary Martin 65.00	48 . . Gloria Jean 65.00
14 . . McGuffey Ana 65.00	33 . . Madaline 45.00	48 . . Susan 30.00
15 . . Cynthia 85.00	33 . . Alice in Wonderland 65.00	50 . . Nanette 35.00
15 . . Rosebud 40.00	33 . . Elise Ballerina 45.00	50 . . Nanette 35.00
15 . . Active Miss 45.00	34 . . Agatha 50.00	50 . . Nanette 35.00
15 . . Christening Baby 30.00	34 . . Scarlet 150.00	50 . . Miss Coty 6.00
16 . . Binnie Walker 40.00	34 . . Renoir 125.00	51 . . Count Dracula 3.00
16 . . Jo 45.00	34 . . Amish Boy & Girl 40.00	51 . . Frankenstein 3.00
16 . . Queen 45.00	34 . . Spanish Boy 35.00	51 . . Wolfman 3.00
16 . . Lissy 45.00	34 . . Spanish Girl . . . . . 18.00 (S.A.)	51 . . The Mummy 3.00
17 . . Groom 40.00	34 . . Suzy 50.00	51 . . Lil Abner 65.00
17 . . Cissy Queen 125.00	34 . . Janie 35.00	54 . . Betsy McCall, 11½" 22.00
17 . . Lissy 45.00	34 . . Rosy 50.00	54 . . Betsy McCall, 22" 26.00
17 . . Billy 45.00	35 . . Cinderella . . . . . 22.00 (S.A.)	54 . . Betsy McCall, 29" 35.00
17 . . Wendy Ann 35.00	35 . . Easter Girl 75.00	54 . . Betsy McCall, 36" 75.00
18 . . Elise Bride 45.00	35 . . Scarlett 40.00	55 . . Kewpie Doll 30.00
18 . . Cisette 35.00	35 . . Alice in Wonderland 35.00	55 . . Miss Peep 20.00
18 . . Cisette 35.00	35 . . Peter Pan Set . . . . . 165.00 set	55 . . Scootles 75.00
18 . . Sleeping Beauty 55.00	35 . . Renoir Child 55.00	55 . . Kewpie Beanbag 8.00
19 . . Aunt Agatha 40.00	36 . . 11" Portretts . . . . . 65.00 each	57 . . Carol 6.00
19 . . Renoir 75.00	37 . . Cowgirl & Cowboy 40.00	57 . . Polly Pond Doll 25.00
19 . . Kelly 45.00	37 . . Southern Belle 40.00	58 . . Ginger 5.00
19 . . Cissette 35.00	37 . . Lady Hamilton 125.00	58 . . Miss Ginger 8.00
20 . . Quintuplets . . . . . . 150.00 set	37 . . Japan 35.00	58 . . Ginger 5.00
20 . . Janie 35.00	38 . . Rumania . . . . . . 18.00 (S.A.)	59 . . Cowgirl Ginger 5.00
20 . . Brenda Starr 45.00	38 . . Finland . . . . 18.00 (S.A.)	59 . . Trike Tike 2.00
21 . . Kitten 25.00	38 . . Godey 65.00	60 . . Sasha . . . . Still Available
21 . . Jaqueline 75.00	38 . . Jenny Lind 50.00	60 . . Gregor . . . . Still Available
21 . . Cissette Ballerina 35.00	39 . . Wendy 50.00	61 . . Sweet Rosemary 12.00
21 . . Lively Huggums 25.00	39 . . Peter Pan 50.00	61 . . Penny Brite 6.00
22 . . Cissette Ballerina 35.00	39 . . Jenny Lind 50.00	61 . . Swinger 5.00
22 . . Caroline 75.00	39 . . Heidi . . . . 20.00 (S.A.)	61 . . Hot Canary 5.00
22 . . Maggie Mixup 55.00	40 . . Renoir 125.00	62 . . Yeah, Yeah & Slick Chick . 5.00
22 . . French . . . . 18.00 (S.A.)	40 . . Lucinda 50.00	62 . . Fancy Feet 9.00
23 . . Sleeping Beauty 115.00	40 . . Southern Belle 40.00	62 . . Kevin 9.00
23 . . Pollyanna 45.00	40 . . Smiley 50.00	62 . . Susie Homemaker 6.00
23 . . Funny . . . . 12.00 (S.A.)	41 . . Renoir Child . . . . 22.00 (S.A.)	62 . . Dawn 4.00
24 . . Wendy 35.00	41 . . Janie 25.00	63 . . Dale 6.00
24 . . Wendy 35.00	41 . . Lucinda . . . . 15.00 (S.A.)	63 . . Van 6.00
24 . . Janie 35.00	41 . . Gainsboro 125.00	63 . . Angie 5.00
24 . . Peruvian Boy 40.00	42 . . Sally 45.00	63 . . Glori 5.00
26 . . Red Riding Hood . 18.00 (S.A.)	42 . . Debutante Walker 50.00	64 . . Gary 5.00
26 . . Polly 45.00	42 . . Jimmy John 50.00	64 . . Longlocks 6.00
26 . . Baby Ellen 30.00	43 . . Ricky Jr. 18.00	64 . . Ron 5.00
26 . . Gretel 45.00	43 . . Ricky Jr. 35.00	64 . . Dancing Dawn 4.00
27 . . Maggie 45.00	43 . . Sweet Sue 35.00	65 . . Dancing Gary 5.00
27 . . African 40.00	43 . . Tiny Toodles 15.00	65 . . Dancing Dale 6.00
27 . . Hawaiian 40.00	44 . . Groom 45.00	65 . . Dancing Van 6.00
27 . . Bride 40.00	44 . . Betsy McCall 25.00	65 . . Dancing Longlocks 6.00
30 . . Thailand . . . . 18.00 (S.A.)	44 . . Whimette 6.00	66 . . Dancing Angie 5.00
30 . . Scarlet 40.00	44 . . New Tiny Tears 10.00	66 . . Dancing Glori 5.00
30 . . Gidgit 35.00	45 . . TeenWeeny Tiny Tears . . 5.00	66 . . Dancing Ron 5.00
30 . . Coco 150.00	45 . . Sally Says 30.00	66 . . Kevin 5.00
31 . . Scarlett 125.00	45 . . Cricket 10.00	67 . . Denise 8.00
31 . . Disneyland	45 . . Margaret Rose 13.00	67 . . Melanie 8.00
Snow White . . . 20.00 (S.A.)	46 . . Freckles 7.00	67 . . Dinah 8.00
31 . . Agatha 125.00	46 . . Hoss Cartright 40.00	67 . . Daphne 8.00
31 . . Pumpkin . . . . . . 20.00 (S.A.)	46 . . Ben Cartright 35.00	68 . . Connie 8.00
33 . . Granny 40.00	47 . . Sweet Sue 35.00	68 . . Longlocks 5.00
33 . . McGuffy Ana 40.00	47 . . Toni 25.00	68 . . Dawn 5.00
33 . . Sheri Lewis 85.00	48 . . So Big 28.00	68 . . Maureen 8.00
33 . . Snow White 55.00	48 . . Baby Donna 20.00	69 . . Dancing Jessica 5.00

291

120..My Candy 2.00
120..Musical Mimi 6.00
121..Mini Martian 5.00
121..Diana................8.00
121..Bimby 2.00
121..Baby Princess 10.00
122..Twin Dandy 4.00
122..Twin Tandy 4.00
122..Popo.................2.00
122..Skeetle.........7.00 (S.A.)
123..Crying Baby ......5.00 (S.A.)
123..Baby Paula ......2.00 (S.A.)
124..Fascination 15.00
124..Mannikin ....5.00 (S.A.)
124..Luisa 5.00
125..9".................22.00
125..Peruvians 22.00
125..6"..................8.00
125..Welsh 50.00
126..Pam 8.00
126..Sparky 2.00
127..Flop Tot 1.00
127..Kitty Coed ......4.00 (S.A.)
127..Sparky 2.00
128..Poland ....3.00 (S.A.)
128..Mexico ....3.00 (S.A.)
128..My Baby 30.00
128..Honeywest 15.00
129..G.I. Joe ......5.00 (S.A.)
130..G.I. Joe ......5.00 (S.A.)
130..Monkee 10.00
130..Dolly Darling 2.00
131..Jamie..............3.00
131..Dolly Darling 2.00
132..That Kid 25.00
132..Daisy Darling...........2.00
132..Dolly Darling 2.00
133..Lily Darling 2.00
133..Music 9.00
133..Peace 5.00
133..Adam 6.00
134..Flower 5.00
134..Peace 5.00
134..Soul 6.00
134..Love 5.00
135..Leggy Sue...........6.00
135..Leggy Nan 5.00
135..Leggy Jill 5.00
136..Leggy Kate 5.00
136..Sweet Cookie 5.00
136..Bonnie Breck 10.00
136..Aimee 18.00
137..7"................12.00
137..8"................7.00
137..9"................8.00
138..Joyce 35.00
138..Roberta.............40.00
138..JoJo 40.00
138..Bright Star 25.00
139..Cindy 20.00
139..Life Size Baby 18.00
139..Cindy 20.00

139..Renee 12.00
140..Perfume Pixie 2.00
140..Yvonne 4.00
140..Cinderella 5.00
140..15"................6.00
141..Molly 8.00
141..Twin Tot 2.00
141..Wee Bonnie Baby 2.00
141..Teensie Baby 2.00
142..Floppy 5.00
142..Anthony Pipsqueek.....7.00
142..Marc Pipsqueek 7.00
142..Cleo Pipsqueek 7.00
143..Baby Precious 4.00
143..New Baby Tweaks 4.00
143..Tiny Baby 2.00
143..Loonie Lite 3.00
144..Penny Penpal 5.00
144..Softy Skin 3.00
144..Bednobs 10.00
144..Pippi Longstockings 12.00
145..Lone Ranger ......5.00 (S.A.)
145..Tonto ....5.00 (S.A.)
145..Baby Wet 4.00
146..Shirley Temple Baby ..125.00
146..Little Princess 65.00
146..Snow White 75.00
146..Judy Garland ......185.00 up
147..22".................35.00
147..Shirley..............75.00
147..18" Shirley 85.00
147..16".................35.00
148..18".................25.00
148..Magic Skin Baby 6.00
148..Talking Tot 20.00
148..Baby Snookie 4.00
149..Baby Gurglee 9.00
149..Peggy 35.00
149..Joan Palooka 22.00
149..Sara Ann.............22.00
150..Mary Hartline 35.00
150..Saucy Walker 20.00
150..Miss Curity 25.00
150..Patty Petite 22.00
151..Posie 20.00
151..Miss Revlon 22.00
151..19" Shirley 65.00
151..17" Shirley 45.00
152..35" Shirley 365.00
152..Little Miss Revlon 14.00
152..Mitzi 8.00
152..Patti 5.00
153..19"................6.00
153..Patti Playpal 65.00
153..Lovely Liz............8.00
153..Tammy 5.00
154..Tammy 5.00
154..Rock Baby Coos 6.00
154..Tammy's Mom 12.00
154..Ted 8.00
155..PosN Pete 7.00
155..Grown Up Tammy 8.00

155..Pepper..............5.00
155..Dodi................7.00
156..Samantha 12.00
156..Baby Herman 6.00
156..Real Live Lucy 6.00
156..Talking Goody
         Two Shoes...28.00
157..Captain Action 4.00
157..Trixy Flatsy 7.00
158..Casey Flatsy 7.00
158..Tressy 6.00
158..Kerry 15.00
158..Filly Flatsy 7.00
159..Baby Flatsy 2.00
159..Spinderella Flatsy 4.00
159..Lemonade Flatsies 3.00
159..Play Time Flatsy 7.00
160..Slumbertime Flatsy ...7.00
160..Nancy Flatsy 7.00
160..Rally Flatsy 7.00
160..Bonnie Flatsy 7.00
161..Candy Flatsy 7.00
161..Brandi 15.00
161..Cookie Flatsy 7.00
161..Mia................15.00
162..Cricket 10.00
162..Velvet 6.00
162..New Tiny Tears 4.00
162..Baby Belly Button 4.00
163..Cinnamon 10.00
163..Busy Lizy 22.00
163..Upsy-Dazy 10.00
163..Harmony 20.00
164..Evel Knievel .....4.00 (S.A.)
164..Look Around Velvet ...6.00
164..Look Around Crissy ...6.00
164..17" Shirleys..25.00-9.00 (S.A.)
165..Pan Am 2.00
165..Jal 2.00
165..BOAC 2.00
166..Little Love 3.00
166..Lovely Liz............3.00
166..Miss Grow Up 4.00
166..Kimberly............5.00
167..8".................18.00
167..8".................18.00
167..Miss America 25.00
167..Steve Scout ....7.00 (S.A.)
168..Crumpet 5.00
168..Blythe 5.00
168..Gabbigale 6.00
168..Meadow 4.00
169..Hy Finance 4.00
169..Sleeping Beauty.......48.00
169..Jeannie 20.00
169..Pamela 6.00
170..Mister Action 4.00
170..Rookies ....3.00 (S.A.)
170..Pamela 6.00
171..Bonnie Jean 4.00
171..Sweet Candy 4.00
171..Debbie..............6.00

293

218..Skipper 5.00
Dog Show...2.00
219..Skipper 5.00
Sledding Fun...2.00
219..Bunson Burnie 2.00
219..Rosemary Roadster 7.00
219..Baby Colleen 8.00
219..Baby Liddle 12.00
222..Sleeping Biddle 8.00
222..Liddle Biddle Peep 8.00
222..Little Middle Muffet 8.00
222..Peter Paniddle.........8.00
223..Liddle Red Riding Hiddle.8.00
223..Sizzly Fridle 7.00
223..Howard Biff Boodle 7.00
223..Freezy Sliddle 7.00
225..Cinderiddles Palace.....4.00
225..Sleeping Biddle Castle ...6.00
225..Babe Biddle Car 4.00
225..Lolli Lemon Kiddle 3.00
226..Lolli Mint Kiddle 3.00
226..Frosty Mint Kiddle 3.00
226..Orange Ice Kiddle 3.00
226..Violet Kiddle Kologne...2.00
227..Lily Of The Valley 2.00
227..Rosebud 2.00
227..Honeysuckle...........2.00
227..Sweet Pea.............2.00
228..Apple Blossom.........2.00
228..Windy Fliddle 8.00
228..Larky Locket 3.00
228..Lou Locket 3.00
229..Lorelie Locket 3.00
229..Lorna Locket 3.00
229..Lilac Locket 3.00
229..Lucky Locket 3.00
230..Heart Pin Kiddle 3.00
230..Lorelie Bracelet 3.00
230..Flower Pin Kiddle 3.00
230..Suki Skediddle.........4.00
231..Teachy Keen 8.00
231..Kiddle Kastle 4.00
231..Baby Small Talk........6.00
231..Alice In
Wonderliddle Castle...12.00
232..Valarie................4.00
232..Talking P.J. 8.00
232..1967 Twist N Turn Barbie 5.00
232..Lavender Kiddle Case 1.00
233..Laverne Locket 3.00
233..Louise Locket..........3.00
233..Hearts Kiddles 7.00
233..Hearts N Flowers 3.00
234..Laffy Lemon 3.00
234..Luscious Lime 3.00
234..Greta Grape 3.00
234..Shirley Strawberry 3.00
235..Anabelle Autodiddle 6.00
235..Sister Small Walk 5.00
235..Lickety Spliddle 6.00
235..Heather Skediddle 4.00
236..Olivia Orange 3.00

236..Lady Lavender 6.00
236..Francie's Bed 5.00
236..Rah Rah Teeny Boppin...4.00
237..Cherry Blossom 5.00
237..Tessie Tractor 4.00
237..Shirley Skiddle 4.00
237..Harriet Helididdle 5.00
238..Lickety Skediddle 5.00
238..Tracy Skediddle........5.00
238..Anabelle Skediddle 5.00
238..Captain Lazer..........10.00
239..Doug Davis 5.00
239..Sgt. Storm 5.00
239..Major Matt Mason 5.00
239..Dainty Deer 3.00
240..Baby Walk N Play 9.00
240..Flossy Glossy 3.00
240..Zoolery Kiddles.....3.00 each
240..Lucky Lion 3.00
242..Tiny Tiger.............3.00
242..Miss Mouse 3.00
242..Funny Bunny 4.00
242..Truly Scrumptious 12.00
243..Barbie Family House 4.00
243..Mr. Potts Set ....9.00 set
243..Lenore Limosine 7.00
243..Henrietta Carrage 7.00
246..Snoopy Skididdle 3.00
246..Donald Duck Skediddle ..3.00
246..Goofy Skiddler 3.00
246..Lucy Skididdler 3.00
247..1968 Kiddle Case 4.00
247..Baby Go Bye Bye 5.00
247..Kiddles Open House 6.00
247..Small Talk Cinderella ...8.00
249..Kiddle Living Room 3.00
249..Callisto 4.00
249..Cookin' Hiddle Set......5.00
249..Living Fluff 7.00
250..Kiddle Mobile 4.00
250..Twist N Turn Francie ...5.00
250..1970 Living Barbie 5.00
250..Barbie 7.00
See Worthy...5.00
250..Barbie 5.00
Yellow Mellow...2.00
251..Playhouse Kiddles 5.00
251..Rosemary Roadster 9.00
251..Good Night Kiddle 5.00
252..Baby Din Din 4.00
252..Lady Lace Tea Party ...6.00
252..Baby Rockaway 5.00
252..Nan & Fran ....10.00 set
253..Wet Noodles 1.00
253..Bugs Bunny Skediddle ..3.00
253..1969 Barbie Case 3.00
254..1969 Barbie Case 2.00
254..Talking Baby Tenderlove .4.00
254..Sing A Song 12.00
254..Baby So High 3.00
255..Tickle Pinkle 3.00
255..Downy Dill 3.00

255..Pocus Hocus 3.00
255..Mother, What Now? 3.00
256..Miss Information 3.00
256..Red Hot Red 2.00
256..Nitty Nan 2.00
256..Lilac Rockflower 4.00
257..Heather Rockflower 4.00
257..Barbie 7.00
Prima Ballerina...3.00
257..Sun Buggy 10.00
257..Rosemary Rockflower ...5.00
258..Barbie 5.00
Club Dress...2.00
258..Barbie 7.00
Skate Mate...5.00
258..Barbie 5.00
Salute to Silver...5.00
258..Walking Jamie 9.00
258..Talking Stacey 9.00
Maxi 'n Mini...7.00
258..Christie...............7.00
Great Coat...5.00
259..Shoppin' Sheryl 5.00
259..Baby Beans 3.00
259..Living Baby Tenderlove .4.00
259..Baby Love Light 6.00
260..Talking Kip 4.00
260..Casper 4.00
260..Cynthia 8.00
260..Baby Play A Lot 6.00
261..Malibu Ken ......6.00 (S.A.)
261..Living Fluff 7.00
261..Living Barbie 8.00
Fashion...4.00
Walk Lively Barbie 7.00
262..Walking Jamie 9.00
262..Ken & P.J. 9.00
262..Pretty Hair Barbie 7.00
262..Live Action Christie 9.00
262..Pretty Hair Francie 8.00
262..Living Barbie 8.00
Silver Serenade...6.00
263..Malibu P.J. ....(S.A.)
263..Malibu Francie ....(S.A.)
264..Malibu Skipper ....(S.A.)
264..Hi Dottie 6.00
264..Barbie 7.00
Silver Blues...5.00
264..Miss America 15.00
265..Mod Hair Ken .....4.00 (S.A.)
265..Tiny Baby Tenderlove ...6.00
265..Peachy 12.00
265..Sweet 16 Barbie........6.00
266..Sunshine Family ......(S.A.)
266..Barbie's 10 Speeder ....(S.A.)
266..Barbie's Horse 12.00
267..Saucy 20.00
267..Stacey 9.00
Maxi N Mini...4.00
267..P.J. 9.00
Fun Flakes...3.00
268..Tanya 4.00

268..Action Jackson..........4.00
268..Spiderman.......2.00 (S.A.)
268..Tarzan.........2.00 (S.A.)
269..Batman.........2.00 (S.A.)
269..Aquaman.........2.00 (S.A.)
269..Robin.........2.00 (S.A.)
269..Superman.......2.00 (S.A.)
270..Dinah-mite...........4.00
270..#1423...............2.00
270..#1431...............2.00
270..MS Fashion...........9.00
271..Riddler.......2.00 (S.A.)
271..Shazam.......2.00 (S.A.)
271..Capt. America....2.00 (S.A.)
271..Penguin & Joker..2.00 (S.A.)
272..Mr. Mxyzptlk.....2.00 (S.A.)
272..Lainie.............15.00
272..Cornelius & Zira...3.00 (S.A.)
272..Astronaut, Dr. Zaius
        And Soldier...3.00 (S.A.)
273..New Born Baby........6.00
273..Sweet & Cuddly........6.00
274..17" Monica...........60.00
275..21" Monica...........75.00
275..18" Monica...........75.00
275..One, Two
        Button My Shoe..12.00
275..Polly Put Kettle On.....12.00
275..5"...............12.00
275..High Button Shoes....12.00
276..5"...............12.00
277..Storybook Dolls.......12.00
278..Storybook Dolls.......12.00
278..5½"..............10.00
278..Muffie.............10.00
279..Muffie.............10.00
279..Lori Ann...........10.00
279..Nappy.............3.00
279..Baby Sue...........3.00
280..Tracy.............2.00
280..Theresa...........2.00
280..Princess...........22.00
280..Joan Palooka........10.00
281..Mousketeer.........22.00
281..Klinker............4.00
281..Playboy Bunny.........8.00
281..Pebbles............3.00
282..Adventure Boy.........2.00
282..World Champion.......10.00
282..Laurel & Hardy........1.00
282..Poppi Fresh Set...2.00 (S.A.)
283..Puss & Boots.........30.00
283..Drum Major..........20.00
283..Pin Up Girl..........12.00
283..Sleepy Head.........4.00
284..Jack & Jill...........1.00
284..Bebe Jetpartout.......8.00
284..Little Audrey.........25.00
284..Lucy Arnez..........25.00
285..Bunny.............20.00
285..Eloise.............30.00
285..18"..............25.00
286..Danny.............5.00
286..Popeye............4.00
286..Crib Angel..........1.00

286..Tatters.............20.00
287..Hamburgler..........2.00
287..Elsie.............8.00
287..Gas Genie..........2.00
287..Dressy Bessie........2.00
288..Little Lulu...........1.00
288..Mary, Many Face..7.00 (S.A.)
289..Dr. John...........20.00
289..Liza.............20.00
289..Judy.............15.00
289..Libby.............15.00
290..L.B.J.............20.00
290..Hildy & Herby.........5.00
290..Spunky & Pip.........5.00
290..TV Jones...........3.00
291..Orphan Annie........18.00
291..Winkin Heidi.........4.00
291..Gingersnap..........20.00
291..19"..............18.00
292..Hug A Bug..........2.00
292..Laurie.............18.00
292..Mimi.............20.00
        Outfits...4.00
293..Baby Lynne..........3.00
294..Roberta Ann.........22.00
294..Debutante Bride......16.00
294..Dr. Casey's Nurse.....5.00
294..Dr. Kildare's Nurse.....5.00
295..Granny.............22.00
295..Polly.............5.00
295..Raggy Muffin........2.00
295..Lisa.............6.00
296..Playgirl...........12.00
296..22"..............12.00
296..Peter Pan..........18.00
296..Mother............20.00
297..Carrie Cries.........6.00
297..Maxi-Mod..........4.00
297..Brother & Sister......20.00
298..Nancy & Kim.......25.00 set
298..Malaika............10.00
298..Wanda.........6.00 (S.A.)
299..Lea.........6.00 (S.A.)
299..Kim.............20.00
299..Baby Ellen..........6.00
300..Cowgirl Annie........2.00
300..Miss Christmas........2.00
300..Dorothy Collins........25.00
300..Baby Skin Doll........12.00
301..Sunbabe............10.00
301..Peter Pan..........5.00
301..Sun-Dee...........15.00
301..Carrie.............4.00
302..Gene Autry.........165.00
302..Connie Lynn.........45.00
303..Cindy.............8.00
303..Cycling Cheri...12.00 (S.A.)
303..Honest Abe..........18.00
304..Needa Toodles.......15.00
304..Toodles............12.00
305..Suzette............5.00
305..Bride Sue..........4.00
305..Sunny Face.........10.00
306..Wish Nik..........2.00
306..Impish Elfy.........1.00

306..Teenie Toodles.........1.00
306..Hee Wee...........2.00
307..Dance Time.........1.00
307..Bride Time.........1.00
307..Angeltime..........1.00
307..Springtime &
        Shoppintime...1.00
308..Schooltime..........1.00
308..Moonmaid..........12.00
308..Baby Pee Wee........2.00
308..Batman Troll........2.00
309..Pretty Portrait.......4.00
309..Educational PeeWee....1.00
309..Kristina............3.00
309..Marika............3.00
310..Fun Time..........4.00
310..Beau Time..........4.00
310..Vacation Time........4.00
310..Prom Time.........4.00
311..Bride Time.........4.00
311..Winter Time.........4.00
311..Date Time..........4.00
311..Party Time.........4.00
312..Connie............5.00
312..Littlest So Soft.......3.00
312..Lovable Lynn........3.00
312..Patti-Cake.........3.00
313..Donna............4.00
313..Magic Meg.........6.00
313..Miss Dollikin.....3.00 (S.A.)
313..Lin.............2.00
314..Loo.............2.00
314..Weepsy...........1.00
314..Thum-Fun.........2.00
315..Janie.............4.00
316..............3.00
316..Calico Lass.........4.00
316..Ellie Mae..........4.00
316..Rusty............15.00
317..Happi-Time Walker....25.00
317..Dondi............35.00
317..Roxanne...........25.00
317..Luann Simms........30.00
318..Lucy.............5.00
318..Lucy.............8.00
320..Composition..........16.00
        Early Non-Walker...14.00
        Early Walker...12.00
    Molded Lashes/Walker...10.00
    Bending Knee/Walker...8.00
        Add 2.00 for Brown Eyes
        Outfits...3.00 to 12.00
324..Ginny Bed..........18.00
327..Ginny Bed..........15.00
327..Jan.............15.00
329..Wardrobe Case.......12.00
332..Pinky Toe..........8.00
333..Littlest Angel........6.00
333..New Baby Dear........30.00
333..Angel Baby.........6.00
333..Miss Ginny........7.00 (S.A.)
334..Jeff.............15.00
334..Ginny............10.00
334..Ginny............10.00
334..Baby Dear.........25.00   295